The Untold Whispers of the World

Nadr Aboukhodr

TUCK-WA

Visit us at www.tuckwa.com

DISCLAIMER

The contents of this book are intended for informational and educational purposes only. Nothing contained herein is intended to be a substitute for professional medical advice, diagnosis or treatment. Always seek the advice of a physician or other qualified healthcare provider with any questions you may have regarding any medical condition, and never disregard professional medical advice or delay in seeking it because of something you have read in this book.

Acknowledgments

All praise belongs to Allah (swt) and everything belongs to Him (swt). Without a doubt, if it wasn't for Allah (swt), not even a letter within this book could have been formulated. May Allah (swt) accept such a small token and may He (swt) bless, protect, and forgive us all. May He (swt) give us strength to always obey and serve Him (swt) until our last breath. Through Allah (swt) may we not give into our evil passions, desires, ambitions, and always reject the accursed Chief Deceiver, Shaytan. Lastly, may we follow the light of the Prophet Muhammad (saww), Imam Ali (as), and the AhlulBayt (as); through their light we will attain optimal nearness to Allah (swt)!

I would like to thank my mother and father who always showed me love and care. Their advice helped me create the best version of myself. To my siblings, cousins and friends, thank you for always encouraging me to write and for your honest feedback. To the scholars who shared their valuable knowledge with me, I am indebted to all of you forever. To my best friend, I am eternally grateful for everything you have done for me; it was more than I could have imagined. Lastly, I thank my local and online community for inspiring me to publish this book. I didn't intend to, but you all convinced me that it was necessary.

My Personal Story

As-Salamu Alaikum wa Rahmatullahi wa Barakatuh.

With the permission of Allah (swt), I would like to introduce myself and share my personal story with you. I was born and raised in Dearborn, Michigan by an immigrant family. My family and I come from humble beginnings. My parents settled in Dearborn in the late 1980s and experienced hardships like many other immigrant families. Despite the adversity, my parents made it work. They took good care of my three brothers and me. I attended the local public schools and in high school I was part of the football team. A memory I will forever cherish because football was and still is my favorite sport. Throughout high school, I worked as a busboy at a restaurant. I dreaded busing tables but it taught me valuable lessons, such as eliminating the ego. Most of my free time was spent with my brothers and cousins. After graduating high school, I was fortunate enough to start my education at a community college. When it comes to religion, I would say I grew up in a moderate religious household. My parents taught us the basics of religion: right from wrong, how to uphold good manners, etc. They also enrolled us in several Islamic and Arabic programs. However, as time went on I realized that what I was taught in the past was a minor fraction of what Islam truly is. Coming to such a conclusion was a journey.

In the beginning of 2011, at 18 years old, I completed my fall semester in college with good grades, but the following winter semester I would drop out of all of my courses. I was going through extreme hardship and I could not continue any longer. I felt very lost in my life despite having plans and goals. Growing up we weren't familiar with mental health. For example, when I used to be uncomfortable in certain situations, I was told to "stop being shy." Throughout my life I always thought I had a shyness problem, but then later I found out it was anxiety. I will never forget that winter; I became severely depressed and anxious. I thought my life was over because of some decisions I made. My anxiety and depression were so bad that I became physically paralyzed from time to time. I was so weak that I could not even lift five pound dumbbells. That year, my favorite football player made it to the championship game and we had a gathering with some family and friends. At the gathering I was physically there but mentally I was not, which kind of ruined the mood of the guests. I was known to be the individual that made people laugh on such occasions, but instead I was dead silent in the corner of the room.

Seeing me in such a state hurt my parents immensely. They offered help in countless ways, such as making me my favorite foods and taking me to nature filled places. They even encouraged me to seek professional help and take medication. I always refused medication, not because I am against it but because I knew it was a temporary solution. Also, from observing family members who were on medication for a period of time, the long-term side effects made me despise it even more. Was that the right decision to take? Everyone knows themselves best. Please do not misunderstand me; yes, I chose such a path, but that does not mean I go around encouraging such a route to others or condemn those who do take medication. I will say this, mentally I suffered. My thoughts were always negative and non-stop racing. The only time my thoughts paused was when I was asleep. After hardship comes ease, even hardship has an appointed term it can't go past. The following months I was feeling like myself again, and decided to enroll back in school part-time. Later that year, my mother returned from Hajj. She was glowing and in a state of tranquility. Seeing her like this impacted me and I asked myself, how can I feel how she is feeling all year around and not only in Mecca? I never really found an answer at that time. However, as the years went by I realized my depression and anxiety were becoming worse. This whole time I was just distracting myself and I never really offered myself a real solution.

As I was transferring to university in 2014, an earthquake struck my mental and physical foundation again but this time it was unbearable. I became extremely depressed and anxious to the point that I was afraid to leave my home. I even had to sleep next to one of my parents every night. If you saw me then, you would think I was a zombie. I was fortunate that I had someone there for me, but being a 22-year-old male sleeping next to his mother wasn't ideal. I would hug her tightly every day because I was terrified, and she would tell me, "One step at a time."

My mother began to notice that I was no longer sleeping next to her as the days passed. She became concerned and asked, "Is everything okay?" I looked at her with a heavy heart and said, "Thank you for everything, but this time I have to do this on my own." For a while, I would sit in my room in the dark reflecting for hours and hours. I would listen to "I Am Near" by Hajj Khalil Jaffer. It was a short video describing how close Allah (swt) is to us. I would shed tears excessively each night because I didn't know what to do anymore. I was losing myself slowly and even the thought of suicide crossed my mind by the whispers of Shaytan, but I knew it was haram and it would devastate my family forever. So, I kept praying and calling out to Allah (swt), and then out of nowhere everything just clicked in my mind. The trial had come to an end! Thankfully, I didn't drop out of university during that time, but I was close to doing so before the semester began.

Anyway, I only had one goal, and that was to earn enough credits to begin substitute teaching. I didn't think I was capable of finishing my degree. As I was sitting in class, I started reflecting on what got me to the point of mental destruction. I asked myself if it could have been a sign, and if it was the best thing that had ever happened to me. That day, I made a covenant with Allah (swt) to stop standing between truth and falsehood. Even though I was doing my basic duties, I was still intentionally doing things that displeased Allah (swt). It's the small things we tend to overlook that can fuel our suffering without even realizing it. It is important to understand how the human soul properly works, and what it needs to survive.

Nonetheless, after my classes I would dedicate some time to study Islam properly at the library. I had to break and rebuild my foundation on Islam. I made it my mission to never feel that point of destruction again. I was fortunate enough to come across a profound lecture series by Hajj Khalil Jaffer titled, "The End of Negative Suffering." This lecture series changed my life. Hajj Khalil Jaffer introduced me to the spiritual side of Islam and to one of my favorite words of all time, Taqwa. Prior to this, despite being enrolled in several Islamic programs and attending lectures, no one had ever spoken about spirituality. They would always focus on the history of Islam, the laws of Islam, and so on. There are different ways an individual can find a solution to their suffering, mine was therapy through religion and becoming God conscious.

As 2015 came along, I felt different! I thought depression was going to strike again, but that year it didn't. I was depressed for almost four years straight, but after I took that pledge with Allah (swt), everything changed. However, I was still anxious but not as severe. I started referring to my anxiety as "anna," and that caught on among my family members. It was funny because they began using it in their own lives, saying things like, "this is causing me anna," or "this place is anna free." Before taking the vow with Allah (swt), my anxiety was so harsh that I couldn't handle speaking on the phone to place an order, or pick up food from a restaurant for myself. Socially, I wasn't able to communicate properly with others. Learning to live in the now helped me have better control over my anxiety because it taught me to slow down the moment, make good decisions, and realize what was at hand wasn't that complex at all. I went from being terrified to speaking to people, to becoming a substitute teacher and controlling classes that had over 30 students. Something I never imagined! I then went on to graduate with my bachelor's degree, which if you remember wasn't even a part of the plan.

In 2016 I began to write and share posts on social media with the intention of thanking Allah (swt) for all that He (swt) has done for me. I had no intent of writing The Untold Whispers of the World, zero. I just wanted to serve Allah (swt), and I really didn't know how, but I always had a knack for writing, so I decided to use this skill to spread His (swt) message. My whole mindset shifted, and it all happened after taking that covenant in 2014. Now, let me be clear what I mean by covenant, it wasn't only something that I said, but I made sure my actions followed as well. I rigorously reflected to understand what the meaning of this world is and my purpose in it, and it boiled down to only two things in my opinion. This temporary world is here to test us and our purpose is to obey and serve Allah (swt) in anything and everything we do, like the Prophet Muhammad (saww) and AhlulBayt (as).

To end, I enrolled back in university in 2017 and completed my master's degree two years later. Something I thought was impossible as well. To be clear, I am not bringing up these accomplishments for boasting reasons, such a trait is out of my character. I mention them to show you that when we are powered by Allah (swt) anything is possible, so long as it is within the boundaries of permissibility. Many of us never unlock our full potential because we are distracted by the Dunya, neglect our Islamic duties, and continue to sin. Having said that, to me, worldly accomplishments are nice and all, but the best accomplishment in this world is to be God conscious, to have Taqwa to the highest degree. Sometimes, I look back and I miss those dark days where I was severely depressed and anxious; I felt so close to Allah (swt), but then I learned that such closeness was dependent on being in such a state. One of the most difficult obstacles is trying to obey and serve Allah (swt) when life is going your way.

People have praised me and have called me special due to my writing, but I am neither special nor worthy of praise. Such remarks may feed the ego and make an individual feel like they're better or "holier" than everyone else. I don't consider myself either of these things. I am nothing but a servant of Allah (swt) and a student of Islam. I hope even this, Allah (swt) accepts from me. I am nowhere near where I need to be, and I have many flaws I have to work on. However, so long as I am breathing, I am determined to put out the best version of myself mentally, physically and spiritually, by Allah (swt), and you should too. A God conscious community can help expedite the reappearance of our beloved Imam Mahdi (atfs).

[1] "Don't submit to this world and what's within it, for surely, without a doubt, death will end us and end it."- Imam Ali (as).

Fi Amanillah,

Nadr Aboukhodr

[1]From "The Soul Cries" by Imam Ali (as)

Contents

DISCLAIMER iii

Acknowledgments v

My Personal Story vii

Reflection 1: Where is Allah (swt)? 1

Reflection 2: Struggling is Unavoidable 3

Reflection 3: Role Models 5

Reflection 4: Reaching Infallibility 7

Reflection 5: I Am Not My Trial .9

Reflection 6: Mental Change 10

Reflection 7: Sin Catcher 11

Reflection 8: Mankind is Flawed 14

Reflection 9: Who is Watching Me? 15

Reflection 10: Becoming Aware .16

Reflection 11: When We Feel Guilty 18

Reflection 12: Ninety-Nine 20

Reflection 13: Double Edge Sword 21

Reflection 14: First Step 23

Reflection 15: Television 24

Reflection 16: I Am Rich 25

Reflection 17: Brainstorm 26

Reflection 18: O'World 27

Reflection 19: Why Me? 28

Reflection 20: Honey 29

Reflection 21: The Chief Deceiver 31

Reflection 22: Fearing Allah (swt) 34

Reflection 23: Experiences 35

Reflection 24: I See Nothing, but Beauty 37

Reflection 25: Do We Commit "Shirk" Today? 39

Reflection 26: What is Your True Intention? 41

Reflection 27: Search and Find .42

Reflection 28: Put Allah (swt) Aside 44

Reflection 29: Handicapped 45

Reflection 30: I Want to Get High 46

Reflection 31: I Have an Exam to Take 48

Reflection 32: Money. 49

Reflection 33: Marriage and Naseeb 50

Reflection 34: Suspend Your Emotions 52

Reflection 35: Only God Can Judge Me 55

Reflection 36: Who is the Strongest Amongst You? 56

Reflection 37: Extravagance 57

Reflection 38: Now You Want to Be Religious? 59

Reflection 39: I Fear Poverty. 60

Reflection 40: Practice Religion in Private 62

Reflection 41: Meet My Friend, Death .63

Reflection 42: Don't Harden Your Heart 64

Reflection 43: What is Islam? 66

Reflection 44: What Am I?. 68

Reflection 45: Working For This Life 69

Reflection 46: I Can't Touch Her. 70

Reflection 47: Do I Believe in Allah (swt)?. 71

Reflection 48: How Do You Measure Them? 73

Reflection 49: Ramadan. 75

Reflection 50: Hidden Intentions 82

Reflection 51: To Struggle 83

Reflection 52: Oppression 84

Reflection 53: Conflicted Soul. 86

Reflection 54: The Checklist 88

Reflection 55: Disagreeing With Allah (swt). 89

Reflection 56: "Religion Was Forced...". 91

Reflection 57: Burden or Blessing? 93

Reflection 58: I Worship Myself 95

Reflection 59: Love 97

Reflection 60: Allah (swt) is Only Known When 99

Reflection 61: Trying to Fit In 101

Reflection 62: When I Am Ready 102

Reflection 63: Jealousy 103

Reflection 64: Oil and Water Can't Fuse 104

Reflection 65: I Can't Cry 106

Reflection 66: Dating 108
Reflection 67: Praying On Time 111
Reflection 68: Music 113
Reflection 69: Our Mind 115
Reflection 70: Today's Information 116
Reflection 71: The Structure of Our Lives 118
Reflection 72: Happiness. 119
Reflection 73: Anxiety 121
Reflection 74: Forgiveness. 123
Reflection 75: The Bigger Picture 125
Reflection 76: Happy New Year. 127
Reflection 77: To Be a Parent 129
Reflection 78: Desires 131
Reflection 79: Suicide 133
Reflection 80: Kindness and Revenge. 135
Reflection 81: Just Be Straightforward 137
Reflection 82: Driven By Allah (swt) 138
Reflection 83: Ambitions and Dream Chasing 140
Reflection 84: Proper Physical Hijab. 142
Reflection 85: Why Are You Angry? 144
Reflection 86: Void Within Me 146
Reflection 87: Friends 147
Reflection 88: Spiritual High. 150
Reflection 89: Heartbreak 151
Reflection 90: Repetition 153
Reflection 91: Ego 155
Reflection 92: Charity 157
Reflection 93: Clothes 158
Reflection 94: Red Cape 160
Reflection 95: She Makes More. 162
Reflection 96: Just Pray 164
Reflection 97: Drama & Rumors 167
Reflection 98: Hollywood 170
Reflection 99: Laid OFF 171
Reflection 100: Flaunting. 172

Reflection 101: Legacy 174

Reflection 102: Cancer. 176

Reflection 103: Ashura. 177

Reflection 104: Divorce. 179

Reflection 105: This Life 181

Reflection 106: Congratulations 183

Reflection 107: The Media. 184

Reflection 108: Opinions 185

Reflection 109: That Feeling 187

Reflection 110: The Future. 189

Reflection 111: Stingy 190

Reflection 112: Masturbation & Porn 192

Reflection 113: Testing His Seriousness 195

Reflection 114: I Want to Get to Know Her. 196

Reflection 115: Logistics 198

Reflection 116: Worldly Fear. 199

Reflection 117: I Am Getting Married. 201

Reflection 118: Vaccine 203

Reflection 119: Pandemic .204

Reflection 120: Our Freewill 206

Reflection 121: Care 208

Reflection 122: Love vs. Attachment. 210

Reflection 123: Confidence vs. Anxiety 215

Reflection 124: It's My Fault. 217

Reflection 125: Addicted to Being Sad 221

Reflection 126: Mutah 223

Reflection 127: Men's Mental Health 232

Reflection 128: An Individual's Image 236

Reflection 129: We Are Not Weak. 237

Reflection 130: Mental Wounds. 238

Reflection 131: Who Hired You?. 239

Reflection 132: What Truly is Hell? 240

Reflection 133: Become a Healer 241

Reflection 134: Ding-Dong Ditch 242

Reflection 135: Self-Growth 243

Reflection 136: What is Our Duty? 244

Reflection 137: Without Allah (swt) vs. With Allah (swt). 245

Reflection 138: Greatest Worry & Least Concern 246

Reflection 139: Belittling One's Problems 247

Reflection 140: We Must Stay Patient 248

Reflection 141: Before You Show OFF 250

Reflection 142: What is Stopping You? 251

Reflection 143: Shaking Hands With the Opposite Gender. 252

Reflection 144: I Wanted to Leave Mid-Lecture 254

Reflection 145: When Our Friends Pressure Us to Side With Them . . . 256

Reflection 146: What if I Fail?. 257

Reflection 147: Crossing a Point of No Return 258

Reflection 148: Morning Prayer (Fajr) 259

Reflection 149: Can We Be Friends? 260

Reflection 150: Is Going to the Gym Haram? 261

Reflection 151: Why Doesn't Allah (swt) Answer Our Prayers?. . .262

Reflection 152: You're Too Extreme 263

Reflection 153: Do it For Yourself. 264

Reflection 154: Why Haven't We Reached Our Full Potential as a
     Community? 265

Reflection 155: About Our Eyes 267

Reflection 156: Why Do I Need to Pray? 268

Reflection 157: Witnessing People Die Young 269

Reflection 158: Asking Allah (swt) For Help 270

Reflection 159: Speaking With an Atheist. 272

Reflection 160: There Are Two Types of Individuals 273

Reflection 161: A Couple Bad Years 274

Reflection 162: Detachment. 275

Reflection 163: They're Religious. 277

Reflection 164: Be Honest With Yourself 278

Reflection 165: Judging 280

Reflection 166: Imam Mahdi (atfs) 282

Reflection 167: Waiting 283

Reflection 168: Supporting Haram 284

Reflection 169: Pain. 285

Reflection 170: Battling Fear as a Community 286
Reflection 171: Comfort 287
Reflection 172: What You Lost 288
Reflection 173: Palestine 289
Reflection 174: Allah's (swt) Command 291
Reflection 175: The Destruction of Society. 292
Reflection 176: Negative Attitude 293
Reflection 177: Shaytan-Ophobic 294
Reflection 178: Heart Hardening 295
Reflection 179: Gambling 296
Reflection 180: Strange 298
Reflection 181: Ask Them 299
Reflection 182: The People of Lut (as) 300
Reflection 183: The Perfect Moment. .303
Reflection 184: Walk Behind Me 304
Reflection 185: Who Has a Better Relationship With Allah (swt)?. . . . 305
Reflection 186: The Test of Life 306
Reflection 187: Religious Family 307
Reflection 188: Life Without Social Media. 308
Reflection 189: Losing Opportunities .309
Reflection 190: It's an Every Moment Thing. 310
Reflection 191: When We First Got into Religion 311
Reflection 192: The Quran. 313
Reflection 193: Focus On the Why 314
Reflection 194: How to Stop Suffering 316
Reflection 195: Playing a Game 318
Reflection 196: The Right Tools 319
Reflection 197: Connecting With Allah (swt) 320
Reflection 198: Your Income. 321
Reflection 199: Alhamdulillah. 322
Reflection 200: Corruption 323
Reflection 201: Impulsiveness. 324
Reflection 202: Making Things Haram 325
Reflection 203: Changing For Someone 326
Reflection 204: It's Haram 327

Reflection 205: Thanksgiving 328
Reflection 206: Insects. 329
Reflection 207: Ghusl 330
Reflection 208: Threatening Your Family 331
Reflection 209: Our Parents. 332
Reflection 210: Saying No. 334
Reflection 211: They Asked. 335
Reflection 212: Starting Our Lives 336
Reflection 213: Certainty 337
Reflection 214: What IF. 338
Reflection 215: That One Time 339
Reflection 216: Letting Go. 340
Reflection 217: Be Specific 341
Reflection 218: Playing Favorites 342
Reflection 219: Paralyzing Yourself 343
Reflection 220: Wearing Gold 344
Reflection 221: Feeling Worthy. 345
Reflection 222: Capitalism 346
Reflection 223: Decision Making 348
Reflection 224: Faith 350
Reflection 225: Political Positions 351
Reflection 226: Modeling the Hijab. 352
Reflection 227: 3-Phases 353
Reflection 228: Alcohol 355
Reflection 229: Representing Islam. 357
Reflection 230: Out of Pity 358
Reflection 231: Taqwa 359
Appendix. 360

They said, "tomorrow…"

However, there came a time where tomorrow never came.

Reflection 1

Where is Allah (swt)?

Passage 1

We have this misconception that Allah (swt) is only present at the mosque or religious occasions which motivates us to act and dress a certain way, for the good of course. Now, obviously "something is better than nothing," but let's not be naive, and just stop there. Sure, out of respect we change our attitude when we enter a place of worship, but why settle? Realistically, Allah (swt) is everywhere. The image you portray should be consistent despite your surroundings. At loss are those who acknowledge Allah (swt), yet still choose to neglect Him (swt).

In the *Quran:

57:4- It is He who created the heavens and the earth in six days (periods) and then established His Dominion over the Throne. He knows whatever enters into the earth, what comes out of it, what descends from the sky, and what ascends to it. He is with you wherever you may be and He is Well-aware of what you do.

58:7- Did you not consider that Allah knows all that is in the heavens and the earth? There is not a single place wherein any secret counsel can take place between any three people without Allah being the fourth, nor five people without His being the sixth, nor any gathering of more or fewer people, wherever it may be, without His being with them. On the Day of Judgment, He will tell them about their deeds. Allah has the knowledge of all things.

67:19- Did they not see the birds above them, stretching out, and flapping their wings. No one keeps them up in the sky except the Beneficent. He certainly watches over all things.

* Quran English Translation by Muhammad Sarwar

Passage 2

Have you ever noticed how some individuals that return from Hajj or Ziyara are still wicked? At these locations they're praying, reciting, conscious of their actions, etc. Blatantly they appear holy! However, as soon as they return home and settle in, they're back to their sinful ways. Why is it that these individuals are only pious at such holy sites? One begins to wonder if this person actually went to Hajj, or were they just physically there going with the flow, and their soul was in another place?

You see, our crucial mistake is that we confine and limit Allah (swt). We put Allah (swt) in a box, and we are convinced He (swt) only exists in certain places. If we are of the belief that the only way to connect with Allah (swt) is to travel to these holy sites, then surely we are wrong. We lack consciousness! For example, suppose we see a police officer while driving, quickly we slow down, put on our seat belts, and toss our phones to the side. We do this because we are aware of the consequences, and we want to avoid trouble. We have this consciousness within us; where is it towards Allah (swt)? Oh yeah, "if I cannot see it, it is not real," right? Also, we don't capitalize on the clear signs that come our way. When death arrives, we do the basic societal norms like post, "rest in peace," mourn, wear black, but nothing too serious. When we see poverty and disaster strike, we say, "I feel terrible," and donate a few dollars, but nothing too serious. Death doesn't exist for you and I to show sympathy only; death exists to expose the reality of this world.

The *Quran states, "And certainly We created man, and We know what his mind suggests to him, and We are nearer to him than his life-vein" (50:16).

* Quran English Translation by Muhammad Habib Shakir

2

Reflection 2

Struggling is Unavoidable

Passage 1

*Quran,

"And We will most certainly try you with somewhat of fear and hunger and loss of property and lives and fruits; and give good news to the patient" (2:155).

According to society the standard nature for human beings is to avoid struggle, and to search for eternal happiness constantly. This world doesn't have the right means nor resources to convey a utopia. Allah (swt) says, "We will most certainly try you," meaning there is no way an individual can escape the struggle. As for happiness, we tend to seek happiness through others and materialistic objects. This is called "temporary happiness." For example, go purchase an item that you desire, and I guarantee the item you purchased will bring you pleasure for a certain period of time, then it's on to the next new product. It's a repetitive system almost like recycling.

Eternal happiness doesn't exist in this world. If eternal happiness and a struggle free life were meant to be in this world, what is left for heaven? Our true goal should be contentment. Having too many options isn't always necessarily a good thing, rather try to adapt to what you have, and make the best out of it.

* Quran English Translation by Muhammad Habib Shakir

Passage 2

When we speak to a family member or a random foreigner, sometimes they will say, "Back home the economy was awful; we struggled a lot. You have an opportunity here in the west, take advantage of where you are and do not struggle like us." Obviously, they're not saying anything wrong, they just want what's best for their child, nephew, niece, friend, and so on. However, such a statement might seem harmless, but in reality it is very dangerous because it plants a negative seed in our mind. They're indirectly hinting to us to run away from the struggle, and that to struggle is bad.

Anyway, many of our parents aren't aware of the difficulties we face in the west. Their greatest concern was financial struggle. Our struggle might be financially too, but there are also numerous barriers we face as well because we are exposed to so much. For instance, many parents tell their children before you even think of marriage you have to be financially secured, or in a promising academic program like medical school.

So, what ends up happening, as the children grow up, they already have in their mind that they cannot get married or engaged until they're in a perfect financial situation. So, they end up delaying marriage because the stigma around struggle is undesirable. Many parents are not realistic and do not take human nature into consideration! Today, many parents set up their sons and daughters to follow their sinful desires without even realizing it. Meaning, to some parents it's like, it's okay if my child sins, as long as he or she will not struggle financially in the future. Ironically, many of our parents got married at a young age in a country that had a terrible economy, right? But somehow still managed to do well for themselves over time. Why should the standard be different for us; why do we have to be in a perfect situation before we can commit to something that is needed and highly beneficial?

To end, don't fear the struggle, instead fear of becoming a sinner. When trying to attain spirituality, all factors must be taken into consideration and accounted for. What the people of the past failed to realize is that struggling is inevitable, and facing it instead of avoiding it makes one stronger because they become more dependent on Allah (swt). Had they been in the strongest economy, or the weakest, their circumstance was already ordained. What they failed to realize is that the struggle they went through was really a trial instead of a burden, gifted by Allah (swt) to find Allah (swt).

Reflection 3

Role Models

Passage 1

One of the greatest misunderstandings we can commit as individuals is taking human beings as our role models when it comes to practicing Islam. Islam is flawless, people are not. For instance, when we see or hear negative comments about someone who is regarded to have high faith we become astonished. Furthermore, sometimes we try to justify their gloomy actions in our personal lives. Meaning, when this individual of high faith commits a sin we assume that it is okay and say, "If they can do it, then we can do it as well."

Our only role models in Islam should be the Prophet Muhammad (saww) and AhlulBayt (as), who are infallible by Allah (swt). Now, ordinary human beings may reach a state of infallibility for a second, minute, hour, week, month, year, and so on, but only Allah (swt) knows what truly lies in their hearts, while the Prophet Muhammad (saww) and AhlulBayt (as) are guaranteed to be perfect always.

Passage 2

We must be careful of who we take as our role models, especially when it comes to religion. One main reason people walk away from Islam is because they weren't able to distinguish between the actions of mankind and the principles of Islam. Meaning, when they see a scholar or a "religious individual" do or say something hypocritical, they become upset with Islam, but the reality of such situations is humans are fallible. So, if they commit a sin or mistake it was because of their own fault; Islam has nothing to do with it. Islam was and still is perfect!

We assume just because an individual is very knowledgeable about religion he or she is supposed to be perfect, but when they do or say something wrong we lose all hope in them. Just because someone is knowledgeable about religion doesn't mean they're free of Shaytan's tactics, or have imprisoned their desires forever. This is what makes us humans; the journey to defeat Shaytan and desires is a long one that requires time, practice, and God consciousness. Matter of fact, when we grow as believers Shaytan attacks us more aggressively. That being said, who should we look up to when it comes to Islam? Plain and simple, the Prophet Muhammad (saww) and AhlulBayt (as), only. However, if someone fails in YOUR "eyes," try to be more understanding. Know that they too are going through their own struggles as well, despite what they know. Don't shame them! Rather, pick them back up and seek the straight path together.

Reflection 4

Reaching Infallibility

In my opinion a state of infallibility by human beings is very reachable, but the question that arises is, how long does this individual want to stay in the state of perfection?

The old aged expression we are normally used to is, "Humans are not perfect." I believe this proverb is an excuse to prevent us from progressing spiritually and connecting with Allah (swt). It is an excuse to keep indulging in the sweetness of the world; an excuse to fuel our materialistic desires. On the contrary, humans can do whatever they put their mind to. Once we are able to perceive that we are in the presence of Allah (swt) constantly, everything becomes different. Once we are able to master our Taqwa (God consciousness) we have no limit, by Allah (swt) of course. Suppose we sin 100 times per day, 20 sins for each human sense (sight, hearing, taste/speaking, smell and touch). At this rate our Taqwa is completely disregarded, but once we begin to understand and believe that Allah (swt) is always watching us, only then do we become awake. Instead of sinning 100 times we cut that number in half, and so on, until we reach zero. The QURAN and PRAYER are two of the most important keys to strengthen your Taqwa, because if you pray you're guaranteed to remember Allah (swt) five times a day. Each day is a new day, our actions of yesterday stay there. They don't follow us to our new day, but the consequences do if we don't sincerely repent. Every day we have the opportunity to be in a state of perfection.

We must train ourselves endlessly to see Allah (swt) in every single thing, no matter how small it is. The Imam (as) states, [2] "In everything I see, I see Allah (swt) before it, I see Allah in it, and I see Allah after it." Only then are we able to reach the level the Prophet Muhammad (saww) describes in a *narration that states, "When I (Allah) make him My beloved, I become his ears to hear, and his eyes to see and his hands to grasp, and his feet to walk. When he asks Me, I grant him and when he seeks My protection I protect him." However, this all goes back to the first question, how long?

* Hadith al-Qudsi
[2] Attributed to Imam Ali (as)

Reflection 5

I Am Not My Trial

Rumi goes on to say, [3] "You, who have lost yourself in a losing encounter, Distinguishing not the other from your own true self; At every shadow you are quick to exclaim: Ah! This is me! By Allah it is not you! Isolate yourself for a while from the crowd, And immerse yourself to the neck in thought. Indeed you shall find that you are one with One, Beautiful, serene and blessed is your self."

We must understand that the trial we are going through is not us. We must differentiate between the two. There is the trial then there is YOU. The *Quran states, "Allah does not impose on any soul a responsibility beyond its ability" (2:286). Let's not lose ourselves within a trial, rather let's use it as means to gain nearness to Allah (swt). Nevertheless, to blame others for our trial is a mistake and a distraction from reaching our true goal. We can either settle in the trial and make it our never ending abode, or we can master it and ask for another one. The choice is for YOU to choose only.

Those who surround us do not define us. We define ourselves. We should realize this now before it is too late. Amir al-Mu'minin Ali (as) states, [3] "I wonder at the man who searches for his lost things but doesn't care to recover his lost self [soul]."

---

[3] Ṭālib ʻAlī Ibn Abī. *Nahjul Balagha: Peak of Eloquence: Sermons, Letters and Sayings*. Tahrike Tarsile Qurʼan, 2009. –p.139

* Quran English Translation by Muhammad Sarwar

Reflection 6

Mental Change

Mental change is difficult, why? Because we have adapted to the same thought process over time, which makes us feel safe. So, we would rather live in our identical thoughts and play the same scenarios over and over. We refuse to step out of our mental comfort zone because it is alarming, plain and simple!

Instead of addressing ourselves, we tend to avoid ourselves. We purposely distract ourselves second by second with: social media, television, music, gym, sports, school, food, friends, family, work, drugs, and so on. Are we really that afraid to face our thoughts, that we frequently keep the environment around us noisy and busy? Are we really that afraid to spend time alone and resolve what we are suffering from, which is preventing us from mentally sprouting?

Have you noticed when we are alone and our environment is noiseless, the thoughts we are suffering from begin to fill our mind rapidly and we are forced to acknowledge them. It usually happens around the time before we fall asleep, but we are mentally drained and physically exhausted to fix anything, so we tend to put it off. Shouldn't we know that no matter how far we run away from our problems, it's our thoughts that we can never run away from.

Mental change takes time, effort, and work, like everything else we tend to prosper in. We have to want to change! We must spend time alone for a long period with no distractions at all, reflect and conquer. We have to face the realities of this world and know the reasons behind it. How do we expect to know Allah (swt) if we don't know ourselves? Let's stop oppressing ourselves with the mundane thoughts of the past and future, and let's start living in the present, and act accordingly to what He (swt) asks for. We owe it to ourselves, not to find ourselves, but to be the best worshippers we can be for ourselves.

Reflection 7

Sin Catcher

"Catching the sin" is one of the simplest strategies one can do. An individual doesn't just sin, there are steps he/she takes to reach the point of sinning. Focus on the sin(s). Study it and observe it thoroughly. Monitor the routine that leads you to the sin. That's the key, because if you don't, and you settle in the realm of the sin, the chances of pulling away become very difficult.

Moreover, discovering what takes you from point A to point Y (Z-The Sin) can be a blur during the birth of this process, but is well worth it in the long run. Suppose you improve just by a measurement of a centimeter, it is better than nothing. The next time around, you are a centimeter stronger. A centimeter doesn't stay a centimeter forever. As you become more conscious of Him (swt), a centimeter becomes an inch, and an inch becomes a foot, and so on. One will get to a point where his home will be point A, and when temptation, desire, and all evils of the world come knocking, they will be ready because they built and strengthened their army of willpower. Wage war on your sins!

Nonetheless, usually when one sins constantly their hearts become hardened. They sin as if it's their second nature, without feeling remorseful, guilty, or a centimeter of regret. Repentance is in their system, but it is buried so deep down and cemented that they forget it even exists. There are those who take pride in their sins. They're proud of their sins. They boast about their sins. They believe they are untouchable, and are naive of the fact that Allah (swt) controls everything. The *Quran states, "They are those on whose hearts, and their ears and eyes Allah has set a seal, and these are the headless ones" (16:108).

* Quran English Translation by Quran Hadi

Example: Marijuana

How to stop sinning? These steps can be used for any type of sin, and is not only limited to the example below.

Let's say my particular choice of sin is smoking marijuana, also known as weed. I smoke weed out of enjoyment; it's not a medical condition. Therefore, anytime I smoke out of a weed pen or "blunt," I am racking up sins. Today is the day I decide to stop because deep down I know what I am doing is haram, and the guilt is eating me alive. However, I keep on failing to stop, why? Because I try to stop when I am in the middle of the war. Meaning, I try to stop when I am around weed. This is why many of us have such a hard time trying to stop sinning.

Moreover, the following day is a new day, I wake up in the morning and the thought of smoking weed comes to mind. That is Battle #1! After thinking about it, I decided that today I am going to smoke weed; I lost Battle #1. Battle #2, my friends hit me up, and ask me if I want to chill and smoke? Am I going to win this battle? No, I am not. I respond with, "yeah I am down." Battle #3, I am now driving to my friend's house and I'm getting second thoughts, "maybe you should go back home" my conscience tells me. I tried to but I couldn't, my desire for weed is overpowering. Battle #4, my friends and I are together now and we finally decide what type of weed we want, now it's time to pick it up. I don't want to be a buzzkill, so I definitely lost this battle. It's WAR time. The drug is being passed around and it's time for me to take a hit, after everything is all said and done and I'm "high," I have decided to stop. But did I really decide to stop, or did my desire just get fulfilled for that day?

Next day comes along, and you guessed it, repeat. I am smoking weed. When we break it down, do you see where our focus should be? It's the small battles, not the war. If I could've just beat one of the four battles, I would've avoided going to war. That's how we stop sinning!

Grab a piece of paper, put your sin of choice on top, and you on the bottom. Draw out a road map, or list all the steps that you have to take before you commit that sin. Once you're able to visualize everything, start going to work! You might fail the first, second, third, fourth, the hundredth time!

However, each time you're becoming a little better and more aware. You're taking mental notes, using the power of prayer and dua, asking Allah (swt) for assistance, etc. Then guess what? Trial one hundred and one comes along and you finally succeed. You were able to stop the sin in its tracks during Battle #1, and it's no longer a temptation. Forget the war, and fight the battles!

Reflection 8

Mankind is Flawed

Mankind is flawed! Mankind has a beginning and an end. The norms of society are created by mankind. Therefore, if mankind is flawed then why do we continue to follow an imperfect system? Why do we allow society to dictate our lives? Society promotes a lifestyle that is unattainable, which leaves us constantly working towards it and distracting us from discovering the truth. The trends that society encourages can make us feel prideful and rare when followed. Truth be told, we are not special. Reflect on the human race and observe how everyone is similar to one another, and stuck in the same realm.

On the other hand, Allah (swt) has no beginning nor end. The religion of Islam is a perfect system. The ultimate Muslim(s) are the Prophet Muhammad (saww) and AhlulBayt (as). Don't become who society wants you to be, or who you think you should be, but be the one that Allah (swt) wants you to be. Doubt enters our hearts when we choose to follow Islam according to our preferences. Follow and serve Islam just like how the fourteen infallibles did. Would you rather be a servant of a man made system, or a perfect system? Your choice. When everything is said and done, no one is at loss or gain, but YOU.

Reflection 9

Who is Watching Me?

Growing up we were taught to fear authority. By authority I mean: parents, an officer, a teacher, and so on. How we behaved depended on who was observing us. This structure is successful until we reach an age of independence (mentally). Afterwards it becomes defective. Reason being, it is nearly impossible for any type of authority to be with us during every moment of our lives.

The *Quran states, "Does he not know that Allah surely sees" (96:14)? Only Allah (swt) is with us in every moment of our lives. Learn and teach to instill ONLY the fear of Allah (swt) in you and others. Acknowledge that you're in the presence of the All-Knowing, the All-Seeing, and the All-Hearing. Isn't it strange that we are able to follow the laws of this world in fear of paying its consequences, but we neglect the consequences of our sins?

* Quran English Translation by Quran Hadi

Reflection 10

Becoming Aware

Passage 1

In this day and age the struggle with oneself is demanding because we own a device that can access anything within seconds. The chances of sinning are very high, especially on social media. Be careful and aware of what you choose to look at, and what you choose to promote. What one chooses to look at is self-explanatory, without a doubt it is between Allah (swt) and themselves. However, what one chooses to promote is between Allah (swt), themselves, and the viewers. Let's say you like or share inappropriate pictures, profanity, places, music, etc. Not only do you put yourself at risk, but also those following/befriending you as well.

On the Day of Resurrection Allah (swt) states in the *Quran, "Till when they reach it, their hearing and their eyes and their skins will bear witness (testify) against them of what they used to do" (41:20). Again, be careful and aware.

* Quran English Translation by Quran Hadi

Passage 2

Before you share something on social media do you ever ask yourself if it will cause others to sin?

This is an important conversation to have with yourself. Sometimes what we share might make us feel good, but we should look at it from the other side as well, and ask ourselves if it is worth it.

Passage 3

One mistake that many of us commit is trying to predict how Allah (swt) will react when it comes to certain actions. For example, we often hear people say, "I don't think Allah (swt) will punish me if I do…"

Our job isn't to think what Allah (swt) will do or not. Such a mentality is misleading because it's based on assumptions, and these assumptions can be fueled by the whispers of the Shaytan.

Islam is clear cut and straightforward! Our duty is to follow what is ordained and leave the rest to Allah (swt).

Reflection 11

When We Feel Guilty

Passage 1

We cannot justify our sins. There is no balance between good and bad. For instance, we tend to sin, and afterwards, we convince ourselves that it is perfectly fine because we do an act of worship as well. We try to find a balance to feel less guilty of our sinful actions. A poet states, "Take no small sin lightly, for mountains are made up of sand."

Passage 2

Sometimes, when we feel guilty we like to make ourselves feel better by psyching ourselves out. Meaning, sometimes we know what we are doing is wrong, but we cannot stop doing it. So, instead what do we do? To make ourselves feel better we do something good, and tell ourselves, "This makes up for it."

This is not what Allah (swt) wants from us. Such a method is incorrect! The only substitute for bad sins is to stop doing them. Let's try not to deceive ourselves!

Passage 3

Feeling guilty isn't always bad! Sometimes we have to make ourselves feel guilty to wake up.

I am sure we can all relate to this scenario. Have you ever spent hours binge watching a TV show? Why is it that we can spend a great amount of time watching these shows, but have a difficult time watching or attending ONE Islamic lecture per week or month?

Sometimes we say we don't like the speaker or topic, but many of these shows we watch are boring in the beginning, however, we force ourselves to watch them because we heard eventually they will become better. Where is this mindset when it comes to religion? Why is it that when it comes to Islamic activities, it's always I have work or I cannot leave the house because of my children, but when it comes to leisure, we go above and beyond to make it work. It's unfortunate because when we plan for our vacations we are very precise, but planning to go to a local Islamic center becomes foreign to us.

We have to have these discussions with ourselves because they put things into perspective. Are we really doing everything that we can to gain nearness to Allah (swt) and become educated about Islam? Most of the time we aren't, and feeling guilty about this is not wrong.

The bottom line is, it's not that we don't have time for religion, it's that we don't see value in religion to make time for it!

Reflection 12

Ninety-Nine

A common misconception individuals state is, "a person doesn't need to practice their religion to have good morals."

For example, an Atheist does good even though he/she doesn't believe in Allah (swt). Let's take a step back! Over time an Atheist chose not to acknowledge Allah (swt) by his/her own free will. But if we go back to our origin (the creation process), *Allah (swt) blew into them from His (swt) spirit while He (swt) was creating them, regardless of what the person has now become.

To conclude, do we learn to adopt good morals or are they already instilled within us, and we are manifesting the 99 names of Allah (swt)? Our morals are already instilled within us! When we do good we are manifesting Allah's (swt) attributes whether we believe in Him (swt) or not! But to reach the highest state of morality we DO have to practice our religion. Morals aren't only limited to "please" and "thank you," or holding the door open for someone. There are moral attributes within you that you're not even aware of yet! You will only unlock them when you gain nearness to Allah (swt). How do you gain nearness to Him (swt)? You practice your religion.

* Quran English Translation by Quran Hadi -15:29

Reflection 13

Double Edge Sword

Oblivious is the one that saves others, but neglects oneself. Allah (swt) states in Chapter 80 of the *Quran:

33. And when the deafening cry comes,
34. The Day on which a man shall flee from his brother,
35. And his mother and his father,
36. And from his wife and his children,
37. Each one of them, That Day, will have concern enough to occupy him.

Do you know what is amusing about mankind? The way they try to give back to Islam. How they do it is questionable sometimes, because it helps the masses while hurting them.

Take for example Muslim sisters who observe hijab and are in the fashion industry. Their intention might be to promote modest wear among women, but many of them do this through the avenue of using themselves as "models." They might be convinced that what they're doing is righteous, but what they neglect is their own inner soul.

Their intention might be pure, but their actions are automatically put through a format where they have to compromise their beliefs to fit a status quo that doesn't really align with the Islam of the Prophet Muhammad (saww) and AhlulBayt (as). The question here is, is it worth it for such individuals to sacrifice their own relationship with Allah (swt) to teach others "how to dress modestly?" This is one out of the many instances; I believe this concept can be applied to politics, business, and so on.

We have to be careful in everything we do, be a little selfish when it comes to your relationship with Allah (swt). Just because we might find a void in society, it doesn't mean we have to quickly fill it. Understand what it comes with first! Don't be the type of individual where others benefit from your actions while you don't. Allah (swt) didn't task us to prove Islam to the world; we have to prove ourselves to Islam!

* Quran English Translation by Quran Hadi

Reflection 14

First Step

Laozi states, "A journey of a thousand miles begins with a single step." Islamically speaking we cannot compare one to another. For instance, if an individual took the time and effort to practice Islam and becomes more conscious of Allah (swt), he/she shouldn't fail to remember the steps they took to reach such a level of conviction. Those who practice Islam correctly, without a sense of pride or ego, will never think they're better than individuals who don't practice Islam at all, or individuals who are in their beginning/constant stage; this is because they frequently remember who they once were, and the ignorance they once had.

On our part we must practice the knowledge that we are receiving. For example, if a believing brother or sister approaches us about our incorrect actions, listen to what they're saying. Don't assume they're judging you, or they believe that they are wiser than you. Their awareness of Allah (swt) may have increased, and when they come to you with knowledge that means they care for you, and want you to become a person of not only good deeds, but high faith as well.

Reflection 15

Television

Are we more conscious of the creation than the Creator (swt)? A simple scenario we can all relate to is watching television and an inappropriate scene comes on.

1. When we are watching with our parents, we quickly change the channel due to the respect we have for them.
2. When we are watching with our younger siblings, we quickly shout out "cover your eyes" or "get under the blanket."
3. When we are watching alone, we quickly become glued to the television.

For number one and two we took action based on our surroundings, and protected our parents/siblings from a sin. However, for number two we failed to realize that a sin has no age limit. Meaning, just because we get older, it doesn't mean we are allowed to openly gaze at whatever we want. For this circumstance, it's best we join our siblings. For number three, how do we have the audacity to protect others, but not our own selves? How do we fail to realize that we are not alone, but we are in the presence of Allah (swt).

Reflection 16

I Am Rich

There are many definitions of wealth. However, the common definition of wealth we are used to is having an abundance of valuable possessions or money. Wealth shouldn't only be measured by a piece of paper, or limited to: status, homes, cars, etc. To others, wealth is quitting a severe addiction, and entering rehab. Wealth is getting out of bed while depression and anxiety try to chain you down. Wealth is providing for your family. Wealth can simply be mowing the lawn and maintaining it. The point is wealth can be anything!

Be considerate of others' definition of wealth. But what is the greatest wealth of all? In my humble opinion, our bank accounts might not be excessive, but I can assure you we are richer than we think. How? Because we are blessed with the knowledge of the Prophet Muhammad (saww) and AhlulBayt (as). We are blessed with a book where Allah (swt) is the author from beginning to end. Now, that is immeasurable.

Reflection 17

Brainstorm

Actions are fueled by desires. Desires are fueled by thoughts. Thoughts are fueled by intellect. When our intellect of Him (swt) is little, our actions become polluted. Once we increase our intellect of Him (swt), our actions can become pure, constantly.

Reflection 18

O'World

Passage 1

O' World, I have to ask, what do you want from me? Is it not enough that you have distracted me from my Lord? I tried to trap you, but little did I know you trapped me. I tried to chase you, but little did I know you were faster than me. I tried to deceive you, but little did I know you deceived me. O' World, how can I defeat you?

Passage 2

Beware of this "Dunya!" Just because it's giving you what you want, it doesn't mean it is your friend. By the time you realize what it has taken in return, it can be too late. How many people lost their way as soon as they got their way?

How many people do you know that were once committed to religion? They looked the part, but as time went on they rapidly changed for the worse, and who knows maybe you and I are next if we are not wary…

But how did this happen? For it was Dunya! It took everything from them. It deceived them to the point they became forgetful of their hereafter. No one is safe from Dunya, except those who are constantly remembering Allah (swt). Come back, before it is too late, because like how you're chasing Dunya, the Angel of Death is chasing you!

Passage 3

When one reflects about this World they will realize that they are just a "renter." There isn't a sense of true ownership in this Dunya; it is as if everything is just an illusion.

Whether it is your physical bodies or your materialistic possessions, you're just renting them for a period of time.

Reflection 19

Why Me?

When our hearts are in a state of torment and our brain isn't tranquil we begin to question our existence. We ask, "why me? Why, why, why?" What we fail to realize is, "when?" When a burden strikes, we become one with it. We cease to separate ourselves from it. Reason being, we believe what we are suffering from has no end, and is going to be prolonged for eternity.

Remembrance of death is one of the many blessings, believe it or not. Next time a burden strikes, pause for a moment, and tell yourself, "What you are going through has an end, guaranteed." Observe how precise Allah (swt) speaks about man in the *Quran, "Some people worship God to achieve worldly gains. They are confident when they are prosperous, but when they face hardships they turn away from (worship). They are lost in this life and will be lost in the life to come. Such loss is indeed destructive" (22:11).

* Quran English Translation by Muhammad Sarwar

Reflection 20

Honey

This world is known to be very sweet and pleasant when one indulges in it, but can it really be compared to the hereafter? According to the *Quran:

1. 6:32-And this world's life is naught but a play and an idle sport and certainly the abode of the hereafter is better for those who guard (against evil); do you not then understand?

2. 9:38-O you who believe! What (excuse) have you that when it is said to you: Go forth in Allah's way, you should incline heavily to earth; are you contented with this world's life instead of the hereafter? But the provision of this world's life compared with the hereafter is but little.

3. 13:26-Allah amplifies and straitens the means of subsistence for whom He pleases; and they rejoice in this world's life, and this world's life is nothing compared with the hereafter but a temporary enjoyment.

4. 16:96-What is with you passes away and what is with Allah is enduring; and We will most certainly give to those who are patient their reward for the best of what they did.

5. 29:64-And this life of the world is nothing but a sport and a play; and as for the next abode, that most surely is the life-- did they but know!

6. 40:39-O my people! this life of the world is only a (passing) enjoyment, and surely the hereafter is the abode to settle.

7. 47:36-The life of this world is only idle sport and play, and if you believe and guard (against evil) He will give you your rewards, and will not ask of you your possessions.

8. 87:16-Nay! you prefer the life of this world, 17-While the hereafter is better and more lasting.

These are the few of the many verses describing the reality of this world and the hereafter.

* Quran English Translation by Muhammad Habib Shakir

Reflection 21

The Chief Deceiver

Passage 1

Do you want to know who the greatest salesman known to mankind is? This salesman does not discriminate; he comes to all. He is the only being that can sell us a product that is malfunctioned, and we know it is malfunctioned, yet we still choose to buy it. If you haven't guessed yet, this being isn't your car or insurance salesman. This salesman is Iblis, better known as Shaytan.

There is no way around it, every day we are going to face the whispers of the Chief Deceiver, Shaytan. This egotistic creature comes in all forms. There are times we are able to recognize him quickly, and then there are times we are not. He can be beautiful and discreet while presenting himself, to the point that it becomes very difficult to refuse him. The **Quran states, Iblis said, "Lord, because you have caused me to go astray, I shall make earthly things attractive to (people) and mislead all of them" (15:39). However, by Allah (swt), he can never control us, but he will constantly try to provoke us. The *Quran states, "Then I-(Shaytan) will certainly come to them from before them and from behind them, and from their right-hand side and from their left-hand side; and Thou shalt not find most of them thankful" (7:17).

The Imam (as) states, [4] "he who loves you forbids you from committing sin." Let's reflect on this statement and look around us, and learn who supports our unacceptable actions that displease Allah (swt). On the other hand, we have to be careful of who and what we support as well, because we might be held accountable on the Day of Judgment for misleading others. To conclude, the *Quran states, "Like the Shaytan when he says to man: Disbelieve, but when he disbelieves, he says: I am surely clear of you; surely I fear Allah, the Lord of the worlds" (59:16).

Beware of this creature; he is out to get you. He can put the illusion of light in a dark, dirty place.

* Quran English Translation by Muhammad Habib Shakir
** Quran English Translation by Muhammad Sarwar
4Attributed to Imam Ali (as)

Passage 2

The Chief Deceiver, Shaytan, isn't one that should be underestimated. Many of us take this ugly creature and his minions lightly, as if they're nonexistent. We have created a naive platform with Shaytan. First, to conquer such an enemy, his abilities must be respected. For instance, before any two sport teams face off they watch film, and study one another. If one team fails to do so, then most likely they will lose the match drastically.

This is how our approach towards Shaytan should be. We have to study him! Shaytan works endlessly. He doesn't know any sick days, nor does he vacation in Florida. He capitalizes on every opportunity! Whisper here! Mumble there! The only time this animal ceases is when we fall into transgression! Sure, our tongues might refuse Shaytan, but do our hearts? Study him! When does he attack? How does he attack? Where does he attack? We already know why he is attacking! Use your past FORGIVEN mistakes to your advantage, to prepare for him now, tomorrow, and forever! This is our film.

To end, Shaytan seems to be a folk tale to many, or a myth, but unfortunately, he is very real! A speaker once shared an interesting story regarding a scholar who had a dream about Shaytan. In this dream, a man asked Shaytan if it is difficult persuading men and women to join him. Shaytan went on to say that there are three types of people. First, there are those that when I try to pull them in, I can't because it is as if I am tugging on weighty chains. They stand their ground firmly. The second type of men and women are less challenging; it is as if I am pulling on a rope. They put up a fight, but in the end they follow me. Lastly, the third type of men and women require the least amount of effort. It is as if I am yanking on a thin piece of string. I hardly jerk the string, and they're here. Finally, the man asked Shaytan which type he is. Shaytan laughed uncontrollably and said, neither...I don't waste my time on you. You come to me! Which type are you?

Reflection 22

Fearing Allah (swt)

We should fall in love with Allah (swt); if only we knew how much He (swt) loves us. It is true, He (swt) is known to be the All-Merciful and the All-Forgiving. So, let's ask ourselves, "How do we have the nerve to take advantage of such love?" Because of fear; we completely lack it. The strategy of fearing Allah (swt) is very important, when we don't have this in our belief system, we are truly setting ourselves up for failure.

However, many of us believe fearing Allah (swt) is bad, but that is not true. Fearing Allah (swt) keeps us aware and sharp. If anything, love can be taken advantage of, but that's not to say we shouldn't love Allah (swt). Rather, when we meet our sins we should battle them with the fear of Allah (swt). This is the strongest weapon in our arsenal that is always overlooked. I never once took advantage of fear, but I always found myself taking advantage of mercy.

We tend to shy away from conversations that deal with fear, and we actually believe that hell is some sort of myth, that it doesn't exist! We have adopted a mentality that we can do whatever we desire, and all we have to do is repent, and everything will be okay; but the Imam (as) goes on to say, [5] "To commit a sin willingly, with hope of forgiveness is the worst of sins." That is one side of the spectrum. The other side preaches that they have already done so much and accepted hell as their abode, as if they're certain hell is comfortable and cozy.

If the love of Allah (swt) isn't enough to cease our sinful ways, then we must depend on fear. It's the reminder that cannot be hidden, and prevents us from following our whim. Are we uncertain of His (swt) message? The *Quran states, "And believe in what I have revealed, verifying that which is with you, and be not the first to deny it, neither take a mean price in exchange for My communications; and Me, Me alone should you fear" (2:41).

---

[5] Attributed to Imam Ali (as)

* Quran English Translation by Muhammad Habib Shakir

Reflection 23

Experiences

Passage 1

There are many routes one can take! To narrow it down, there is either a worldly route or a hereafter route, more commonly known as the straight path. The worldly route is based on desire, whim, and so on. It is a much easier path to take compared to the route of the hereafter because one is only taking themselves into consideration. On the other hand, the straight path is a bit more challenging because one has to factor Allah (swt) into every thought and action, but is much more rewarding.

Every individual living today has an advantage on their side, known as history. It is true, history does repeat itself! Before one makes a decision they should research the history of their decision. They should consult their elders who might have taken that same decision in their past. One doesn't need to act on their decision to discover the outcome of it. History will give you an idea of the matter. For those who have made arrangements with the worldly route, are you curious to know what the people of the dead utter about such a direction?

*Quran,

23:99- Until when death overtakes one of them, he says: Send me back, my Lord, send me back;

23:100- Haply (perhaps) I may do good in that which I have left. By no means! it is a (mere) word that he speaks; and before them is a barrier until the day they are raised.

Do you still question the worldly route and where it leads to? If that's the case, let's find out what the Chief Deceiver Shaytan says about the worldly route. The *Quran states, "And the Shaytan shall say after the affair is decided: Surely Allah promised you the promise of truth, and I gave you promises, then failed to keep them to you, and I had no authority over you, except that I called you and you obeyed me, therefore do not blame me but blame yourselves: I cannot be your aider (now) nor can you be my aiders; surely I disbelieved in your associating me with Allah before; surely it is the unjust that shall have the painful punishment" (14:22). Glory be to Allah (swt), we have the worst creature ever created admitting this. Yet we still choose to befriend him and his journey? Certainly we are not physically asleep, but we aren't awake.

* Quran English Translation by Muhammad Habib Shakir

Passage 2

Experiences, they say to know what you want you must experience it. However, there are many experiences in life that we don't have to go through first hand. We can learn about them from multiple different platforms.

This idea that we only learn through experiences shouldn't sit well with us. In fact, the aftermath of many experiences brings a great amount of hardship that we could've easily avoided had we learned from others.

Why do we have to put ourselves through certain situations to find out the outcome of something when we could've simply researched it? This is where the challenge lies, convincing our curious soul that such experience is harmful for us without needing to experience it. Save yourself sometime, ask before you act!

Reflection 24

I See Nothing, but Beauty

Glory be to Allah (swt) for blessing us with trials to gain nearness to Him (swt). Had we known the value of such trials we would call for them. When you look at the history of the Prophets (as) and Imams (as), you'll discover that they faced the most difficult and challenging trials.

Do you want a trial of patience? Look at Imam Ali (as) who waited 20+ years to become caliph of the Ummah. Do you want a trial of wealth? Look at Prophet Sulaiman (as) who used all his wealth to relay the message of Allah (swt). Do you want a trial of an oppressive government? Look at Prophet Musa (as) who split the sea, only to drown the tyrant Pharaoh and his men. If you want a trial of orphans, look at Imam Hasan (as) and Husayn (as) who lost their mother Lady Fatima (as) at a young age. If you want a trial of losing a child, look at Prophet Ya'qub (as) who lost Prophet Yusuf (as) for years before reuniting with him. If you want a trial of an unfair and unjust system, look at Imam Musa al-Kazim (as) who was imprisoned for countless years for no legitimate reason. Do you want a trial of morality and manners? Look at the Prophet of Islam, Muhammad (saww), and how he treated human beings while spreading the message of Islam.

The standard of how burdensome one's life may get has already been set. The worst of trials have already happened to our beloved Prophets (as) and Imams (as). The trials we face today aren't going to be anything new. Let's research how they responded to their trials, and make the connection with our own personal trials that we face. Now I am not trying to take anything away from the events and hardships an individual encounters today, but rather I want to focus on how we should respond to such experiences. On the day of Ashura (the greatest trial/tragedy known to mankind), after witnessing his (as) family and companions massacred, after being in critical pain, Imam Husayn (as) still went on to show contentment and gratitude towards Allah (swt). Do you see the difference between him (as) and us?

Nonetheless, after such a profound perspective some individuals will say, "How can we be compared to the Prophets (as) and Imams (as)? They are infallible and we are not, they have knowledge of the unseen." If that's the argument here, then what do you say about Lady Zaynab (as). She wasn't a Prophet (as) or Imam (as), or even part of the fourteen infallibles, but had reached such a high state of consciousness of Allah (swt) that she was able to say, "I see nothing, but beauty."

Reflection 25

Do We Commit "Shirk" Today?

Passage 1

During the period of Prophet Ibrahim (as) the people of the time were known to be idol worshippers. In Islam this is known as shirk, which is the practice of polytheism, or in simpler terms, associating partners with Allah (swt). Such a sin isn't acceptable. Do we commit shirk today? By Allah (swt), I am going to relay simple scenarios that we can relate to. From there what you conclude is between Allah (swt) and you. It's time for prayer, according to the Adhan (call for prayer) prayer is regarded to be the best of actions, "hasten to the best of actions." It's our duty to let go of our worldly affairs and worship Allah (swt). Now, I am not going to focus on the things we cannot drop due to certain circumstances, rather I am going to focus on the things we can easily drop, but we choose not to.

1. It's time for prayer but the festivities on my cell phone, video games, television, etc., are amusing. The game is on! I cannot miss a play.

2. It's time for prayer, however, the gathering I am currently at is fascinating. Laughter is in the air; there are snacks everywhere! There is no way I can leave. I don't want to miss anything.

3. It's time for prayer, but I have a difficult exam tomorrow; I must continue to study. My worldly future depends on this exam. Forget about my eternal future.

4. Prayer is at 7:10 pm but the movie starts at 7:00 pm, and the team wants to go eat and shop after. I'll try to pray when I get back.

5. It's time for prayer but I wonder who is going to pump the iron at the gym? It's my responsibility!

6. It's been time for prayer, I just got off work. I already delayed prayer due to my job. However, I am not satisfied or content with how much I made today. So I have to delay prayer more and voluntarily go to my other job to chase the world more. I cannot go home and read the Quran, pray, grow spiritually, and sit with my family because I see no physical reward in that. As long as there are hours in the day, I have to milk each one to the max so I can collect green paper.

So ask yourself, "On a daily basis how many things do you willingly choose over Allah (swt)? How many things do I worship before Him (swt)? How many partners did I put on the same level next to Him (swt)?" Live your life revolving around Allah (swt), and not a day will go to waste. Do otherwise, and every day will be a loss.

Passage 2

Our commitment to Allah (swt) must be stronger than what we desire. For example, how many times have you delayed prayer because you were in "study mode," or because you had an "important" outing with your friends to the movies or dinner?

To discipline your soul, you must do the opposite of what it desires. Meaning, sometimes the vibe is good, the gathering is chilling, and prayer hits, so you tell yourself, "I don't feel like praying right now and killing the mood." I know many of us can relate to such a scenario. It's so important we choose Allah (swt) in these matters, because from this Allah (swt) notices our commitment, and from there He (swt) will begin to reveal Himself (swt) more to us. Sometimes we brush off such things, but they're so crucial when it comes to spirituality.

Prove your commitment to Allah (swt) by actions, not just words.

Reflection 26

What is Your True Intention?

In modern day, when society sets a trend we become inclined to follow it, whether we have pure intentions or not. For instance, when it comes to Islam many of us take it as a trend instead of a way of life. With any trend comes competition; with competition comes boasting, which can lead us to fall in a state of riya. [6] "Riya means to falsely make oneself appear to be virtuous, good natured or a true believer before people for the sake of earning their respect and admiration, or for the purpose of gaining a good reputation among them."

A *scholar once said, "Shaytan will use anything; he will even use religion to mislead a person." How can we relate such a profound statement to our everyday lives? Simple, before you do anything you must constantly ask yourself, why? I will use myself as an example. What is the reason I am sharing this post? Am I sharing it to receive excessive "likes" and praiseworthy comments? Am I sharing it to get a certain person's attention? Am I sharing it to show off the knowledge I have, or how creative I can be with regards to the poetry I write, or the pictures I draw? Am I sharing it to make a profit?

On the other hand, am I sharing it to benefit others? Am I sharing it strictly for Allah (swt)? What is my non-mysterious straight forward intention/reason behind me sharing anything? The Imam (as) states, [7] "When words come from the heart of anyone, they will find a place in the heart of another." Don't act out of desire, keep your heart obedient. Before you do anything, if 99.9% is for Allah (swt), and the rest is for your own personal gain, stop right there and try again another time, even if the ounce of ego in you is as small as a seed. We may be able to fool anyone, but we can't fool Allah (swt).

[6] "Diseases of the Soul: Pretending Virtuousness (Riya)." *Al-Islam.org*, 18 Aug. 2019.
* From a lecture by Hajj Khalil Jaffer.
[7] Attributed to Imam Ali (as)

Reflection 27

Search and Find

What if our daily actions are haram (forbidden), but we are not aware of it? What if the way how we present ourselves is un-Islamic, but we do not perceive it? To be straight forward, I am writing this reflection with the intention to raise awareness regarding our duty as Muslims who are striving to perfect themselves. This reflection isn't intended to hurt, offend, or condemn anyone. I have no authority to do such a thing. I truly care and fear for my brothers and sisters in faith, just like how I care and fear for myself. Anyway, every moment we are blessed with we can either guard against evil, or indulge/promote it. To give everyone the benefit of the doubt, including myself, sometimes we don't know what is considered haram (forbidden), halal (allowed), and makrooh (disliked). We truly do things out of innocence at times, which is understandable to a certain point.

Having said that, Glory be to Allah (swt) who blessed us with resources to gain nearness to Him (swt). Depending on the respected Marja' you follow, it is a must that we visit their books, websites, lectures, and so on. It's our duty to research what is permissible and non-permissible. This is when our freewill should come into play. Isn't it ironic that we get opinionated when it comes to fatwas (a ruling on a point of Islamic law given by a recognized authority) that are not in our favor? When a doctor diagnoses you with a sickness, do you question them? Me neither. That same concept should be applied when it comes to certain fatwas scholars issue. They know more than you and I; they have countless years of knowledge under their belt that is based on the teachings of the Quran and hadiths (narrations) by the Prophet Muhammad (saww), and AhlulBayt (as). Lastly, we might be doing something that we think is completely meaningless, but we truly might not know the reality of the act, and how harmful it is to our souls. A minor example for women, it is noted that using cosmetics publically is problematic. For men, there has been a misunderstanding regarding what is allowed and not when it comes to interacting with the opposite gender.

Research what your respected scholar says about these matters and more. Do not take the word of your forefathers. We might be collecting sins without even knowing it.

Reflection 28

Put Allah (swt) Aside

Have you ever heard someone say "put Allah (swt) and religion aside"? This phrase is commonly used by many, especially when it comes to business. We cannot separate Allah (swt) from our daily lives at any point, it just doesn't work that way, and whoever believes they can, they're being foolish. This is Allah's (swt) world, and we are living in it. It is not the other way around! He (swt) is the Creator, while we are the creation.

Allah (swt) is not an OPTION! Whether we like it or not, we have to take Him (swt) into consideration. We are temporary, while He (swt) is everlasting, and yet, we have the nerve to say put Him (swt) aside. We cannot remove Allah (swt) from any equation because He (swt) is the equation, while we are the variables. Let's stop such egotistic chatter, it is embarrassing! Let's renew our vows to Allah (swt) before it is too late.

To what extent does Allah (swt) have control over us?

*Quran,

"And He it is Who takes your souls at night (in sleep), and He knows what you acquire in the day, then He raises you up therein that an appointed term may be fulfilled; then to Him is your return, then He will inform you of what you were doing" (6:60).

* Quran English Translation by Muhammad Habib Shakir

Reflection 29

Handicapped

Typically when we come across an individual who is either: deaf, visually blind, mute, or physically paralyzed, we quickly begin to sympathize with them. Without a doubt it is not wrong to sympathize for those who are handicapped! May Allah (swt) protect/strengthen them, and bless those who care after them.

However, for the moment let's view those who are disabled from a different perspective, and try to uncover the blessings within their disadvantage, or maybe it is an advantage? You can decide. First, we can all agree that all kinds of suffering must come to an end. *Quran, "Every soul shall taste of death..." (3:185). Second, after we taste the inevitable, we are resurrected and tried based on our intentions and actions. Third, any human being would hope their intentions and actions were pure and not sinful to avoid punishment. Lastly, during the Day of Resurrection Allah (swt) states in the *Quran, "Until, when they reach it, their hearing and their eyes and their skins will testify against them of what they used to do" (41:20). *He (swt) also says, "On that day We will set a seal upon their mouths, and their hands shall speak to Us, and their feet shall bear witness of what they earned" (36:65).

Having said that, if our limbs and senses are going to testify against us, I wonder how many sinful scenes a visually blind person avoids due to their condition? I wonder how many vulgar words a deaf person avoids due to their condition? I wonder how many backbiting situations a mute person avoids due to their condition? I wonder how many forbidden affairs a physically paralyzed person avoids due to their condition? The intention of this reflection isn't to take away anything from those who are handicapped, or try to belittle their disability, rather it's a chance to discover hidden blessings from a different perspective.

* Quran English Translation by Muhammad Habib Shakir

Reflection 30

I Want to Get High

Disaster is inevitable! We are bound to face difficult trials and dark tunnels. As disaster strikes, we run! We run to our comfort zone. We run to our safe haven. We run to our "high." Basically, we run to something that makes us forget the pain and sadness for the moment. We all have a different "high," for some it can be: drugs, alcohol, music, shopping, and food. For others, it can be: family, friends, career, school, books, hobbies, and more. Some good, some bad. All these "highs" have something in common, but first, by definition a "high" is something that makes one feel excited and forgetful of the moment. Anyway, what they all have in common is that they all come to an end at some point.

Let's take music for example, suppose an individual is feeling down. They depend on their favorite song to lift them back up. However, their favorite song only lasts a maximum of five minutes. Meaning, the individual feels better about themselves for a good five minutes. So what does he or she do next? Either replay or move on to another song. Do you see the problem here? The individual is relying on something that has an end. Another example, I am going on vacation. I am so happy to get away from the responsibilities and hardships of life. However, as soon as I get back from my vacation, I feel down again, and wait until my next vacation to feel good again. Again, I am depending on something that has an end.

We must stop running to this world for our "high." When difficulty hits, run to Allah (swt). Depend only on Him (swt). We must stop distracting ourselves with materialism. We must understand the creation of man. When Allah (swt) created us, He (swt) programmed us to feel tranquil when we remember Him (swt), not through materialism. *Quran, "Those who believe and whose hearts are set at rest by the remembrance of Allah; now surely by Allah's remembrance are the hearts set at rest" (13:28).

Look at history, there are many who have accomplished more than you and I. They have reached a status and wealth that one can only dream of, but when you ask them, "How do you feel?" They will tell you, "Something is missing." So what do they do? They move on to the next big thing. They set new status goals and try to accumulate more wealth, believing that will fill in the void. If only they knew, mankind will never be satisfied until he or she remembers their Creator, and OBEYS Him (swt). We have to stop running in circles, and start following the path that leads us to Allah (swt). By Allah (swt), I wonder how mankind would behave if the veils of time were removed. Meaning, if we knew how long we had until our last breath, how then would we behave?

* Quran English Translation by Muhammad Habib Shakir

Reflection 31

I Have an Exam to Take

Majority of men and women are very selfish. They will not do an act unless they receive some type of reward back. We all have taken an exam before at some point in our lives. When exam time comes around, we are there on time because we see the reward within it. We know by taking this exam, it will bring us one step closer to achieve our "goals/dreams."

Also, we are aware of the consequences if we miss or fail the exam, and where it leads to. So we are very cautious, very careful to achieve this ONE worldly affair. We set a bunch of alarm clocks and tell our friends and family members to, "Make sure I am awake around this time!" WHERE is that same mentality when it comes to prayer? Obviously, such a mentality exists within us according to the exam example, but why do the majority of us fail to have such a mentality when it comes to prayer? Because we cannot see the reward of prayer. Also, we cannot see the consequences of delaying and missing prayer. If our eyes cannot perceive it, we won't believe it. We spoke about "exam time," let's go back one step to preparing for an exam. We spend the whole night reading, highlighting, note taking, and studying, because we know there is something on the line. Where is that same mentality when it comes to the Quran?

Now, I am not trying to provoke anyone to lock themself up in a room and pray a hundred times, and read the whole Quran in one day. Rather, question yourself. Ask yourself, "Do I really believe in Allah (swt)?" And if you do, "To what extent do I believe in Him?" Logically speaking if we had 100% certainty in Allah (swt), which is the greatest reward ever, then reading the Quran and praying would be more valuable to us than air. However, if it's not at 100% it's okay, but what's not okay is oppressing yourself. Meaning, when you have endless resources to get it to 100% but you choose to be arrogant.

48

Reflection 32

Money

Not to say acquiring money is wrong, but there are those who have taken money as their God. Financially speaking, when you ask someone, "How much money do you want to make?" Their initial response is always, "Enough, enough to be able to live a comfortable lifestyle and to stay stable." Such a statement is flawed! Reason being is that our state of comfort and stability shouldn't come from wealth, rather it should only come from Allah (swt). We must understand that if we become rich it's not only because we worked hard for it, but it is because Allah (swt) allowed it, and He (swt) is testing us to see how we are going to use such wealth. *Quran, "You shall certainly be tried respecting your wealth" (3:186).

That being said, are we going to use it for His (swt) sake or are we going to hoard it, become greedy, use it on forbidden worldly affairs, excessive materialism, and desires? The more you have, the more you're accountable for! Obviously the test of a rich person is more difficult than a poor person. Be careful what you pray for and how much you pray for, because Allah (swt) will answer.

Use your time wisely in this world and try to suspend chasing unnecessary worldly affairs. Meaning, if one has prayers to make up, use your time for that instead of chasing something that brings no value to you after you die. By Allah (swt), I am not trying to say don't seek and provide, rather take the proper measurements and earn only what you need. From person to person needs might differ, but the overall idea is that when we begin to chase money while neglecting our Islamic duties, the money does more harm than good. The Imam (as) said it beautifully, [8] "What a companion your money is, that it only benefits you once it leaves you."

* Quran English Translation by Muhammad Habib Shakir
[8] Attributed to Imam Hasan (as)

Reflection 33

Marriage and Naseeb

The word "naseeb" loosely translates to destiny or fate. Naseeb is commonly misused, especially when it comes to marriage. For example, there are those who marry an individual that consumes alcohol, and they have knowledge of this, but they marry the alcoholic anyway. When struggle arrives in the marriage, or the marriage fails, the first thing they say is, "Naseeba, it was written for me." Does mankind actually believe Allah (swt) will set them up for failure in such a way? Never! To marry an alcoholic was the individual's choice. That was not naseeb! Sure, maybe crossing paths (at school, work, mall, wedding, social media, etc.) with the alcoholic might have been naseeb, but to marry him or her was the individual's choice. This example is not only limited to alcohol, it can be used for almost everything.

Speaking of marriage, we cannot let our emotions cloud our judgment. We have to know who we are going to marry on all levels, not just on an emotional level. Based on common observation and history, in my opinion, I believe there are three types of marriages.

1. The couple whose main goal is Allah (swt). This marriage has a high chance of being successful because their focus has no limit, it is never ending.

2. The couple who have two different main goals. For instance, one partner's focus is Allah (swt) and the other partner's focus is worldly affairs. This type of marriage may face struggle in the present, but will most definitely struggle in the future, because after the couple completes their "bucket list," and their children have grown up, they will hit a plateau during their old age. Sure they can tolerate each other and whatnot, but their marriage dies out and lack of purpose enters the marriage. Of course, it doesn't always lead to a divorce, but at the same time the marriage isn't reaching its full potential.

3. The couple whose main goal is the world and completely neglects Allah (swt). A prime example of such marriages are celebrity marriages. We are all well aware of their ways, and the result of their ways.

Be cautious of those who don't fear Allah (swt), and don't waste your time trying to change them. I can't change you; you can't change me! You can only change yourself; I can only change myself! To conclude, stop basing an ideal marriage on a two hour movie and 30 second commercials. Marriage is a beautiful covenant, and for it to reach its full beauty, cement Allah (swt) as the main common goal.

Reflection 34

Suspend Your Emotions

Emotions are mischievous if one doesn't stay alert. Imam Ali (as) states, [9] "I warn you of the world. It has decorated itself with deception and deceives with its decoration." Let's try to connect this statement to emotions. The majority of human beings' thought process is only emotionally driven; we conceal the part of our mind that deals with logic. Such a process can be destructive! We go through hardship and pain when we could have easily avoided it through a moment of reflection.

In many cases people tend to introduce strong emotions early on in a potential relationship before it has gotten "serious." By "serious," I mean the Islamic definition, not societies'. This reflection is about the steps an individual takes when they develop an emotional connection for someone before it gets serious, and why it is not okay. Let's start off at the root of a potential relationship, the very beginning, when an individual has the intention to get to know someone. This process starts off with the eyes. Meaning, the first thing an individual looks for is attraction. When they find someone who meets their physical preferences their emotions begin to boil. They probably haven't said a single word to the individual, and yet, they're slowly becoming emotionally attached to them because they're creating different situations in their mind about possibly being together.

Now let's say the two individuals agreed to get to know one another, so they begin the process. Dull questions are asked such as, "What is your favorite show, color, food, etc.?" They agree on many basic things and have very little differences, but they aren't asking the serious questions. After sometime they realize the conversation between them is flowing, and right then and there they conclude that they're "the one." At this point emotions are flaring and erupting. They continue this same repetitive process for a long period of time. Now emotions are deeply invested between the two, and they still haven't gotten serious.

Having said that, several months go by and the man is emotionally connected to the woman; she's emotionally connected to him as well! However, after the infatuation phase has passed the man realizes the woman is saying or doing something he disapproves of. First time he lets it go because he is not sure how she will react. Emotionally they're in heaven, and he doesn't want to be the one that messes that up, so he ignores it. On a side note, this is what usually happens in some relationships. One person doesn't mention what they're not okay with not because they can't, but because they're afraid. They're afraid of conflict, because with conflict the chances of losing the individual increases. So they avoid it and suppress how they truly feel, because many times when a person loses someone they're emotionally tied to self-destruction enters their world, and they don't want to go through that.

Anyway, back to the example. The second time around she does something different that he is not okay with. Third, fourth, and fifth, and he turns a blind eye to everything. Before he knows it there's a huge wave of things he is not okay with in front of him. He wants to marry her and get serious with her, but now he is having second thoughts; however, instead of ending things he decides to continue because he is emotionally connected to her.

Now, suppose he did address the first thing he wasn't okay with, and they did resolve it, but what about the other things that continued to come up? Is he trying to mold and change a person to his liking, or is he trying to find a potential spouse that he already shares similar views and goals with? This is why it's important to be on the same page from day one! One must skip the whole forbidden flirtatious phase and dodge igniting the trigger for emotions. Yes, the man is avoiding conflict, but in reality he is building internal pressure as well! According to science, when pressure exceeds its limitation something must explode. An explosion may lead to destruction, and destruction leads to death, if not physical death, then mental death, which consists of "what ifs," curiosity, and so on. One doesn't have to go through this process to see the end.

If we emotionally and LOGICALLY think, we can see the end of anything, or get a hint of it before getting there; it is only when we become emotionally driven, that we become blind. To end, it all began with an emotional spark on the inside. Do you now see how something so beautifully decorated can be really deceiving and deceptive at times? To avoid this process I urge everyone to try to suspend their emotions during the process of getting to know someone for marriage, and communicate with one another about real life scenarios. You don't want to be emotionally invested in someone only to later find out that they're not your type, because it will be hard to disconnect from them. I have heard situations where couples end their engagement or marriage after a brief time for this reason; they knew the potential spouse wasn't for them, but they introduced their emotions too early and built a strong connection that was hard to walk away from at that time, even though they knew they needed to. They decided to push through, and eventually separated when it got too bad. Emotions and feelings aren't enough to save a relationship! There is a proper time to introduce your emotions, and it definitely is not in the beginning.

[9] Ṭālib 'Alī Ibn Abī. *Nahjul Balagha: Peak of Eloquence: Sermons, Letters and Sayings*. Tahrike Tarsile Qur'an, 2009. –p.487

Reflection 35

Only God Can Judge Me

There are those who believe death is only for the old, as if death hasn't been claiming many youth nowadays. They live a sinful carefree life as if they're promised "no end." When approached and told, "Your actions are detrimental," they say, "only God can judge me." They stand between truth and falsehood. For instance, brothers who plot their lives based on their animalistic desires; they know what they're doing is forbidden, but they still do as they please. Or sisters who wear their hijab to their liking, exposing their hair significantly as if they're unaware. Many of us are making a mockery of our religion when we purposely act ignorant. In the *Quran, Allah (swt) states, "And do not mix up the truth with the falsehood, nor hide the truth while you know (it)" (2:42).

You see, the thing is Allah (swt) created us with a mind, and this mind is able to think and process information logically! When Allah (swt) gave us the rubric to life through the Quran, the Prophet (saww), and AhlulBayt (as), stating what He expects from us, He (swt) also included the consequences of each action. So when an individual dies and passes, what do they expect is going to happen if they lived a life of a sinner? My point is, yes, "only God can judge us," but Allah (swt) gave us the material to be successful; if we don't follow it, we cannot assume salvation is still guaranteed and do as we please. That is wishful thinking!

Don't take advantage of the mercy of Allah (swt). Constantly, individuals say, "We want to change our ways," or "we are trying and we regret our sinful actions," but the very next moment they publicly flaunt their sinful habits. They offer only lip service! To those people, the *Quran states, "And when they meet those who believe, they say: We believe; and when they are alone with their Shaytans, they say: Surely we are with you, we were only mocking" (2:14).

* Quran English Translation by Muhammad Habib Shakir

Reflection 36

Who is the Strongest Amongst You?

Who are the strongest men and women amongst you? To narrow it down, they're not those that can physically lift heavy weights at the gym. Nor are they those that have accumulated wealth extravagantly, or those that have loud voices, or those that use their fists to frighten others. Not even those who hold positions of power. The strongest men and women are those who guard against evil! The ones who are able to say, "NO," and suppress their desires.

For instance, I am going to present a simple scenario of one of many desires we can all relate to.

Scenario: My friends are having a get together. With my friends comes trouble; they don't physically harm anyone, but at the same time I know what they're doing is wrong. They indulge in unsupervised mixed gender gatherings, they curse, they listen to music, they backbite dramatically, their tongue only whispers worldly affairs, and Allah (swt) and his message is never mentioned. Unfortunately, groups like this are considered "good friends" nowadays. I guess if they don't consume alcohol, don't engage in drugs, and don't go to forbidden places, they're considered good. To be clear, both sets of friends aren't good to be around! Wrong is wrong, there's no in between. Anyway, back to the scenario. We say, "These are my friends; I like them, and they like me." But ask yourself, "Who do I like more? Do I continue to meet with them or do we go our separate ways?"

To connect with Allah (swt) one must be able to give up those unlawful matters we desire sometimes! The *Quran states, "Whoever desires the gain of the hereafter, We will give him more of that gain; and whoever desires the gain of this world, We give him of it, and in the hereafter he has no portion" (42:20). Choose wisely!

* Quran English Translation by Muhammad Habib Shakir

Reflection 37

Extravagance

There is one sin in particular that we might have not been aware of, and that is "Israf" (extravagance, wasteful spending). The *Quran states, "Do not squander wastefully. Surely the squanderers are the fellows of the Shaytans and the Shaytan is ever ungrateful to his Lord" (17:26-27).

There's this mentality among us, that if an individual doesn't spend excessively they're considered stingy or cheap. We have to use Allah's (swt) rizq wisely! With all due respect, does a bride need an expensive ring and wedding to solidify her marriage? Does a man truly need to collect multiple cars as if he's hosting an auto show? Do we need the latest cell phone each year to talk and text the same people? Does a family of five need a ten bedroom home to live comfortably? Islam encourages us to dress and look good, but not to the extent that an individual spends 200 dollars on a belt to hold up their pants! Do we really need to spend 500 dollars on shoes, or 1000 dollars on a purse? Are "I worked hard," "I can afford it," "I like it," good enough reasons to buy such items? I am not here to say what is wasteful or what is not; we are just here to entertain our thoughts, and InshaAllah you can come up with your own conclusion.

However, the question that always comes to mind is, "Who am I to own such items at that rate?" Even if I give back, it still doesn't make sense to me, especially when we study the lives of the fourteen infallibles. One in particular is Imam Ali (as), when he (as) was asked, [10] "Has Allah prohibited you to eat better kind of food?" He (as) replied, "No, but I want to eat the kind of food which the poorest of this realm can afford at least once a day. I shall improve it after I have improved their standards of life. I want to live, feel and suffer like them." Now, I am not saying go practice poverty, but what I am saying is we should practice humbleness and humility externally as well.

That is one aspect of the spectrum, but the other side is more important, and one we tend to overlook. We fail to realize that such belongings have the power to feed our never content, competitive ego. It makes us feel a type of way when we own these things. We can easily become deeply attached to such materialism, which makes it hard to give up when the time comes. Why should we put ourselves in such a position? We are supposed to put ourselves in ideal situations to succeed, not in ones that might deter us from the straight path when it counts most.

I end with a narration by the great Imam Ja'far al-Sadiq (as),

[11] "Do you think if Allah has bestowed someone with wealth, it is because he is His beloved? And if He has given less to someone it is because he is low? No! It is not so. Whatever wealth is there, it all belongs to Allah. Allah gives it to whomsoever He wishes as a trust and He has permitted the trustee to eat, drink, wear clothes, marry, and ride from it, (but) in moderation. If he has excess he must distribute it among the poor and fulfill their needs. Then whoever follows the Divine commands, whatever he has eaten, drunk, worn, married and riden in moderation; all this is lawful for him and if he does not act upon it, everything is Haram."

* Quran English Translation by Muhammad Habib Shakir
[10] Ṭālib 'Alī Ibn Abī. *Nahjul Balagha: Peak of Eloquence: Sermons, Letters and Sayings*. Tahrike Tarsile Qur'an, 2009. –p.187
[11] Shirazi, Sayyid Abdul Husayn Dastghaib. "The Thirty-Second Greater Sin: Isrāf." *Al-Islam.org*, Ahlul Bayt Digital Islamic Library Project, 18 Jan. 2013.

Reflection 38

Now You Want to Be Religious?

There comes a time in everyone's life when they get tired. They get tired of standing between truth and falsehood. They get tired of being hypocritical, and the hypocrisy that surrounds them. They know the reality about this world but they choose to follow their "low desires." As Imam Ali (as) once said, [12] "Yes by Allah (swt), they had heard it and understood it, but the world appeared glittering in their eyes, and its embellishments seduced them." On the other hand, there were those who wanted to follow the truth. They wanted to seek the straight path, gain nearness to Allah (swt), detach from this world, reach a state of spirituality, but they became discouraged. Meaning, they got bombarded with unnecessary comments. Family and friends always bringing up their past, and saying, "Now you want to be religious? You were doing this yesterday," or "stop kidding yourself, religion is for the old; live your life right now," or "we already did so much, there is no hope for us," and more. The reason people attack those who are trying to find Allah (swt) is because they love this world. They have befriended Shaytan, and when it comes to sinning, "the more the merrier" is ideal for them, so they can feel less guilty.

The sad thing is there are cases where even parents stand in the way of their children when they're trying to strive for the straight path. However, Allah (swt) always warns us; the truth is there, it's our duty to search for it and act upon it. The *Quran states, "And We have enjoined upon man goodness to parents. But if they endeavor to make you associate with Me that of which you have no knowledge, do not obey them. To Me is your return, and I will inform you about what you used to do" (29:8). Do not let anyone get in the way of you and Allah (swt). Even if your sins cover the whole earth, from the east to the west. Sincerely repent, and obey! Your greatest proof is the elderly. Look at them well, and how they behave as they know death is approaching. Don't waste your youthful years being rebellious.

* Quran English Translation by Muhammad Habib Shakir
[12] Ṭālib ʿAlī Ibn Abī. *Nahjul Balagha: Peak of Eloquence: Sermons, Letters and Sayings*. Tahrike Tarsile Qur'an, 2009. –p.316

Reflection 39

I Fear Poverty

One of mankind's greatest fears is poverty. The feeling of being poor terrifies mankind to the point they're always in a state of worry. They become desperate for wealth, and their faith in Allah (swt) disappears. They tend to put their Islamic duties on the side, and feed their conscience, which is filled with never ending scenarios on "how to dodge poverty." We have to understand the role of the Chief Deceiver, Shaytan; his main duty is to sway us away from the straight path to Allah (swt). As Allah (swt) mentions in the *Quran, "Shaytan threatens you with poverty" (2:268). To be clear, I am not encouraging anyone to not seek a livelihood; on the contrary, seek a livelihood, but we shouldn't become extremely troubled if we go through a financial crisis. Rather, we should embrace such conditions because Allah (swt) didn't forget us. If we experience poverty, it is a trial from Allah (swt), and anything from Allah (swt) is a blessing. Meaning, such trials can strengthen our certainty and faith by increasing our dependence on Him (swt), and destroying our arrogance, or the trial can reroute our lives towards Him (swt), and the hereafter. Maybe we were too attached to money!

On the other hand, there are those who have taken others as their provider. For instance, they worship their employer and give all thanks to them. They're actually of the belief that if it wasn't for their employer they wouldn't be financially secure. Such a mentality is incorrect. Every drop of permissible provision is from Allah (swt). Allah (swt) just uses the employer as a means, a funnel to get it to us through them. Allah (swt) states in the *Quran, "And there is not a thing but with Us are the treasures of it, and We do not send it down but in a known measure" (15:21).

Lastly, there are spouses who want to have children, but they choose not to because they're not "financially ready." They're haunted by thoughts about how they will attend to their children when their financial condition is not much. The same thoughts we face today the people of the past faced as well, but during that time they would kill their children due to fear of not being able to provide for them. Then *Allah (swt) responded, "And do not kill your children for fear of poverty; We give them sustenance and yourselves (too)" (17:31). Reflect on the second part of the verse, who gives you sustenance/provision?

* Quran English Translation by Muhammad Habib Shakir

Reflection 40

Practice Religion in Private

Isn't it ironic? When it comes to the religion of Islam society enjoys concealing it. People will express their thoughts by saying, "Keep religion between Allah (swt) and you," or "do that in private." However, it is encouraged to promote: sinning, extravagant materialism, mixed gatherings, vulgar music, academic achievements, stylish clothes, couples and family portraits, food, vacation time, and so on. Why do people enjoy advocating worldly affairs, but when it comes to Islam, keep it behind trapped doors? Imagine we live in a world where Islam is publicized. Meaning, instead of having mundane provocative billboards, we have billboards that read, "Did you say *salawat today?" Or even electronic billboards that present the times of the five daily prayers. We live in a time that discourages the remembrance of Allah (swt).

Furthermore, I was blessed to attend a religious event. Usually before an event begins, or if technical difficulties arise, or if the organizers choose to pause the event, a random individual will say "salawat" for the time being until the issue is resolved. However, during this particular event "the pause" was a bit lengthy. So, the salawat began, first, second, third, fourth, fifth, and so on. By the time the sixth salawat came along, the people of the crowd began to become irritated. They were upset over the excessive salawats! Had we known the benefits of one sincere salawat, our lips wouldn't utter anything else. One reason we fail to realize the importance of such a phrase is because we say, "Keep religion in private." Majority of us worship Allah (swt) with our tongues only, and not with our hearts!

We have to encourage an Islamic environment. I don't mean this in a way where we brag about our actions, but rather, people shouldn't feel embarrassed or discouraged to pray in public when needing to.

* Salawat: Asking Allah (swt) to send His (swt) blessings to the Prophet Muhammad (saww) and AhlulBayt (as).

Reflection 41

Meet My Friend, Death

Typically when someone speaks about death, people quickly assume he or she is sad, depressed, unhappy, dark, and so on. Death is one of those topics we shy away from frequently. Anytime death is brought up, negativity is connected with it. Such a perspective is incorrect! Without a doubt we should befriend the Angel of Death. Who else by the will of Allah (swt) can take a soul and transport them on the path to the hereafter (which is "better and more lasting" *Quran, 87:17)? Who else is able to link an individual back with their loving and merciful Lord (swt)? Who else is able to keep an individual cautious of sinning when he is remembered? What a great companion this creation is; we should embrace him! We should speak about him more often.

Imam Ali (as) states, [13] "I am as fond of death as a baby is fond of his mother's breast." Such a level of comfort is astonishing! In addition, Imam Ja'far al-Sadiq (as) was asked, [14] "Is the believer upset upon death and doesn't want it to happen?" He (as) replied, "At first he might show some grief and wail, but the Angel of Death will tell him, 'O' friend of God, don't fret, by God…I am kinder to you than your father.'"

SubhanAllah! Our perception of death must change for the good.

* Quran English Translation by Muhammad Habib Shakir

[13] Ṭālib 'Alī Ibn Abī. *Nahjul Balagha: Peak of Eloquence: Sermons, Letters and Sayings*. Tahrike Tarsile Qur'an, 2009. –p.277

[14] Rastani, Shaykh Amin. *Death and the Barzakh: Stages Between Dunya and Resurrection*. MIZAN INSTITUTE, 2018.-p.7

Reflection 42

Don't Harden Your Heart

Let's not harden our hearts; the heart is a beautiful organ that will guide us to the straight path when cared for properly. The *Quran states, "He (swt) it is Who sent down tranquility into the hearts of the believers that they might have more of faith added to their faith" (48:4).

In my opinion, in some cases the mind is reliable, but not as reliable as the heart. To put it into perspective, if we reflect within ourselves we will realize that the mind has multiple characters within it, and if the mind is not controlled properly it can lead us to the path of self-destruction. The mind faces constant enemies, like the ego and the whispers of Shaytan. For example, have you ever sat in a gathering and your mind began judging a random person you don't know on its own? Then when you separate yourself from your thoughts and ask yourself if you truly feel this way about this individual, it is always a "no," for me at least. Next time you are around others put this **experiment to a test.

In addition, have you ever realized when the opportunity of sin arises, your heart quickly shuts it down and you get a strong solid feeling in your heart that this is wrong, but our mind doesn't do that. From my experiences, it plays two roles; it tells me that this is wrong, but at the same time it encourages me to sin. The mind doesn't deliver a solid answer until trial and error takes place. It needs conviction for it to make a solid decision, but even then it can work against you because it is always curious, and that is why we sometimes make the same mistakes over and over. The heart is not like that! Next time you're tested with a sin pause for a moment, and listen to the answer of your heart, then compare it to the answers of your mind. Separate the two, and you'll notice a difference!

Having said that, it is hard for the heart to stay in such a helpful state when an individual is disobedient to Allah (swt), and we can prove this. In the beginning stages of an individual's life, when they sin, immediately they are filled with sadness and regret, and quickly turn to Allah (swt) for forgiveness; but what happens when they continue doing that same sin the second, third, and fourth time around? At that point they're allowing a section of their heart to harden. Meaning, that specific sin they acted upon doesn't appear inappropriate to them anymore. Rather, it becomes a norm to them and they don't feel remorse towards it. Excessive sinning is a form of disbelieving in Allah (swt)! Let's not allow our hearts to harden; let's not allow ourselves to perceive falsehood and try to justify it.

* Quran English Translation by Muhammad Habib Shakir
** From a lecture by Hajj Khalil Jaffer.

Reflection 43

What is Islam?

The struggles the religion of Islam faces aren't only emerging from the outside anymore. Rather, a new more public movement is growing on the inside. Our own brothers and sisters are modernizing and practicing secular Islam. Their main goal is to "fit in," by any means necessary! They will compromise the teachings of their religion just to prove to the creation that "they belong." Majority of men and women view Islam as boring and restrictive, which is incorrect.

Not to blame the people of the past or point any fingers, but the version of Islam that they relayed to the newer generations mostly consisted of praying, fasting, and hell. For many, worshiping Allah (swt) is observed as a chore instead of a blessing. In a sense this is why some of the Muslim population are seeking alternatives, and searching for freedom in this world. However, their type of freedom is in disguise! Meaning, in reality they're becoming slaves of society as they follow the trends of this world. So, are they really free?

Now what is our responsibility? Our duty is to examine the essence of Islam. Islam means submitting one's will to Allah (swt). Furthermore, there are [15] five fundamental beliefs called Roots of Religion! Three are known as Roots of Islam: Tawhid (Belief in Oneness of God), Nubuwwat (Belief in the Prophets), and Qiyamat (Belief in the Day of Judgement). The last two are known as Roots of Faith: Adl (Justice of God) and Imamat (The successorship of the Prophet). Moreover, there are ten Islamic practices: Prayer, Fasting, Zakaat, Khums, Pilgrimage known as "Hajj," Jihad which means to struggle or strive, Enjoining Good, Forbidding Evil, Tawallah (Showing love and support to those who walk on the path of Allah (swt)), and Tabarra (Disassociating from the enemies of Allah (swt)). This is freedom!

This is what makes a HUMAN BEING whole! We have to spread this Islam to our: parents, siblings, friends, and all. It is heartbreaking that we are losing a great number of brothers and sisters to this temporary world. This isn't our world; this world is an illusion. Forever doesn't exist here! The hereafter is our final destination. Once a man came to a great leader and said, [16] "You have taken your country a couple hundred years back." The leader replied, "I'm looking to take it back 1400 years…to the time of Prophet Muhammad (saww) and Imam Ali (as)."

[15] Rizvi, Sayid Sa'eed Akhtar. "The Seven Responsibilities." *Al-Islam.org*, Ahlul Bayt Digital Islamic Library Project , 4 June 2015.

[16] Attributed to Sayed Ruhollah Khomeini (ra)

Reflection 44

What Am I?

I am the brother who prays on time and fasts occasionally as well. My tongue does not curse and only tastes halal. I do not consume alcohol nor do I abuse drugs. I am the brother who doesn't listen to vulgar music nor do I hang out willingly at places where I am exposed to mixed gatherings, like nightclubs. I do put my hand on my chest as I greet the opposite gender, and I lower my gaze too. I am a brother who doesn't chase materialism. I want to live a humble life, nothing extravagant, but what am I?

I am a sister who recites Quran and memorizes supplications. I am the one who stops my friends from gossiping, and backbiting too. I do not flaunt myself; matter of fact, I do wear a hijab without showing a single strand of my hair, and I do dress modestly as well. I do not promote the use of makeup or nail polish publicly. Did I mention that I do not meet with men privately too? I am ambitious; I do have goals and dreams, but if they don't line up with my beliefs then to each their own. I do not want a lavish wedding, I would rather save up my wealth for something useful instead of spending it all in one day, but what am I?

To the world, I am extreme, delusional, close-minded, obsessed, and more; but to Allah (swt), I am...

Reflection 45

Working For This Life

The Imam (as) has a profound statement that is well known; he (as) says, [17] "Work for a better life as if you will live forever, and for a better end as if you will die tomorrow." Unfortunately, we as individuals only take the first portion of this saying. We are constantly striving for only "forever"! We have to begin to incorporate "dying tomorrow" in our day to day lives.

When we ask any individual, "How are you?" After they reply with "Alhamdulillah," they quickly follow up with "I can't wait until..." We are always in a state of "I can't wait," waiting to graduate, to start a career, get married, vacation, have kids, and so on. Such a mentality is a distraction from reality! We must train ourselves to live in the moment, the now. Picture this, someone comes up to you right now and hands you a note. The note reads, "So and so, I am death, and tomorrow I am going to claim your life, *mm/dd/yyyy at 5pm." Will "I can't wait until..." matter anymore? Majority of us will go mad, but on the other hand there are those who won't because they balanced their lives out. They didn't just strive for their future only, but they prepared for their hereafter as well. Preparation for the hereafter is an every moment action.

[18] "Each breath taken by a man is a step closer to his death," Imam Ali (as) says. To many, the message of Allah (swt) is farfetched, but to the few, Allah (swt) states, "Therefore be patient; surely the promise of Allah is true..." **Quran, (30:60). Work for this world and hereafter, simultaneously.

---

[17] Attributed to Imam Ali (as)

* Plug in the following day from when you're reading this reflection.

** Quran English Translation by Muhammad Habib Shakir

[18] Ṭālib 'Alī Ibn Abī. *Nahjul Balagha: Peak of Eloquence: Sermons, Letters and Sayings*. Tahrike Tarsile Qur'an, 2009. –p.844

Reflection 46

I Can't Touch Her

I remember when I was younger this used to confuse me a lot, and I am sure it is something that many people are still confused about until today. I blame culture for this matter because in religion it is as clear as day! Growing up I was told that I can't touch a girl who wears a hijab in any way, no high fives, shaking hands, hugging, etc. But if a girl doesn't wear a hijab, it is okay, I can shake her hand.

That is absolutely incorrect! Being able to touch someone or not doesn't depend on them wearing a hijab. In Islam, a man is not allowed to touch a woman at all unless she is "mahram to him"; hijab has NOTHING to do with it. Also, a woman is not allowed to touch a man unless he is mahram to her. To be clear this doesn't mean we are allowed to touch people from different faiths; this rule applies to everyone.

Having said that, who are mahram to females? Husband, father, grandfathers, great grandfathers, sons, brothers, nephews, paternal and maternal uncles, and father-in-law.

Who are mahram to males? Wife, mother, grandmothers, great grandmothers, daughters, sisters, nieces, paternal and maternal aunts, and mother-in-law. For technical cases like stepfather or half sisters, please refer to a scholar.

To end, even if you grew up with your cousins and they're like your sister or brother, you still cannot touch them. It doesn't matter what anyone is like to you, what matters is what Allah (swt) decreed. These are the small types of sins that we always tend to overlook, or we think they're meaningless, but when we keep committing the same sin over and over, it no longer stays small...

Reflection 47

Do I Believe in Allah (swt)?

Stop for a moment and ask yourself, "Do I believe in Allah (swt)?" If you don't, it is okay…for now! We all struggle with this prominent question. We go back and forth, and yet coming to a consistent conclusion might be difficult.

Nowadays some of us are rebellious because we don't believe or fully believe in Allah (swt). Sure, verbally we might say we do, but our hearts utter, "Who is Allah (swt)?" This happens because we go all these years as children and Allah (swt) is not mentioned properly. Then out of nowhere, when we reach a certain age our guardians come along and tell us, "It's time." Time for what? Time to do your Islamic duties. So, we agree and proceed to do them not knowing for who or why we are doing these acts. As if we are robots! As we get older, hardship and struggle enters our lives, and this "God" that is supposed to rescue us is not around. Afterwards, we get disappointed, and conclude that Allah (swt) doesn't exist, and we start revolting instead. When people ask, "Why are you behaving in this manner?" We won't admit that we don't believe in Allah (swt) because such a response is crossing boundaries according to society. Instead we shrug off the question and continue our ways. With this process we have taken Allah (swt) as a concept instead of a way of life.

To be alive we must have certainty. To have certainty we must prove His (swt) existence. Imam Ali (as) states, [19] "The foremost in religion is the acknowledgment of Him. The perfection of acknowledging Him is to testify to Him. The perfection of testifying Him is to believe in His Oneness." This is how we should relay Allah (swt) to ourselves and others.

Before we start addressing praying, fasting, heaven and hell, we must answer the question of, "For whom are we performing these duties and why?" We have to stress on the who and why, not on the how, what, when, where, but the who and why. Now to be clear, our limited minds aren't fully capable of answering who is Allah (swt), but it's capable of proving His existence and realizing who He is through His attributes. Who else reflected His attributes better than the Prophet Muhammad (saww) and AhlulBayt (as)? This very moment if you don't believe in Allah (swt), it's okay. If you believe in Him (swt) 50%, it's okay. If you believe in Him (swt) 99%, it's okay. What is not okay is not taking advantage of the endless resources available to us that can increase our certainty in Him (swt) to 100%. That is arrogance! Currently we are all capable of reaching 100%. Don't accept 0%, 50%, or 99%! We shouldn't be ashamed of asking questions. Leave no doubt!

[19] Ṭālib 'Alī Ibn Abī. *Nahjul Balagha: Peak of Eloquence: Sermons, Letters and Sayings*. Tahrike Tarsile Qur'an, 2009. –p.299

Reflection 48

How Do You Measure Them?

All praise belongs to Allah (swt), The Loving One.

When you look at an individual, how do you measure them? Meaning, in your opinion what brings value to this person? It is unfortunate that humanity has ruined the worth of a human being. Humanity goes on to endorse that an individual's importance depends on their career, wealth, and status. If one doesn't meet a certain criteria, they're considered a failure.

I ask, how is that fair? We all originate from different foundations and struggle with trials and tribulations that many are unaware of. We shouldn't accept this system! This is the reason why many feel worthless at times, because they don't meet the standards of "society." It is up to us to destroy this stereotypical scheme and support all, despite one's current position in life. For instance, an individual's greatest accomplishment of the day might be getting out of bed and stepping outside. To them this act is very meaningful, but to others this person is considered a "bum" if that is their highest achievement. We must be thoughtful of others, and encourage all as well. Everyone moves at a different pace! Just because someone doesn't line up with a certain speed it doesn't make them a failure. On the contrary, we are failures when we put people down.

When you're feeling prideful and egotistical, remember what you are! When it is all said and done we are pieces of dust. The *Quran states, "And Allah created you of dust, then of the life-germ" (35:11). When you're feeling depressed and down, remember who you are. You're the one that is mentioned in the *Quran, "He it is WHO shapes you in the wombs as He likes" (3:6). You're the creation of Allah (swt), The Almighty, The Great! [20]"Within you is enfolded the entire universe!" By Allah (swt), at times we feel like we are stagnant, but this is untrue. Allah (swt) is near, and He (swt) is constantly guiding us, but the guidance He (swt) is projecting is unfamiliar to us because we desire this world more. Shift your focus to Him (swt) ONLY, and perceive how this realm reveals itself to you. [20]"What you seek is within you…if only you reflect."

* Quran English Translation by Muhammad Habib Shakir
[20]Attributed to Imam Ali (as)

Reflection 49

Ramadan

Passage 1

Gold Rush Ramadan

So...Ramadan is approaching. Ramadan is known to be one of the most significant times of the year. As Allah (swt) states in the *Quran, "O you who believe! Fasting is prescribed for you, as it was prescribed for those before you, so that you may guard (against evil)" (2:183).

It is unfortunate that many of us have destroyed the essence of Ramadan. Meaning, when you ask today's generation, "What is it that you favor about this holy month?" They'll reply with, "The feast every night, hanging out until sunrise, and the company." It is tragic that we have taken Ramadan as a "lounge" nowadays. Some of the gatherings we wait for eagerly are filled with gossip, backbiting, drama, and more. We prepare a great amount of food, that not only can feed our families but communities as well, just to see it all thrown away at the end of the night. We presume we are generous, but in reality we are wasteful. The number of men and women who don't fast has increased. Their reasons have become more mundane over the years. For instance, it reached the point that many refuse to fast because they're afraid to lose their physique that they have been sculpting all year. As for many business owners, they flourish because of Ramadan, but when it's time to give thanks to Allah (swt), some become greedy.

We perceive this to be the norm of Ramadan, but this is the evil we must be guarding against. Ramadan is much more than an empty stomach, parched throat, and dry lips. Use Ramadan to increase your consciousness of Allah (swt), and to become a FAITHFUL individual. The Chief Deceiver Shaytan and his minions are imprisoned during Ramadan. We are blessed with the Great Night of Power! We have countless opportunities to cleanse ourselves, and to cement a permanent path leading to Allah (swt). Seek sincere forgiveness! The choice is ours! "Surely Allah does not change the condition of a people until they change their own condition;" *Quran, (13:11).

* Quran English Translation by Muhammad Habib Shakir

Passage 2

Ramadan Food Stands

To be clear, the intention of this reflection isn't to shame anyone, but rather it is simply to introduce a different perspective so we may reflect on it. Entertain the thought, that's all! I kindly ask while you're reading, don't just think about yourself, but take everyone into consideration as well.

To begin, whether we like to admit it or not there has been a massive influx of businesses. We are treating Ramadan as a gold rush, and everyone wants a piece of it. Once upon a time it was only bakeries catering to the masses for a few hours before sunrise, but now it is: lounges, food stands, festivals, pastry shops, etc. People have argued that extending hours helps generate more cash which can be used for paying bills, giving to charity, creating jobs, etc. Are we trying to justify our actions to make MORE money, or are we really trying to give back? Mind you, many of these businesses operate normally through the month of Ramadan, and are also running all year round. Do they really need the extra income? Think of their employees who are forced to come back to work until sunrise after already working the whole day. They don't get to spend much time with Allah (swt) or their family. They truly miss out on reaping all the benefits of Ramadan.

During a month where we are supposed to connect with Allah (swt), we are chasing work instead. I get it, we want to get ahead on the bills and whatnot, but is it worth potentially losing moments that may increase our consciousness of Allah (swt)? With the overflow of businesses and events taking place we are creating more options. With options come many distractions! In addition, the settings are not controlled; so when we do have these social events where mix gatherings take place, how do we know lustful gazing, flirting, touching isn't happening? Instead of being cautious we created venues that potentially can increase the chances of sin. It is as if we shot ourselves in the foot! Also, teenagers are telling their parents one thing and doing another to get out of the house late at night.

The Messenger of Allah (saww) has said, [21] "I warn you in relation to eating too much because surely this act poisons the heart by making it hard (no emotional feelings), and makes your body parts lazy and lethargic (tired) in relation to obedience of Allah, and it deafens the ears from hearing advice and good counsel." To end, it is not Ramadan that is fading away, but it is our understanding of what Ramadan truly is.

[21] Shirazi, Naser Makarem. "Discourse 13: Two Despised Characteristics: Eating Too Much and Looking at Others." *Al-Islam.org*, Ahlul Bayt Digital Islamic Library Project , 3 Oct. 2012.

Passage 3

Zoom in on Ramadan

Ramadan begins next week, right? I thought last year's (COVID-19/2020) Ramadan was very special compared to other years, even though we were in a lockdown. That being said, there weren't those extra activities going on after Iftar like festivals, food stands, lounging, etc., instead the majority of individuals were spending their time attending lectures online. It was nice to feel that sense of spirituality again within our community; it was quiet, and sometimes the human being needs silence around them so they may reflect properly. However, we can all admit that over the past few years Ramadan has been loud through the influx of distractions, which can cause a great amount of harm, especially when it comes to spiritual growth.

Now, why do we continue to bring this topic up every year? Are we purposely trying to be annoying? Are we against individuals and businesses making money, the nightly gatherings, and whatnot? Of course NOT, none of that! But we are against the excessive distractions during Ramadan. I want to ask you, who mainly runs these food stands? The youth! What is saddening is, these food stands have become a place to hangout for boys and girls, and some stands even play music. Instead of telling the youth, "Hey maybe this isn't the time to try to make money, let's focus on strengthening our religion and spirituality," we glorify and applaud their actions, and label them as "young entrepreneurs." Just consider how time consuming this might be for the youth, and where this time could've been spent instead.

I hate to say this and I hope to God I am totally wrong, but I think we are getting to a point where some of us view Ramadan not as a time to become God conscious, work and restore our faith, but a time for personal gain, only. This isn't only about the youth, it is about all of us, and I think as a community we have opened up a door that is no longer controllable. As the years go on, more and more businesses are being established during Ramadan, people have now realized the monetary gain to the point where they announce their service months before Ramadan even starts, so they can grab a piece of the pie just in time.

I am not speaking out of hate; I am speaking out of care and love, and this isn't the true essence of Ramadan. Sometimes I wonder if I am really fasting, or just starving myself for a month…What does it mean to truly fast?

Passage 4

30 Day Muslims

Why is it that when Ramadan ends many of us return to our old ways? Because we have adopted the poisonous mindset that being a "30 Day Muslim" is better than nothing. Such a mindset is limiting because it is as if you're telling your brain, "You just have to get through these next 30 days, and then you can return to your norm."

This label that many of us seem to support during Ramadan every year is deceiving because we are encouraging people to settle! Why should we settle when we all have the potential to reach a great level of connection with Allah (swt)? We have to treat the straight path as a journey, not a one month trip.

The process of change does not occur if we are not willing to give up haram for good! For instance, there's a difference between someone who voluntarily commits a haram act and someone who aggressively fights against a haram act, then falls into it. People say, "Someone can change within a second, that's why we say better than nothing." That is not true! Maybe that second can motivate us, but true change takes hard work, planning, trial and error, practice, consistency, and time.

Let's be creative and throw away such toxic phrases! If we turn to Allah (swt) one month out of the year, is it really better than nothing? Are we truly being productive to the best of our capabilities? We shouldn't accept this "better than nothing" option! Our goal is to build a foundation to obey and serve Allah (swt) throughout the whole year, and so on. Instead, let's try to say words that have a long term effect!

Passage 5

Ramadan Nights

I believe many people have great intentions, but I don't believe every opportunity is worth capitalizing on. That being said, the intention of this post is to introduce different perspectives so we may entertain our thoughts, and I am not here to focus on just one event; I think the whole "nightlife" during Ramadan has become intriguing to say the least.

Consumer

The "nightlife" has become very distracting, and takes away from the true essence of what Ramadan is. I believe from a consumer perspective when we see everything going on during these nights it automatically awakens our curiosity, because that is how we are wired. Mentally, the process isn't simple anymore. It's no longer going to your local bakery before sunrise and getting something modest, then heading home. Now because of the endless options we have, it's more of I want to try this stand tonight and this other one tomorrow, and lets meet up here, and so on.

This type of noise might not be haram, but it is dangerous because it is loud enough to keep us distracted so we don't reap the full benefits of this holy month. I understand to each their own, and we have to control ourselves, but when we create something that is so attractive it is difficult to do so, especially if one hasn't worked on themselves properly.

Stand Owner

From a stand owner, organizers, and employees perspective, I wonder how it feels to be in their position. How time consuming is it for them to prepare each night? Most likely most of these individuals have day jobs or go to school. Is it really possible to truly take advantage of this holy month while catering to the wants of people? Let's be honest with ourselves! Are they not Muslims too? Also, last year several stands didn't close during the Great Night of Power, and many of these stands have a good amount of employees, and they're young. Instead of saying this is wrong; we continue to applaud them for being "entrepreneurs."

Where is the silver lining? Now I know many of these people put themselves under such circumstances willingly; but the point is, this urge to have a "nightlife" during Ramadan also hurts stand owners, organizers, and employees from a spiritual standpoint, not so much their pockets though. Price gouging is at an all time high during Ramadan, but that is for another conversation.

Empty Mosques

Furthermore, people have made the assumption that the "nightlife" has caused the mosques to be empty. I don't believe that is necessarily true because prior to Ramadan people were barely going to mosques anyway. Individuals have expressed that the mosques and scholars have failed us due to their lack of creativity in drawing in crowds, but is that accurate? This is false because there have been great programs in the past, and I am sure there will be in the future as well.

People will flock in groups and wait hours for food and dessert, but have a hard time sitting through a lecture, why? Because the truth is we don't see the joy when it comes to religion. Experiencing such joy requires an individual to put in the work, and then Islam becomes attractive. But to blame this place or that person are just excuses. We have to blame ourselves because the programs are there. I have seen centers incorporate sports, food, Islamic plays, trivia, and even have addressed those crucial topics, but people hardly come.

Also, keep in mind that these new upcoming generations aren't being raised by immigrants where religion and good parts of culture were stressed on. The generation of today is being raised by those who are born in this country, and some of them may have adopted the western culture and norms, which may have led religion to the backseat in their households.

It is impossible to compare the generation from 10 to 20 years ago to now. I think we are beginning to truly see the effects of living in the west. Just look at other religions and how they responded over time. We shouldn't overlook the influences of advanced technology either...

Final Thoughts

To end, is this the new norm during Ramadan? I hope it isn't because trying to become closer to Allah (swt) has become more challenging, especially in this month. I wonder what the future of Ramadan looks like here in the west. Are big corporations going to start getting involved? Who knows, but the attention is there. Is Ramadan going to turn into a Hallmark holiday? It may! I personally think this is a door that should have stayed closed, because this is just the beginning. Not every opportunity is worth capitalizing on, especially in a temporary world.

Reflection 50

Hidden Intentions

Do you know what is magnificent about Allah (swt)?

It is how He (swt) knows that many of us only come to Him (swt) in desperate times, and are going to stop coming to Him (swt) when our situation improves. Yet, He (swt) still blesses us with what we pray for, and doesn't turn us away.

Now imagine we truly invested our time building a real relationship with Allah (swt)...

Reflection 51

To Struggle

The word "jihad" precisely translates to struggle in the way of Allah (swt). There are two types of jihad; the lesser jihad and the greater jihad. After a certain battle the Prophet (saww) said to his companions, [22] "We are returning from the lesser jihad, and heading back towards the greater jihad." What?! Anyone would think the greater struggle lies within war, but what do we know compared to the City of Knowledge (saww)? In my opinion, you see, in battle the chances of death are high. A soldier is only thinking about one thing...survival.

Now, what is the greater jihad? It is the struggle between one's own soul. The battle that consists of, You vs. You! We all have desires. We have good ones, and really bad ones. We live in a time where our bad desires can easily be fulfilled. Whatever it is we desire, we have an outlet for it. The people who are victorious are the ones that look at their bad desires and say, "I will not fulfill you for the sake of my love, Allah (swt)." This is honor, being able to do whatever we want but choosing to say "NO" to our animalistic nature.

Our greatest failure is that we limit Allah (swt)! Meaning, look at our controversial actions, the really disgusting ones. Had an individual that we respect been in our radius, like a guardian, we would not dare to portray such behavior. Reason being, we truly believe Allah (swt) is not everywhere; we are convinced His (swt) existence is only at a place of worship. To conquer our greater struggle, we must begin to realize that we are in Allah's (swt) presence at every single moment. We are never alone!

[22]Attributed to the Prophet Muhammad (saww)

Reflection 52

Oppression

Oppression is tragic; there are many forms of oppression. The form that we are most familiar with is the actions of a tyrant against his people. When we get news that the people around the world are experiencing destruction through: poverty, hunger, war, shelter displacement, etc., it is heartbreaking, and really gets one to ponder! Why is it that we are able to live in a relaxed comfortable environment while others live in such a struggle that is catastrophic? Why was I fortunate enough to be born and live in a land that has minimal worry? There is no way our only goals are to achieve a higher academic education, gain wealth, build a dream home, and live happily ever after with our family. If it is not happening to us, it is not our concern, right? Do we just brush the deaths of our brothers and sisters under a rug and turn a blind eye?

Sure we can do that, but there is one thing every human fails to remember! Before many individuals choose to disbelieve in Allah (swt) because of oppression they state, "Why does Allah (swt) let such and such occur?!" They blame the actions of the people on Allah (swt). The true question is, why didn't mankind just follow what Allah (swt) has prescribed? It would have been heaven on earth! Anyway, every human fails to remember that we belong to Allah (swt) and to Him (swt) we shall return. Doesn't man understand that one day he will take his last breath? How foolish are the power hungry to actually believe that their actions won't be accounted for? In this world all kinds of oppressors might seem strong and invincible, but by Allah (swt), in the next, they will pay their dues in full.

No worries my brothers and sisters, their term is fixed, but so is ours. If we don't do at least the bare minimum, which is spreading awareness against oppression, because we are afraid to lose the deceiving ornaments of this world, then know that Imam Ja'far al-Sadiq (as) states,[23] "...And not helping the oppressed (is a greater sin)." Don't be afraid to speak out against any kind of oppression! Worst case scenario is death, but the misconception about death is that it is the beginning, not the end…

On the other hand, oppressing ourselves is very common as well. Typically, oppression against ourselves occurs when we know what is good and right for us, but we choose to act otherwise, and ignore all visible signs. In addition, being stuck and attached to past situations, and anxiously waiting for the future can be very harmful as well. Lastly, depending on the creation instead of the Creator (swt) is an action we must avoid at all cost!

---

[23] Shirazi, Sayyid Abdul Husayn Dastghaib. "The Thirtieth Greater Sin: Not Helping the Oppressed." *Al-Islam.org*, Ahlul Bayt Digital Islamic Library Project, 18 Jan. 2013.

Reflection 53

Conflicted Soul

When our inner soul is conflicted it is because it's hanging on to two ropes that are each pulling it in the opposite direction. For example, think of a person pulling your right arm and another individual pulling your left arm at the same time as hard as possible. Ouch, right?

Rope A represents this world and rope B represents the hereafter. Now, if I want to feel better I have to let go of one of the ropes. What most of us do is we let go of rope B (the hereafter) and cling on to rope A (this world), because it gives us that instant gratification! We aren't willing to be patient and invest and build our hereafter; we want our reward now!

When people are conflicted in this way they have to find a source to blame it on; the first thing they do is declare that their problem originates from religion because they feel religion restricts them, and prevents them from who they really want to be. They say, "My problem is with praying, my problem is with fasting, my problem is with hijab," and so on. They're convinced that if they stop a certain Islamic duty they will feel a sense of relief because they have been choked up all this time, and they might feel that relief, but it's very temporary! It's not the long lasting relief that is only offered through submitting to Allah (swt) completely.

Now, the question that must be asked is, when we analyze our lives in this way, why is it that religion is the first thing tossed out of the window? Why don't we reflect more and say, "Maybe my problem is with what comes with rope A." Those who have let go of rope B aren't happy, and deep down, they know that the decision they took wasn't a good one. So, they ignore the feeling until it fades away, and then they become numb to it. This internal struggle is very common; it's not rare. Every human being goes through it; it actually hit me hard at 19 years old!

Clearly I am not perfect, and I struggle on a daily basis; but what influenced me to let go of rope A was that I saw the highest potential of those who have sucked the life out of this world. I saw the ceiling and it wasn't all that interesting, but on the other hand, I have yet to see the ceiling of an individual fully committed to Allah (swt), even if I had the power to look beyond the entire sky.

Reflection 54

The Checklist

We have to get in the habit of holding ourselves accountable at the end of each day. Create a mental checklist and realize where you went wrong. For example:

1. Did I use profanity today?
2. Did I dress immodestly?
3. Did I lower my gaze?
4. Did I listen to music?
5. Did I miss prayer?
6. Did I...?

Knowing our weaknesses and addressing them will eventually lead us to success and a better connection with Allah (swt). The state of perfection isn't impossible; in fact, it is very attainable. Stay in the moment, stay God conscious, and you will make better decisions. We easily can go from committing 100 sins to 0 sins per day if we work hard. To you and me these actions might be small because we are used to sins being something extreme like stealing, but that is not the case when it comes to spirituality, the smallest actions matter. Think about it...

On the other hand, what did you do today to help increase your faith? For example, today I am going to:

1. Pray on time.
2. Read the Quran, even if it is one verse.
3. Not lash out at my parents.
4. Avoid my friends who enjoy drama, gossip, and slandering others.
5. Donate to charity, even if it is a penny.
6. Stand and spread awareness about oppressors.

Evaluate yourselves frequently!

Reflection 55

Disagreeing With Allah (swt)

Passage 1

Many of us disagree with Allah (swt) openly, and sometimes we might not be aware of it. Meaning, there are some of us who come across verses from the Quran and draw up our own negative conclusion without taking the proper measures to seek the truth. We begin to use sentences like, "How can Allah (swt) allow…?!" and so on.

In addition, some of us even decide to leave Islam as a whole, or try to reform it to our liking based off several verses that we dislike. People try telling such individuals, "At least read the before and after verse just to get a better understanding," but one verse was enough for them to shake their whole foundation. Out of 6,000+ verses, it only took one verse that was taken out of context by society for them to say, "I am done with Islam!" Did they attempt to search for a strong explanation of the verse by credible resources? Probably not!

When we don't understand something, especially when it comes to religion, we have to do the proper research and ask those who are knowledgeable.

Passage 2

Do you know what is frustrating? It is when people interpret the Quran to their liking, and they spread it based on their opinion. Please, if someone comes and speaks to you about the Quran, I don't care how eloquent they may sound, ask for their credentials. Then ask for the source that backups their "statement." Then ask them as well if they have studied in an Islamic Seminary, and also ask how many years.

After you do all of that, then take into consideration what they're saying, and fact check it through credible resources. The things I am hearing from people are ridiculous. People are really out here corrupting young minds, and they have ZERO credentials. This is pure arrogance!

Reflection 56

"Religion Was Forced…"

"Religion was forced on me!" "I was forced to wear a scarf!" "I was forced to pray and fast." "I was forced to attend Saturday school." We hear these common remarks frequently. Force! Force! Force! Many individuals blame their deviation from Islam because their parents "forced it" on them. However, is it really a matter of force or is it a battle of worldly desires fueled by the Chief Deceiver, Shaytan?

Let's rewind for a moment and logically reflect about this scenario. Parents always want the best for their children! The best: education, clothes, food, friends, activities, etc. The best gift parents can give to their child is the knowledge of Allah (swt) and Islam, and don't forget, they're also aware of the consequences of sinning. So, that is why our parents pushed strongly for religion and were overprotective at times. They wanted to set us up for a heavenly hereafter instead of...! But, as we grew older and this world started to display its ornaments, and these decorated ornaments are against our religious beliefs, we became frustrated, and uttered the words, "Religion was forced on me."

If the veils of paradise were to be removed and we were able to perceive heaven, not one of us would say, "Religion was forced on me." Instead, we would give praise to those who tried to guide us to the straight path! It is a matter of perspective. We have many individuals who are leaving Islam because it was "forced" on them. That is a very flawed excuse! Fine, if we want to use such an excuse when we were younger and weren't cognitively developed, so be it; but we have individuals who are in their late teens, twenties, thirties, forties, and so on, who can differentiate between right and wrong that state the reason for their questionable behavior is because religion was "forced" on them.

That is false! It isn't about force; it is about, "Nay! You prefer the life of this world" *Quran, (87:16). It is about your evil desires! It is difficult for you to give up your desires for Allah (swt) and Islam. To be successful our love for Allah (swt) has to exceed our love for our desires. But to play it out, suppose religion was "forced" on you, what is the debate? At the end you're being forced into something magnificent. It is a win-win situation!

* Quran English Translation by Muhammad Habib Shakir

Disclaimer: Force in this context does not equate to abuse or trauma, whether verbal, physical, emotional, or mental.

Reflection 57

Burden or Blessing?

The *Quran states, "Do the people think that they will be left to say, 'We believe' and they will not be tried" (29:2)? Know that what you're going through is merely a trial, and all affairs should be transferred fully to Allah (swt). Every trial has a beginning and an end. No trial lasts forever! We are all tried, however, our greatest mistake is that many of us look at these trials as a burden, and ask, "Why me?" In reality when you reflect on such trials, it is only then you will realize it is an opportunity! All trials are an opportunity to gain nearness to Allah (swt). All trials are blessings because they cement a platform for us that guides us to Allah (swt).

What is our purpose in life? The *Quran states, "And I did not create the jinn and mankind except to worship Me" (51:56). Meaning, to worship Allah (swt) not just through our Islamic duties, but in all actions. Sometimes mankind drifts away from the straight path because they start feeling overly dependent on themselves, and fail to remember Allah (swt). Because Allah (swt) loves them so much, He (swt) blesses them with a trial so mankind can remember Him (swt).

Remember, our end goal isn't this world, but it is the hereafter! We look at these trials as a heavy load, but at the same time when we start reflecting we realize that because of such a trial we have become more dependent on Allah (swt), and conscious of Him (swt). When we put it together, instead of asking "why," one begins enjoying the trial and embracing it because we are getting closer to our Creator (swt). We are not at loss; the only individuals who are at loss are those who aren't truly obeying and serving Allah (swt). The only way an individual becomes alive is if he is connected to Allah (swt). Other than that, they might seem awake, but really, they're in a state of "sleepiness." Look around you! We think all these individuals are having the greatest time of their lives. We presume they have everything, but looks are deceiving. Many of them lack Allah (swt) in their lives. They're preparing for this world, while we are preparing for the hereafter, our permanent home; our true abode. The **Quran states, "And this life of the world is nothing but a sport and a play; and as for the next abode that most surely is the life-- did they but know" (29:64)!

Before I conclude, I would like to share a life lesson by Imam Musa al-Kazim (as). A man who found light in the midst of darkness, Imam Musa al-Kazim (as) was treated unjustly by an oppressor and was sentenced to prison for several years without any legitimate reason. When he (as) first entered prison, he thanked Allah (swt) because he always wanted to worship Him (swt) alone.

* Quran English Translation by Sahih International
** Quran English Translation by Muhammad Habib Shakir

Reflection 58

I Worship Myself

Who is it that you glorify? Many of us go about our lives worshiping everything but Allah (swt). We idolize: our spouse, our children, our professions, our wealth, celebrities, technology, etc. However, the most common form of worship mankind commits in my opinion is, "the worship of oneself." We have taken our souls as Gods. Our own souls are being praised instead of Allah (swt)! We nurtured our ego, and coated it with pride, and called it power and confidence. Polytheism comes in all shapes and molds. For instance, simple acts are hard for us to do because we believe that we are remarkable, and above all.

Like apologizing FIRST to someone who we hurt, or cleaning after others. Many of us refuse to participate in such noble acts because we assume it might hinder our social status. We have built this image of ourselves that doing such acts is considered abnormal. In particular, some people are infatuated with their physical beauty, "I am so...I can't do that!" Okay, but what makes you think that you're so fantastic? Your hair that will eventually turn gray, or your skin that will wrinkle? Others say, "I have an excessive amount of wealth, I am better than that! I will have someone do it for me because I won't." Are you referring to the same wealth that doesn't follow you to your grave? We have countless opportunities to worship Allah (swt), but instead we choose to worship ourselves! Majority of individuals behave in such a strange selfish way! They only take measures that benefit them. During their struggles they depend on Allah (swt) fully, but once the rain stops and the sun is shining, and Allah (swt) guides them to their destination, they start perceiving themselves as a God. They start saying, "I and only I worked hard to get where I am today," forgetting Who (swt) controls all affairs. They refuse to give back to Allah (swt).

For example, have you ever come across a doctor who sponsors a few patients and treats them for free? Or a pharmacist who sponsors free medication? Or a dentist who sponsors free cleanings/fillings? Or a lawyer who sponsors free cases? Or a mechanic who sponsors a free oil change? Or a restaurant owner who sponsors free food? So on and so forth! Very rare. They perceive themselves as "self made." So all the luxury of their "hard work" belongs to them, and none to Allah (swt), and the people. Everything is a transaction, rarely we find anyone doing an act strictly for Allah (swt). If you want to create a better world, obey and serve Allah (swt)! If you want to create a corrupt world, worship yourself. Where are the people that want to do Allah's (swt) work in this life? Be the difference! There is no God, but Allah (swt).

Reflection 59

Love

Love is an interesting topic. Men and women do questionable things in the name of love. You find some individuals go throughout all their lives searching for love. From one person to another, and so on. Searching for a strong, vigorous, full of energy feeling towards someone. Of course it is not bad to love, or be loved, but how society portrays love is detrimental.

Take for example Shakespeare's Romeo and Juliet. This famous play has reached countless individuals. As we know, the story concludes by Juliet appearing dead to Romeo, but really she is in a state of unconsciousness. So Romeo poisons himself to death. Juliet wakes up to find Romeo dead, and then she stabs herself to death. Mind you, the first time we came across this play was during high school. Anyway, what is the final message in this play? Many people find this play beautiful, but in reality it is deceiving. The message this play gives off is, if you don't end up with your lover then death is the answer. Again, society is embedding such behavior in a person's mind at a young age.

This action is not only limited to this play, we find such behavior in movies, shows, books, etc. For many of us the definition of love is surreal. It is too Hollywood! We watch two actors who are ACTING produce a love story, and we say, "That's what we want." When we realize expectation isn't met, we fall into depression and even contemplate suicide. Search, "What is the number one cause of depression?" This is the flawed system that we were taught. This is why the divorce rate is very high. Two people meet each other, they assume they're in love, they're attracted to each other, say the right words, but really, they're infatuated with each other. Once infatuation disappears, it is goodbye.

Now, what is the love that we should be seeking? The love that directs us to Allah (swt). The love that encourages us to stay away from sin; not that type of love that engages in sin, and uses the excuses of, "I love you" or "eventually I am going to marry you" to justify their actions. The love that motivates us to pray, fast, recite the Quran, practice good morals, and become God conscious. That is love! The same love that the Imam (as) describes when he (as) says, [24] "Every time I look at Fatima (as), my worries and sadness would disappear." This is the love that is built on a foundation revolving around Allah (swt). Make all your decisions based on who or what can bring you closer to Allah (swt), especially when it comes to choosing a significant other.

[24] Attributed to Imam Ali (as)

Reflection 60

Allah (swt) is Only Known When

Some intense obstacles we face daily are worrisomeness, nervousness, and unease. Men, women, and children of all ages suffer from some type of anxiety. How can we control such common human nature? How can we transition from anxious to tranquil? Once we start prioritizing Allah (swt) in our lives! Once we start telling ourselves that, "This very breath I just took is not possible unless Allah (swt) allowed it." Many of us don't view our lives in this scope. Many of us wait until our lives are perfect to feel tranquil.

It is essential that we build a relationship with Allah (swt), a strong vivid connection with Him (swt). It is unfortunate that Allah (swt) is only known during Islamic Pilgrimage, Ramadan, and Ashura. It is unfortunate that Allah (swt) is only known when a father, mother, or child dies. It is unfortunate that Allah (swt) is only known during weak health, poverty, and exams. This is why we will never truly understand who Allah (swt) is to us, because we only go to Him (swt) in the time of need, not want.

A *scholar once stated that an individual's relationship with Allah (swt) is based on their daily prayers. Meaning, if you don't pray, or you dislike praying, or delay prayers, or prayer feels like a burden, then this is the relationship one has with Allah (swt). For instance, I'm not sure why, but many of us assume morning prayer is optional, as if it is not mandatory for us to be up before sunrise. Think about it, we have already committed a sin before our eyes have opened by intentionally snoozing. Do you choose Allah (swt) or the sweetness of sleep?

To end, once a man was experiencing intense grief at the loss of his son. Imam al-Sadiq (as) tells the man, [25] "You are grieving at the minor affliction, and heedless of the major affliction. If only you prepared yourself for the place your son passed to, your grief would not be so intense. For your affliction at having neglected the preparation for the hereafter is much greater than the loss of your son." The best way to prepare for the hereafter is to connect to Allah (swt).

* From a lecture by Hajj Khalil Jaffer.

[25] Reyshari, Muhammadi. "Affliction." *Al-Islam.org*, Ahlul Bayt Digital Islamic Library Project, 18 Jan. 2020.

Reflection 61

Trying to Fit In

When do we draw the line? Many of us go about our lives trying to present a case for the human race that we belong as Muslims. We water down Islam from it's true message to fit in, when we should really be proving to Allah (swt) that we are worthy to be called Muslims.

We witness it all the time, the message of Islam being compromised for the sake of pleasing the creation. Why do we have to forcefully accept the ideologies of others, and if we don't we are considered arrogant and evil. We should be able to say respectfully, "I don't agree with this matter because Allah (swt) states..." Unfortunately, the mindset of today preaches to accept falsehood regardless of what the divine truth is. Basically, as long as everyone is happy we are okay. Now, let's look at history; let's look at the individuals who didn't compromise their faith, and directed all their power to Allah (swt). The Messenger of Allah (saww), one man, one mission, and one Lord. Today, we account for two billion Muslims. Imam Husayn (as), 72 champions, one mission, and one Lord. Today, over millions of people visit him (as) yearly on Arba'een, only. By Allah (swt), look at the outcome of those who lived to please strictly Allah (swt). Do you not ever wonder the full potential an individual can reach if they obeyed Allah (swt), only? By the will of Allah (swt), Prophet Musa (as) split the sea!

We have to work on pleasing Allah (swt) only, because such a journey alone requires a lifetime. The *Quran states, "To each among you, We have prescribed a law and an open way. If Allah had so willed, He would have made you a single people, but (His plan is) to test you in what He hath given you: so strive as in a race in all virtues. The goal of you all is to Allah; it is He that will show you the truth of the matters in which you dispute" (5:48).

* Quran English Translation by Yusuf Ali

Reflection 62

When I Am Ready

"When I am ready!" How many of us have used or still use this phrase?

- "When do you want to start worshiping Allah (swt) and learn about His (swt) message of Islam?"
- "When do you want to start praying, fasting, and reciting the Quran and Dua?"
- "When do you want to go to Hajj?"
- "When do you want to wear a hijab and dress more modestly?"

When? When? When? "WHEN I AM READY?" Such words are secretly disguised by the Chief Deceiver Shaytan to keep us astray.

Thus far, have we ever been ready for anything? Don't we have to work hard, discipline ourselves, learn, study, and practice for us to be ready? This strategy that we use on other matters should be applied to religion as well. If we are waiting until one day to "magically" become ready, then surely we are naive. Look how much time we put towards academics and entertainment! Have we put a quarter of that time towards Islam?

What is stopping you from entering the gates of Islam? Is it your sins that Allah (swt) already forgave you for? What is it? Whatever it may be, be the difference...strive for READY!

In a world where one can be anything, especially here in the west (we don't worry about genocides, gunfire and bombs, electric outages, and unclean water), why not be a pious Muslim? The *Quran states, "And whoever turns away from My remembrance - indeed, he will have a depressed life" (20:124).

* Quran English Translation by Sahih International

Reflection 63

Jealousy

Many of us suffer from jealousy and the method of comparing ourselves to others. These two characteristics have killed more humans than any war known to mankind, in my opinion. They're recognized to be a mental death trap. These were the traits that prevented Shaytan from bowing down to Prophet Adam (as). "I am fire; he is clay," Shaytan said. These qualities originate from our animalistic nature. They reside within all of us, but we can control such nature by becoming more conscious of Allah (swt). Society goes on to label individuals with such attributes as "haters," but that is not the case in my perspective. We are not "haters," we are just not aware yet. How can we transition from darkness to light? Many individuals say:

- "Why is he or she wealthy, and I am poor?"
- "How are they already in graduate school, and I am still taking my basic requirement classes?"
- "Why are they healthy, and I am weak?"

At first hand, such statements are presumed to be envious, but in reality it might be out of innocent ignorance. What we lack is the knowledge to understand that Allah (swt) has a different plan for everyone. Each plan is specifically tailored to the individual at best, which consists of either keeping the individual close to Allah (swt) or routing them to the path of Allah (swt). For example, how many people do you know that when they were living a standard life, they obeyed and served Allah (swt), but as soon as they became wealthy they became sinners?

To end, O' you who are fortunate to possess the luxuries and treasures of this world, don't be eager to boast and gloat your credentials. Do you not take into consideration that you're the one that might be provoking the jealousy of the people?

Reflection 64

Oil and Water Can't Fuse

We have to separate Islam from our culture! Culture is known to revolve around traditions, customs, arts, etc., while religion is submitting to Allah (swt). Many of us live out our lives by combining the two, which leads to excessive confusion. Also, we tend to favor and practice our cultural beliefs instead of our religious obligations more. Nonetheless, some cultural acts are considered right but are religiously wrong.

A simple and common scenario that we can all relate to is the physical interaction with extended family members like: first cousins, an uncle's wife, or an aunt's husband, and so on. Culture says when you greet them, you should: high five them, shake their hand, hug them, kiss them, and if you don't you're deemed to be disrespectful. But from a religious perspective, touching anyone who is non-mahram to you is considered forbidden. We must separate our religion from our culture. Even when it comes to dress codes, compare the differences between cultural and religiously driven clothes. These are minimal examples. On a larger scale, in some culturally motivated households, the treatment of spouses is unjust. The man is a king and his wife is a slave, and vice versa. When we fail to separate cultural norms from religion, we get people expressing that "the treatment of spouses in Islam is oppressive," but that is not true because when you study Islam properly you will notice marriages flourished. Read upon how Imam Ali (as) treated Lady Fatima (as), or how Sayed Ruhollah Khomeini (ra) treated his spouse. There are many cases where undesirable actions were derived from culture, but religion faced the consequences because we didn't distinguish between the two.

To end, this world and its societies are deceiving, and if we are not aware we will get lost within it. As I was watching a television show, a commercial came on about driving under the influence of alcohol, and how police are aggressively pushing to prevent such behavior, I thought to myself, "that's awesome." The very next commercial was an advertisement for an alcoholic beverage company. Do you now see how this world works? They feed you good with evil at the same time, trying to deceive you, and stopping you from reaching your ultimate goal; that is the case for us as well, when we follow our religion and take cultural acts that contradict Islam.

Reflection 65

I Can't Cry

I cannot cry for Imam Husayn (as) nor for his family and companions. As I sit in the lecture hall I hear men, women, and children of all ages weeping, but I cannot. As the reciter describes the tragic events that took place, I look around and realize only my head is held up high. I cannot help but ask, "Why do I not share a connection with Aba Abdillah al-Husayn (as)?" Why does my heart feel rigid and solid towards him (as). Every year many of us are troubled with this matter, to the point that it discourages us from attending anything Ashura related. There are clear signs for those who cannot shed tears for the "Legend of Karbala" if they reflect, in my opinion.

You see the thing is, truly crying for Imam Husayn (as) is a precious gift from Allah (swt) reserved for the believers. This beautiful reward that rejuvenates the soul isn't just handed out to anyone. One must earn it. Sure, generations of people have cried and cried, but many of them imitate and perform a mocking act that they're aware of. It is not pure. Purely weeping is from the heart, not the eyes only. We must reserve time alone to contemplate and ask, "Why can't I cry?" Within an instant we will come to a conclusion; "I am not able to cry because I intentionally indulge in the sins of..." Sinning destroys an individual more than any kind of terminal disease. Furthermore, we want to know who Imam Husayn (as) is within ten days, only. If we spent all our lives studying this profound man, we still would not know him. If we want to know him (as) we must try to mimic his (as) God consciousness all year round, so that we may purely tear for him (as). A "ten day Muslim" isn't possible. We don't function in this way. To get a full experience of Ashura we must take the time to prepare our hearts, not when Ashura starts, but when it ends, the day after. The journey starts then!

Nonetheless, ask yourself, "Why am I crying for Imam Husayn (as)?" On paper Imam Husayn (as) has a happy ending as we know. Sure, the people of this world betrayed him, but when it is all said and done, his end is, "leader of the youth in paradise." Next time we want to weep for Imam Husayn (as) we should cry for ourselves as well because we are blessed with this great life lesson (Ashura) that exposes this world, yet we still cannot perceive it for its reality because we purposely let it's temporary ornaments blind us. What is your end? Cry for yourself!

Reflection 66

Dating

Passage 1

Dating is not for us! Sure, social media brings people together, but it's also manifesting the sins of this world. Of these sins is physical interaction between men and women. It seems harmless because the culture of the west promotes it as a norm, but in reality, it is not the standard in Islam. Unfortunately, many of us are inheriting this western ideology, and are using the argument of "we are in love" to support it. All kinds of individuals are flaunting their sinful behavior on social media when it comes to relationships, without any respect to Allah (swt). How does one justify such forbidden actions?

It seems nowadays we have zero tolerance for modesty! Many say, "I am going to do whatever I want, and I don't care what anyone thinks." Fine, adopt such a mentality, but be aware of who you are challenging, Allah (swt)! Why do we belittle such sins like: holding hands, hugging, kissing, flirting, etc.? Also, having a "fatiha" or * "toulbeh" doesn't mean we can begin crossing boundaries with someone who is still non-mahram to us. Just because our parents have become publically aware of our relationship, that doesn't mean we can do whatever we want now; it is still about what Islam says.

Do we not learn from past relationships of others? How many couples do you know that came together in a non-permissible fashion, and their end was disastrous? Let's put into perspective of what typically happens:

- Step 1: Get to know each other.
- Step 2: Become infatuated with each other.
- Step 3: Fake love/attachment.
- Step 4: Crossing forbidden boundaries for a few minutes of pleasure.
- Step 5: Needs have been satisfied, time to eject.
- Step 6: Sadness/depression/hurt/hate/regret begins.
- Step 7: Repeat with another person.

These steps could have been easily avoided if one chose the route of Islam. Unfortunately, the saying in the west is, "try before you buy." Meaning, before you marry anyone you must be verbally flirtatious, or you must physically interact with them to find out if you're serious about them. Mind you, jumping from relationship to relationship might seem fun in the short run, but it is emotionally destructive in the long term. On the other hand Islam states, it is not wrong to get to know someone, but the potential couple must abide by the rules of Islam. These rules are meant to protect us! An acceptable approach in my opinion is:

- Step 1: Seek someone based on compatibility.
- Step 2: Ask about the individual.
- Step 3: Light and non-flirtatious communication to find out if the interest is mutual.
- Step 4: Take permission from the guardian.
- Step 5: Get to know each other under the supervision of the parents, like at the girl's home, or in a proper public setting. Have logical and spiritual conversations about real life scenarios and important topics.
- Step 6: Come together and make a decision on how to proceed.

If this approach doesn't work, it's okay. At least it ends on good and respectable terms, unlike the other method. Sisters and brothers, don't sell yourself short investing in a foundation built on corruption. Surely pleasure fades while consequences remain, and dues must be paid.

*A formal ceremony to ask the parents of the potential bride for her hand in marriage.

Passage 2

Sweet Talk

This is a real problem amongst men! Now I am not saying women don't do this either, but it's mostly infamous with men. Many men sweet talk women to get what they want. They're of the belief that they know how to "spit game," but really they're being manipulative.

To get with a girl they will tell her anything and everything that she likes. For example, they will say, "I love you," or make false promises to achieve their goal. And after they're done, they label themselves as, "the guy who knows how to pick up girls." Oh really? You lied through your teeth to get what you want! You really know how to treat someone, huh? They don't take into consideration the damage and hurt they have caused, but Allah (swt) does.

Also, sometimes we meet people and they might seem impulsive and unstable, maybe they recently went through a traumatic experience. When such individuals cross your path, don't try to talk them up and take advantage of them. Instead, protect them and offer them help as if they were your own kin.

To stop such behavior we must become God conscious; it's easy for someone to hide their intention from the creation, but impossible from the Creator (swt). You shouldn't play with the hearts of people, even if they're not from the same background as you, a human being is a human being.

Reflection 67

Praying On Time

Take a moment and gaze at yourself. Do not let the image you perceive deceive you! Our smooth unwrinkled skin and non-gray hair can be misleading. Meaning, such youthful physical traits can fuel our rebellious nature and encourage us to neglect the Angel of Death. We must separate ourselves from our physical figure, and understand death doesn't discriminate, and comes for all ages.

One way to prepare for the Angel of Death is to steer away from sin. This can easily be done if we perform our five daily prayers on TIME! Notice how the word TIME is strongly emphasized. Human beings are like technology; if technology doesn't receive its daily electrical charge, it becomes unproductive. For instance, when we don't plug our cellphones in charge, it shuts down, and becomes useless. Now, if we don't pray, and receive our daily boost, we will become inefficient from a spiritual standpoint. We might still be productive regarding our worldly affairs, but when it comes to battling our sins and the hereafter, truly we are at loss.

Having said that, praying on time has a whole different effect on us. To put it into perspective, envision that our prayers are like force fields. For example, our first force field goes up after completing morning prayer, but as the day goes on this force field starts to weaken. It needs to be recharged and strengthened during noon prayer to protect us, and the same for the following prayers, but what do most of us do? We decide to delay prayer and tell ourselves, "In one hour I'll get up," or "after studying this slide," or "after this show," etc. This increases the chances of sinning, because our force field is deteriorating as time goes on.

We shouldn't belittle praying on time; the protection it brings is indescribable. We can eliminate almost all of our sins by receiving the reminder of Allah (swt) at the appropriate time. Imam Ali (as) states, [26] "The first *sujud means I was once mud and clay, and as I raise my head from sujud, it means I came to this world from soil. The second sujud means I will return again to the soil, and as I raise my head from sujud, it means on the Day of Judgment, I will rise up from the grave, and be summoned."

[26] Qara'ati, Mushin. "Bowing Down {Ruku'} and Prostration {Sujud}." *Al-Islam.org*, Ahlul Bayt Digital Islamic Library Project, 13 Sept. 2015.
* Prostration to Allah (swt).

Reflection 68

Music

Passage 1

Music! Next time before we reach for the radio knob, let's pause for a moment, and actually reflect on what it is we are pumping into our ears. Without a doubt, we can all agree that any kind of music can alter our mood. We can go from extremely happy to sad within seconds. We shouldn't accept such a controlling platform! Music has been around for a long time. However, it took a wrong turn during the mid-1900s; the music industry switched its focus from poor to unacceptable. The irony is we find ourselves accepting and promoting such forbidden tunes. When you really narrow it down, you realize that we only have two kinds of music artists. On the left we have those who speak about: drugs, intercourse, violence, money, weapons and so on. While on the right we have: relationships, love, heartbreaks, despair, etc. Now of course, there are a handful of artists in the mix who mention prominent issues, but even their work is questionable sometimes. For example, we don't need to hear profanity every other word to get the point across.

Focusing on the left first, the left is very popular among all ages especially the youth. By nature, human beings are a product of trial. They like to experience things first hand. For instance, suppose we take a young child and expose their foundation to music that emphasizes on drugs. Let's say the child grows up and becomes an addict. However, society is confused about how this happened with this child; they were never exposed to drugs at all. Sometimes verbal exposure has a greater effect than physical exposure. Music opens doors, and paints images in the mind that are too tempting to pass up. Now the right! The right is mischievous. The question is, why listen to music that puts us purposely in a state of misery? For example, suppose someone goes through a terrible experience with an individual. Instead of trying to forget this individual through the gateway of Allah (swt), they rely on such music. This leads them to more suffering, developing strong hate, remembering memories, and to never let go. We don't need to go through endless experiences to understand this is a flawed system.

Logic and reflection can answer many questions. Many of us say, "Music is life." Definitely not! Music is a maze with no exits. It's a trap for false desires, hopes, sins, and unattainable expectations. Where do we draw the line? Personally, avoid music completely. Suppose you listen to music that isn't a part of the left or right, avoid it too because there is a high chance it might lead you to the music of the left or right. We are people of caution, not desires. Don't let yourself get used to such recitation! Fight it! If you need something to listen to while driving, here are some alternatives: Quran, Dua, latmiyat/nasheed, poetry, LECTURES, etc. If none of these are appealing, listen to the sound of your breathing, and know it isn't possible unless Allah (swt) wills, and then maybe things which remind us of Him (swt) will become appealing. Challenge yourself! Go a day without music, and then compare/evaluate yourself to how you feel when you do listen to music.

Passage 2

I was asked what type of music is permissible...

I am not qualified to say what type of music is permissible. However, I will say this, music does play with our emotions in my opinion. I found that it puts us in a state of sadness, even when we might not be sad at all; or a state of over excitement, which can lead to impulsive actions, and is extremely dangerous. It does alter our minds and has a huge effect on us! It's a controlling mechanism. We should stay away from music that speaks about: drugs, intercourse, impermissible relationships, violence, etc. The main reason why many people cannot let go of their past relationships is because they continue listening to music that reminds them of it, which leaves them stuck in such a state.

Reflection 69

Our Mind

One of the greatest challenges we face regularly is the battle of the unseen. The battle of the unseen takes place in our mind. No one is aware of it, but us. However, such battles can be conquered and beat through reflection, consciousness, and time. The mind is constantly suggesting to us different types of thoughts that can either be good or bad. A *scholar once said, "We are not our thoughts, and we must separate ourselves from our thoughts."

For example, suppose I am always thinking about consuming alcoholic beverages. Day and night I am wondering how it tastes, how it feels to be drunk, and hung over. Does this make me an alcoholic? No, these are animalistic thoughts recommended by my mind, and fueled by the whispers of the Chief Deceiver, Shaytan. If we capitalize on our thoughts, then we become them! However, if we keep fighting our thoughts off, it is unlikely we will engage in them; but if we don't, we will start believing that these immoral acts are a part of our nature, and eventually indulge in them. So it is a matter of convincing oneself. Meaning, tell yourself, "Just because I am thinking of... and it is all taking place within me, it doesn't mean that is who I am."

Unfortunately, our immoral thoughts will never fade away forever, but our thoughts can become like the wind and just breeze by, when we work on increasing our consciousness of Allah (swt). To end, this might come as a surprise, but be aware and extra cautious of such immoral thoughts when you're in a state of happiness and excitement. Such a state blinds one's true vision, and inclines them to become rebellious while ignoring consequences! Surely a state of happiness and excitement is a trial as well.

* From a lecture by Hajj Khalil Jaffer.

Reflection 70

Today's Information

Knowledge is not about how much you know, but it is acting upon what you know! We can sit here day and night reading books, articles, and posts about Islam and how to become a devoted worshipper. We also have the luxury to attend lectures and watch online videos as well! But why are we still failing instead of succeeding? For example, when it comes to certain topics we have plenty of information about them; we have answers to why it is "haram," why we should stay away from it, the side effects of it, and so on, yet we still indulge in it. Many of us play the unaware card on purpose. How do we let our souls use such poor excuses? With the technology we have access to currently, acquiring information about anything shouldn't be an issue. Maybe many years ago it would have been a problem, but nowadays? Come on…let's be honest with ourselves.

The information that we are taking in is increasing our knowledge, but when we don't act upon it, it is as if we didn't obtain anything, and then we are confused as to why we haven't changed. We have narrations about the Prophet Muhammad (saww) and AhlulBayt (as) which are profound, they describe how they lived their lives. We examine such information and all we gain out of it is being in "awe." This information doesn't exist for our amusement; it is present so we can learn from it and implement it in our lives. For instance, you think the tragedy of Karbala occurred so we can tell our children bedtime stories? Of course not! The lessons of Karbala should be applied in our everyday lives!

Nevertheless, many of us have a sole intent of acquiring information to debate, argue, and challenge others. It is as if we are the official attorneys for Islam, and were appointed by Allah (swt). If your intention is to prove others wrong, and label it as, "I am speaking the truth," then by Allah (swt) you're deceiving yourself! We shouldn't speak with the notion to demonstrate to people that we are knowledgeable, or to frustrate them to get our point across. We should only speak with the purpose of bringing individuals nearer to Allah (swt). To end, [27] "Knowledge is associated with action. Therefore, whoever knows should act [upon it] because knowledge CALLS for action"- Imam Ali (as).

[27] Ṭālib 'Alī Ibn Abī. *Nahjul Balagha: Peak of Eloquence: Sermons, Letters and Sayings*. Tahrike Tarsile Qur'an, 2009. –p.908

Reflection 71

The Structure of Our Lives

In today's age, we have adopted a destructive life structure! Instead of constructing an organized system where Allah (swt) is at the highest, we have accepted a system that isolates us from Him (swt). Meaning, take a simple paper for example, at the very top there is a title that is big and bold! Suppose this title represents Allah (swt), and all subheadings that follow the title represent different categories for an individual in their life. Assume the fifth category is money. When we follow such a structure, we are not going to settle to acquire unlawful wealth in any way, by any means necessary. Rather, we are going to seek the guidance of the title on top, and follow what Islam states regarding what is permitted and not while one is trying to attain a livelihood. Other categories can be: relationships, friends, food, etc. This system protects an individual because everything falls under the banner of Allah (swt).

Unfortunately, that is not the case for many of us because we tend to replace the title that represents Allah (swt) with worldly affairs. How many times have we heard the expression, "Put Allah (swt) and religion on the side," or "religion is something, and this is something else." It is very common to attempt to separate Allah (swt) from our daily lives to satisfy our desires. We make excuses to push our personal agenda, but there is one thing that we fail to realize. When we don't have this constant consciousness of Allah (swt) at every moment, then we are willingly inviting the Chief Deceiver, Shaytan into our lives. This world is a battle of good versus evil, and if we divorce our lives from Allah (swt) then our end is clear, apparent, and well known. To end, The *Quran states, "He is the First and the Last, the Evident and the Immanent: and He has full knowledge of all things" (57:3).

* Quran English Translation by Yusuf Ali

Reflection 72

Happiness

Passage 1

Happiness is a mischievous word because it is presented with no boundaries. How many times have we thought a certain "thing," or individual was going to bring us happiness, but did the total opposite. It is not wrong to be happy, what is wrong is taking it out of context. Happiness is simply just an emotion, and emotions change from time to time; it is human nature! Happiness is not a way of life, but society promotes it as if it is, and that is why we have individuals spending their whole lives searching for permanent happiness.

"Do whatever makes you happy," they say, but at what cost? Suppose what makes me happy is a sin? So am I supposed to indulge in such sin to achieve my dose of happiness? Such a motto is flawed! Do not fall in the trap of trying to achieve "constant happiness" by any means necessary, because it can cause greater harm to you than good. What we expect out of happiness cannot be attained in this world in my humble opinion!

Having said that, what should we search for? First, tell me, how can a mother or father attain endless happiness if they lost a child? How can you and I search for never-ending happiness with all the oppression that goes on in the world? How can one who is disabled achieve permanent happiness when they're viewed as an outcast? We must understand who Allah (swt) is! He (swt) will not create "something" that can only be attained by a handful of people, and not all. This is unfair, and the All-Just (swt) is not unfair! Meaning, the parents, the oppressed, and the disabled will probably never achieve "constant happiness" per the definition of society, but they can attain tranquility! This is the state we should be searching for, and it is reserved with Allah (swt).

Passage 2

Question: Do you define happiness as?

1. Way of Life
2. Just an Emotion

Have you ever seen someone happy when death claims one of their family members, or when sickness enters their lives? As a matter of fact, we cannot even stay happy if we do bad on an exam! How can it be a way of life?

I think many of us confuse a peaceful state of mind with happiness. When we lose a loved one, we can be sad and tranquil at the same time, but can one be sad and happy at the same time? Have you ever seen someone who is joyous and filled with laughter at a funeral?

The point is, if you're searching for happiness as a way of life here, you'll never find it. It's like entering a never-ending maze! Don't treat happiness more than it is, it's just an emotion. Some people go on long quests to search for eternal happiness in this world, and they become disappointed because it doesn't exist in a world that's created specifically to TEST you.

Passage 3

A real challenge is obeying and serving Allah (swt) when you're happy, and when life is going your way. It is easy to seek Allah (swt) when you're sad and down, but do you desire Allah (swt) the same when you're happy?

Reflection 73

Anxiety

Anxiety is a common condition among many people. To be in a state of unease, worry, and having racing thoughts is normal. However, what is not normal is having the resources to completely stop such a state or slow it down, yet not taking full advantage of them. Now, to be straight forward, I am not addressing severe anxiety that requires medication prescribed by doctors. Rather, I will be concentrating on the beginning stages of anxiety, which is the step much before severe. Many of us can dodge severe anxiety if we take proper action from the start, but unfortunately, instead of tackling the issue, we get lost in it as if we are in a maze; however, even a maze has a route out when one follows accurate directions. To abolish/stabilize anxiety within us, one must follow the light that guides us to Allah (swt).

First and foremost, when it comes to anything, there are rules one must adhere to. Whether it is at a job, school, public place, at home, etc. So, what is one main rule for a human being? It is to fully understand what we can and cannot control. To understand we are limited and not limitless. To understand we are confined by boundaries and time. This one simple law, if we follow it, can relinquish us from anxiety. Meaning, many of us fear tomorrow, we are afraid of the future. Others live in the past, they cannot let go of yesterday, and several of us are disturbed by both. To make things simpler, I will try to present a scenario of how a student behaves leading up to taking an exam; this is something many of us can relate to. When exam season rolls around, many of us begin having anxiety attacks, and playing endless "what if situations." We worry, worry, worry, and worry some more, and it's not until we have taken our exams that our worrying slows down. Then we worry again until our grades are posted, and it's not until we see a passing grade that we become pleased with ourselves. Now, how can we relate this to real life? In a nutshell our attitude is dependent on certain variables and elements. We don't become anxious-free until we fully witness our "lifeboat" sailing smoothly, but are we really free or are we temporarily distracting ourselves?

If mankind just followed the rules of his nature set by Allah (swt), suffering becomes conquerable, but mankind doesn't. You see, if we practiced patience instead of investing our energy in worrying, we wouldn't be addressing anxiety greatly in this context; however, because mankind sometimes willingly disregards Allah's (swt) signs and communication, he is left with distress by his own hands. Know your role, and practice your part!

Disclaimer: This post should not be taken as medical advice; it is a mere reflection.

Reflection 74

Forgiveness

Truly repenting is probably one of the easiest things we can do. To the point where before you finish reading this sentence, if you had asked Allah (swt) to sincerely forgive you, you would be forgiven. It is that fast! Think about it, what other relationship offers an individual a clean slate at any given time? We don't even have such a relationship with ourselves. How many times do we beat ourselves up over past sins? If we really knew how merciful Allah (swt) is, we would be amazed. *He (swt) says, "O' son of Adam, if your sins were to reach the clouds of the sky and then you would seek My forgiveness, I would forgive you." This profound statement is speaking to you and I. Now to be clear, this doesn't mean to purposely live a sinner's life, and do whatever we want, and then when it is all said and done it is time for a change. Rather, in my opinion it is speaking to those of us who say, "I want Allah (swt), and I want to be on the straight path, but I have already done so much, and I know I am going to hell." Let's be honest, if your career was to be a sinner, and your shift was 24 hours long, 365 days a year, your sins still wouldn't be able to reach the clouds of the sky.

But is that really the case here? Something so easy, yet it is barely utilized? The truth of the matter is many of us do not want to truly repent. By truly repenting I mean giving up our sins, and trying our hardest to not rekindle them. For many, a sinner's life is more entertaining and amusing than truly repenting. The people of Prophet Nuh (as) were once sinners as well, and then it rained, and it didn't stop raining, and they were gone. The people of Prophet Hud (as) ignored his holy message, and continued to be sinners, and then a terrible tornado destroyed them, and only the good were saved. The people of Prophet Salih (as) did the same thing, and an earthquake ended them. The same thing happened to the people of Prophet Shu'ayb (as), and plenty more.

Our problem is we take these legends as "fairy tales." Many of us dislike the approach of fear when it comes to calling an individual to the straight path, but what is one supposed to do when the approach of love is constantly being taken advantage of? To be clear, I am not saying to tell someone off the bat, "If you don't do this or that, you will go to hell." However, do tell them that there is a punishment, make them aware of it; it shouldn't be left out completely. In addition, in no way am I trying to say Allah (swt) is not loving, caring, or forgiving, but based on history, we are naive if we believe that His (swt) punishment is not true. Balance your life between love and fear. Don't let one overcome the other, and begin the process of truly repenting. Us, the followers of the Prophet Muhammad (saww), let's not let our arrogance overtake us. With so many facts, how can we?

* Hadith al-Qudsi

Reflection 75

The Bigger Picture

Our focus shouldn't be narrow; we have to take the bigger picture into consideration. Many individuals go about their lives doing what is best for them in the most selfish way possible. Harm is of two kinds; first, to one's self, and second, to society. Allah (swt) states in the *Quran, "O you who believe! Do not go near prayer when you are intoxicated until you know (well) what you say" (4:43). Many individuals make the excuse of consuming alcohol because of this verse. These people have taken the Quran without proper and scholarly interpretation. (DISCLAIMER: Consuming alcoholic beverages is forbidden at all times!) Anyway, to draw a better point about narrow focus versus bigger picture, let's assume that a random individual is a "narrow thinker," only for this scenario.

Scenario: One day, after witnessing heavy advertising about alcoholic beverages, and hearing stories of what consuming alcohol does to a person by others, this random individual decided today is the day! He says, "Today I will go out and have my first drink, but first I have to see if it is allowed." He opens up the Quran and searches for intoxication, and comes across the verse mentioned above. To himself he says, "Everything checks out. I am allowed to indulge in alcoholic beverages; I am just not allowed to be drunk while I pray. Perfect!" As the night goes on he is drinking, drinking, and drinking. All the way up to here, he is a narrow thinker! So according to his narrow thinking, this is all okay! But then what starts happening? He becomes intoxicated, and he is not in a state of awareness anymore. Slowly he starts gazing at the opposite gender, and the rest is history. He might have committed zina (unlawful sexual intercourse), or even adultery. Such stories are very common in the world of alcohol. Then he gets in his car and starts driving, he swerves and crashes into another car that had a family of five in it. The crash was so bad that he killed them all, but he lived. These are all sins that Allah (swt) directly forbids in the Quran. Now do you see what narrow focus leads to?

Had this random individual looked at the bigger picture from the start, he wouldn't have needed anything to tell him directly that alcohol is forbidden, and that he should stay away from it. Another good example is about music. Many people approve of music because their favorite singer or rapper utters a few lyrics that are somewhat good to them; but when you look at the bigger picture, this same rapper or singer has hundreds of immoral songs, and their venues bring many evil and wicked acts together. Do you really want to support such a channel in any kind of way? Whether it is purchasing a ticket to a concert, or increasing their views online. Nonetheless, the point of this reflection isn't to condemn the obvious, but rather to reflect wisely on the bigger picture before we act.

* Quran English Translation by Muhammad Habib Shakir

Reflection 76

Happy New Year

It's that time of the year again, where we reflect on ourselves and make a list containing our "New Year's Resolutions." What we want to take into the New Year, and what we want to leave behind. January 1, XXXX is known to be "reset mode" for many individuals. It is ironic that we wait for a specific day to start over, when Allah (swt) gives us this option at any given time. Today, humanity has created their own religion, and if one doesn't adhere to their trends, then they're considered an outsider. They're the norm, and everyone else is bizarre. What is this religion? It is liberal Islam.

Liberal Islam comes with personal opinions instead of taking the way of the Prophet Muhammad (saww) and AhlulBayt (as). We pick and choose what we favor and leave aside what we don't, like a food buffet. But the demand here is not trying to explain what it is, but rather how did we get to this point? One way, in my opinion, is that we aren't able to distinguish between the many paths we have. We have the western lifestyle, we have the traditions and cultures of "back home," and we have Islam. What we want is a little bit of each one. The best of these three worlds! However, this is not possible because each one of these categories are enormous enough to be their own way of life. So what do we begin to do? We start to incorporate all three together, and mash them up, and now we have a whole new religion based on liberalism and secularism; this new religion allows us to pray and fast, but disregards modesty, and allows us to read the Quran, but interpret it to our liking, etc. Every day brothers and sisters are leaving true Islam for this version of "religion." Maybe because it is easier and endorses "freedom," but is it legitimate?

Reset now, and imagine yourself on a trail that has three different paths labeled: western lifestyle, culture and traditions, and true Islam. Now walk towards only Islam, but approach it in a way like how we approach college. For example, in college we cannot take upper level courses unless we fulfill certain prerequisites. This is why many individuals depart from Islam, because they dive into it from the top rather than climbing up the ladder, and taking it step by step. To be straight forward, I am not saying to completely disregard one's culture or lifestyle, but if culture or lifestyle says one thing and Islam says another, follow what Islam says! Make Islam the official and only guideline of your life. So what if you fail? Get up and try again, and again, and again. Let's not compromise our beliefs for temporary illusions. We will regret it! We have to take advantage of our youthful years and seek Allah (swt)! Nothing is more beautiful than a young individual that can have anything, but instead he or she chooses Allah (swt). Fall in love with Allah (swt). So what if the majority of the world isn't seeking Allah (swt). Don't follow them! It is stated in the *Quran, "And if you obey most of those in the earth, they will lead you astray from Allah's way; they follow but conjecture (assumptions) and they only lie" (6:116).

* Quran English Translation by Muhammad Habib Shakir

Reflection 77

To Be a Parent

To be a parent is a blessing! Hopefully in the future we will all experience the blessings of parenthood, but one must ask, "With everything going on in the world, from racism to hate, to oppression to sinning, can we really raise a child in this time?" Most definitely, but we have to be prepared. There are proper steps that we can take that will benefit our children in the future, and I am not referring to financial steps, rather steps that all the wealth in the world cannot buy. The number one mistake parents make is they wish well for their children, but not for themselves. We witness this all the time. Parents want the best for their children, so they put them in an Islamic school to be taught how to pray and to learn about Islam, but the parents themselves don't even pray, or know anything about Islam. What message does that give off? A contradicting one…maybe? This is one reason why many individuals today aren't on the straight path. For example, a boy's first role model is his father. The father works hard and puts food on the table, but completely disregards religion. The boy may come to a conclusion that because my role model doesn't practice Islam, why should I? It is not needed!

Another mistake parents make is implementing fear in their child. What type of fear? The type of fear that does not last. The only type of fear that lasts is the fear of Allah (swt). A child might fear getting punished by their parents when they're young, but do you really think this process works when the child hits their teenage years, or older when they're alone, when it really counts? When you teach a child to fear Allah (swt) only, and be conscious of Allah (swt), then they can take that everywhere with them. They cannot take you and me with them! For example, when a teenager is offered to try drugs, do you think the fear of his or her parents finding out will stop them? No, because they can easily convince themselves of ways they can hide it from their parents, with the help of the whispers of Shaytan.

But when you teach them Allah (swt) is near, and that He (swt) is closer to you than your jugular vein, and that one day all your actions will be asked about, I guarantee they will think twice! It is easy to disregard a parent, but it isn't easy to disregard the All-Seeing (swt). Lastly, the choosing of a spouse is very important. Choose a spouse that views life the same way you do, because if you don't you will cause great confusion for the child. For example, suppose the father is into religion but the mother isn't, what route should the child take?

Reflection 78

Desires

Passage 1

What is it that you DESIRE? Is it the desire for: wealth, power, success, pleasure, relationships, freedom, likeability, or…? To have permissible desires is not wrong, whats wrong is becoming slaves of our desires. Many individuals have no boundaries, whatever desire comes to mind, they will try to fulfill it by any means necessary. To live such a life is harmful! Imam Ali (as) states, [28] "O' people what I fear most about you are two things - acting according to desires and extending of hopes. With regards to acting according to desires, this prevents one from truth; and with regards to the extending of hopes, it makes one forget the next world." One of the most difficult things to do is telling oneself, "NO." It is harder than any exam you will ever take, and heavier than any weight you will ever lift.

What is one supposed to do when they really want something, but the religion of Islam states it is not allowed? You want a challenge, there's one! Who is the most honorable amongst us? Allah (swt) states in the *Quran, "…surely the most honorable of you with Allah is the one among you most careful (of his duty)" (49:13). Not careful just when it comes to praying, but careful in all aspects. Envision that you're putting a puzzle together. If one piece is missing the puzzle becomes incomplete. We all have the potential to become the greatest believers, but what stops us? Desires! If we don't control our desires, this piece alone will forever keep us incomplete when we are trying to seek Allah (swt). To overcome our desires it is important to reflect. You must pause and rigorously reflect on what it is you want from this life, and no, I am not referring to your bucket list, goals, dream career, and wedding; but actually think of what it is you want from this life. Think tirelessly! What is it that you desire?

---

[28] Ṭālib 'Alī Ibn Abī. *Nahjul Balagha: Peak of Eloquence: Sermons, Letters and Sayings*. Tahrike Tarsile Qur'an, 2009. –p.398
* Quran English Translation by Muhammad Habib Shakir

Passage 2

Control your desires before they control you, because if you don't they will transform you into a beast. A beast is constantly on the hunt, but is lost at the same time. He or she runs wild, but eventually runs themselves into the ground. Become God conscious and fear God, for that is what's best for us!

Reflection 79

Suicide

What leads an individual to take their life? Many people believe this practice occurs randomly. Meaning, an individual casually wakes up one day and decides it's their time to go. When in reality that is far from the truth; there is a process that leads a person down such a path. If we take the time to study the nature of human beings, it becomes clear. We are also of the belief that suicide is only reserved for those who don't have anything. This is not accurate; any of us can be victims of suicide if we are not careful. You will notice that suicide is not only limited to those with poor lives; rather history tells us the rich, the famous, the knowledgeable, and so on have fallen to suicide! Even those who have advocated against suicide have committed suicide. Why? What is the pattern?

In my opinion, the first thing that leads an individual to the process of suicide is believing that this life is easy and relaxed. This is mankinds' greatest mistake. Such a mentality is destructive! From the start we must accept that this life is filled with hardship, and it only becomes easier when we use the proper resources to overcome difficulties. For this to work we must prepare for our dark days during our light days.

Second, the concept of love and happiness. At a young age we are taught and told to invest all our time in love and happiness, and to try to achieve such strong feelings by any means necessary. The only problem is we aren't told and taught how to prepare if the source of our love and happiness leaves us, or how to say "NO" to it if it goes against Islam. This is the case for many people; they excessively love a person, or material things, and they find great joy in it, but once they lose the person, or their wealth for example, they fall into a state of extreme sadness.

Third, we tend to disregard the message of Allah (swt), and the actions of His (swt) noble messengers. For instance, take for example a couple in a forbidden relationship before marriage. Let's fast forward to the day they break up, and both are heartbroken and miserable. How many of us have witnessed couples go through this? In this case, had the individuals listened to the message, stayed patient, cautious, and avoided sin, they wouldn't be in a state of distress from this matter. There are countless scenarios like this that they could've learned from, but we tend to disregard them. Sometimes our actions lead us to our destruction, period.

Fourth, when death comes after a parent or child many individuals become outraged. I am not saying it is wrong to grieve, but death to all is one of the first things promised by Allah (swt). Meaning, we should be preparing for death, but what do most of us do? We neglect it, and when loss occurs, we aren't able to grasp it because of our lack of preparation, so we lose ourselves.

Fifth, the expectations and standards society pushes on people is damaging. If we don't meet their expectations and live up to their standards, we are considered failures in our mind. This isn't correct; in this world there is only one set of criteria that should matter, and that is the one ordained by Allah (swt).

To end, many individuals who are suffering mentally are embarrassed to seek proper help because it is deemed to be "weak," or because it is against the norms of their culture. Whoever speaks in this way about those trying to help themselves, may Allah (swt) forgive them because they are doing more harm than good. That being said, if you or anyone you know is suffering from suicidal thoughts, please seek the proper help.

Disclaimer: This post should not be taken as medical advice; it is a mere reflection.

Reflection 80

Kindness and Revenge

Kindness is a trait that many of us lack. We are rude, disrespectful, inconsiderate, and mean sometimes. The way we speak to each other is utterly revolting, even in a "playful" manner. Many times, when brothers get together they spend their time "ripping" on one other. Grown men! After they completely annihilate each other, they end with, "I am just kidding…you know I love you," or "stop being a little girl," if someone takes offense. I am sure sisters have their own similar version. When we don't filter out such "vain talk" from our system, we slowly adopt a hostile personality and welcome negativity into our lives. Beware of those who spill curse words often. Having said that, it is not okay to verbally abuse anyone whether you're a: parent, teacher, spouse, boss, etc. Making a mockery or humiliating someone isn't a form of discipline. One has to be strategic and fair while punishing someone. If we just go off on an individual, and begin to yell at them, this builds resentment within the person. We shouldn't leave such an impression on anyone, even if we hold a position of power, whether it being physically, mentally, or socially. Spread kindness and good energy.

Furthermore, why do we adore seeking revenge? Just because someone hurt us, it doesn't mean we have to hurt them back. Why do we fight each other over the most mundane things? If we leave our "right" to Allah (swt), we are not considered weak. Just because someone looked at you the wrong way, or said something improper to you, it doesn't make you weak if you choose to walk away. On the contrary, it is a sign of strength!

I remind you of the ²⁹ narrations about Imam Ali (as) and Husayn (as). A woman once cursed Imam Ali (as) in front of his face! She lost her husband and children at war, and she blamed Ali (as) for it. Anyway, when she cursed him (as), how did the Imam (as) respond? He began to buy her groceries, cook, clean, etc. He never told her I am Imam Ali (as); it wasn't until her daughter came and asked her if she knew who that man was, that she found out. After finding out the lady became very remorseful. In another instance a man told Imam Husayn (as), "May Allah curse you and your father." How did he (as) respond? He offered him shelter. These are the strongest warriors in history, and yet, they showed mercy; we can too!

[29]Attributed to Imam Ali (as) & Husayn (as)

Reflection 81

Just Be Straightforward

It is essential to be straightforward with others. Many of us like to run in circles or play "mind games" before we get to our point. This is one of the root causes for suffering in my opinion, when we live our lives according to probabilities. Such cases occur a lot between men and women.

For example, the male and female speak for a long period of time, and then when one wants to take it to the next "phase," it is only then he or she learns that they were viewed as a "friend/brother/sister" the whole time. If we go about our lives in this manner, it is as if we are gambling. Do not gamble your time away when it comes to matters where using your free will is highly recommended. Time is very significant in a temporary world! Use it wisely.

We shouldn't avoid asking those tough questions because it isn't time yet; we shouldn't wait a couple months to a year to feel "comfortable" about asking certain questions. This isn't a form of patience in this scenario. We have many individuals who wait a lengthy period just to find out if they're on the same page with another person. Assuming one does get rejected, isn't it better to get rejected after investing a small amount of time, instead of waiting months to a year to find out about the rejection?

To be direct is not only limited to the example above; rather incorporate straightforwardness within yourself in general. It will save you time and hardship! The *Quran states, "I swear by the time, most surely man is in loss" (103:1-2).

* Quran English Translation by Muhammad Habib Shakir

Reflection 82

Driven By Allah (swt)

Look! Look around you! Look how "they" have separated Allah (swt) from our lives. He (swt) is not allowed to be mentioned in our public schools, and He (swt) must be hidden at our jobs. Yet, everything else that Shaytan approves of is promoted. From certain organizations to social gatherings, it is acceptable, but if we take a stand and say, "NO! We are against this!" We are considered "bad people," and close minded. Why do we face this contradiction? Why are we forced to accept the Shaytan's scheme, but must avoid Allah's (swt) system, why? Because the Shaytan's plan keeps the people lost and wandering, but Allah's (swt) system guides the people and awakens them. This awakening is what the disbelievers are frightened of.

Think about it, why don't they offer courses about religion during our time at elementary, middle, and high school? We can take numerous electives, but religion isn't one of them? I guess learning about different shades of colors in art is more important than learning about Allah (swt). Why don't they implement the presence of Allah (swt) and the concept of God consciousness at an early age? Why do we have to rely on costly private schools and weekend programs to learn about Allah (swt)? What's strange is that schools and others will acknowledge corrupt: dictators, lawyers, politicians, doctors, businessmen, musicians, models, athletes, etc., who participate in drugs, fornication, alcohol abuse, encourage violence, and more. Where is the logic? For example, a rapper whose lyrics are completely out of line is given the "keys to the city" in some areas? What does this do to some? It motivates them to be and act like such individuals, because they're the ones who are being recognized. So we obsess over their lives, and we try to mimic their lives, just so we stay lost, which is completely fine to the disbelievers.

The evil that occurs in this world can decrease if Allah (swt) instead of the Shaytan is introduced. Our true awakening depends on the acknowledgement of Allah (swt), and once that is done we will be relieved of the shackles and chains that tie us down. A nation or community driven by Allah (swt) is very powerful.

Reflection 83

Ambitions and Dream Chasing

Passage 1

Originally, this reflection came with a picture; the image showed a man at the age of 17 versus 102. Before reading about this subject, search for a random image online that fits the description to connect to the topic to the fullest.

What is ambition? Ambition is a strong desire to do or to achieve something. To have ambition can either be great or dangerous, depending on how we use it and what our end goal is. Our ambitions become unsafe when we allow it to become greater than Allah (swt). Meaning, when we chase our goals and fail to remember our duties to Allah (swt). Unfortunately, this is the case for many of us. This drive that we have within us, we adore it! We convince ourselves it is a good thing because it makes our family proud, or it makes us feel happy because we are bettering ourselves.

However, ambition can be a form of distraction from the truth. There are many ambitious people who presume they're doing well, but in reality they're not. They give back to the world and have completed their list of aspirations, but what have they done for their souls in the hereafter? At times it is difficult to take our "hereafter soul" into consideration because we are young and feel invincible, but we must break away from such a thought process. Imagine the description mentioned above. On the left, we have a 17-year-old teenager who has no wrinkles and his hair is jet black; he looks very youthful. On the right, we have a 102-year-old man with gray hair and many wrinkles. They're the same person, but in different stages of their lives. I present to you this picture not for entertainment, but to show you your finale. With time, old age will overcome you! What brings serenity to an old man or woman isn't what they have accomplished in this world. Rather, it is what they have done for their next.

Passage 2

As I was sitting in a scholar's lecture a while ago, he said something that stuck with me. It was along the lines of how blessings can become nightmares.

As I reflected on this I asked myself, "How is that possible?" Then one thing came to mind, and that was the concept of "chasing our dreams."

Now I am not saying don't chase your dreams, but when your dreams begin to cross into the boundaries of "haram," then is it really worth it anymore? Sometimes we get caught up in our dreams because we are achieving some success, we become excited and feel accomplished, but when you boil it down, such a dream might be a nightmare in the hereafter.

Now that is terrifying…

Reflection 84

Proper Physical Hijab

Within the past few years the "physical hijab" for women has evolved into a fashion statement, and has drifted away from its essence. A woman's hair is sacred, and is considered one of the two beauties by the Messenger of Allah (saww). When something is sacred it is our duty to protect it, but nowadays that isn't the case. Many sisters are following this new trend where they wear their hijab very loose, and show the front of their hair as if they have a hoodie on. It is very common now; there was once a time that if a single strand was exposed sisters would quickly tell one another to cover up, but now it is encouraged for a sister to wear her hijab in a way that reveals her hair.

Furthermore, this fashion statement might seem harmless, but in reality it is very dangerous because it is causing great confusion. Once a teenage boy expressed to me that one of his female classmates wore her hijab in such a style, and as they were communicating he was saying that he didn't know where to look, because he was taught all his life that if someone who observes hijab accidentally exposes her hair, he should quickly turn around.

Nonetheless, for every occasion there is a certain dress code. For example, at work, school, events, and so on. If one doesn't adhere to the dress code, there are consequences. Wearing the proper physical hijab is the dress code Allah (swt) ordained on women in Islam. There is countless evidence stating it is required, but that is for another time, InshaAllah. Anyway, this is one reason why some women wear their hijab to their liking or don't wear it at all, their argument is that there isn't a clear cut picture of how one should wear their hijab in the Quran. The second argument is that wearing a hijab puts them at a disadvantage career wise, but if that were true how did a woman who observes hijab compete at the Olympics? How do countless women who observe hijab hold high positions in their careers? Lastly, it makes them feel unsafe, but if that is true, then only those who observe hijab would get attacked. If someone gets attacked, the problem isn't with the victim, but it is with the attacker. Also, nowadays many people are becoming more familiar with the hijab; those who observe hijab are in commercials, shows, movies, etc.

We mix all these arguments up and get the fashion hijab we have today, where one is standing between truth and falsehood. After everything is said and done, the critics either cheer the sisters for their fashion hijab, or they begin telling them, "If you're not going to wear it right, take it off!" Though for some odd reason many sisters believe that taking off the hijab is basically a free pass to everything and anything. The Day of Judgment isn't limited to certain people, it is for everyone. Even if one doesn't wear a hijab, it doesn't mean they can do whatever they want. Actions aren't bound by a piece of cloth! Hijab or no hijab, we all have a duty to Allah (swt).

To end, the purpose of this reflection isn't to judge anyone or anything along those lines. Nor is it to encourage someone to take off their hijab if they wear it while exposing their hair, because that isn't a solution either. The reality of the matter is we need to look deep within. Is it really about hijab or is it about your certainty in Allah (swt)? Or are you controlled by your desires? Or is your goal not to seek the straight path and gain nearness to Allah (swt)? If your foundation is rejecting Allah (swt), you will reject what comes with Allah (swt), even if it is a small percentage because something is not adding up. For example, if a teacher gives his students a study guide for an upcoming test, the students will use the study guide to succeed. If Allah (swt) is telling us to do "1,2,3," so we can gain nearness to Him (swt), why aren't we doing it? All hijab is at the end of the day is a powerful weapon to gain nearness to Allah (swt). Everything lies within this one question, do you want to gain nearness to Allah (swt)? Everyone must answer this deep question. When it is all said and done, we all stand alone on the Day of Judgment. All this is a fair warning…

Reflection 85

Why Are You Angry?

Why are you angry? What are you angry about? Why do you feel the need to express your anger through yelling or hitting? Why are you being disrespectful? Why can you not just try to understand what he or she is saying? Ask yourself these questions…

Anger is an emotion instilled within us! Everyone exercises this emotion despite how soundless they may appear. To be angry is not wrong, but towards what is where the issue lies. For instance, being angry about oppression, sinning, or failing is a good form of anger, because a person is trying to improve themselves and those around them. It is a step forward. Unfortunately, this is not the case in many situations; our anger takes us a step back. We use our anger to get our point across, to spread fear, and more. We yell, we shout, and we fuss just to show the person we are going off on, that "I am the dominant one." When we are angry we get an adrenaline rush, we start boiling, and we feel powerful. Such a state can become addictive like a drug if one doesn't control it. There is great reward with such control. The Imam (as) [30] refers to anger as a ball of fire, but if swallowed, it is sweeter than honey.

A difficult moment is when you're on the verge of snapping, but you're trying to stay calm. Anyone can snap, but not everyone can stay calm. So how do we stay calm? It is important to study this emotion. For example, we always focus on what makes us happy, and disregard other emotions. To master our anger we have to focus on what makes us angry. Taking deep breaths and counting up to ten is beneficial to an extent, but it cannot help you master your anger. To really master your anger depends on your awareness of Allah (swt). Allah (swt) states in the *Quran, "Have you not considered that Allah knows all that is in the heavens and the earth? There is not a single place wherein any secret counsel can take place between any three people without Allah being the fourth, nor five people without His being the sixth nor any gathering of more or less people, wherever it may be, without His being with them. On the Day of Judgment, He will tell them about their deeds. Allah has the knowledge of all things" (58:7). We are never alone, Allah (swt) is right there next to us. So when we are degrading an individual, or screaming at our parents, siblings, or spouse, know that Allah (swt) is making a note of it, and know He (swt) will ask you about it on the Day of Judgment. We shouldn't only fear disappointing the creation with our actions, but rather we should also fear disappointing Allah (swt).

On the other hand, we cannot tell others to control their anger or "CALM DOWN" when they haven't been taught how to do these things. We have to be cautious while dealing with an angry individual. We cannot allow the Chief Deceiver, Shaytan to take over by whispering words to us that will add fuel to the fire and further provoke them.

Let's all try to have honey!

* Quran English Translation by Muhammad Sarwar
[30] Attributed to Imam Ali (as)

Reflection 86

Void Within Me

There is a void in all of us, an empty state that makes us feel hopeless. We try to fill it up with lifetime milestones, but it does not fade away. We become wealthy, yet the void still exists. We earn a degree and pursue a career, but it is still there. We get married and have children, but we still feel hollow. We achieve all our New Year's Resolutions, but it is still there. Also, there are many of us who rely on drugs, alcohol, music, and entertainment to fill this void, but is it working? No...why? Reason being, we are trying to fill this void with temporary solutions, when it requires a permanent one. Wealth, children, and entertainment are temporary; it is only Allah (swt) that is permanent.

We must understand the creation of mankind. The creation of mankind depends on Allah (swt) just as much as mankind depends on air to survive. To be straight forward, if we are not actively seeking Allah (swt) we might encounter a few joyful moments throughout our lives, but in reality we are slowly falling apart. Take a simple plant for example, when you nourish it, water it, and place it in light, it grows and flourishes! When you do otherwise, and expose it to toxins, it withers away. Human beings work the same way, especially when it comes to their relationship with Allah (swt).

Reflection 87

Friends

Passage 1

[31] "Tell me who your friends are, and I will tell you who you are," the Imam (as) states. Who we associate ourselves with is very important. Many of us do not take this factor into consideration, but our friends can be one of the reasons we either gain nearness to Allah (swt), or drift away from Him (swt). Today we call anyone a friend! A friend to many of us are those who show us a good time. They go with us to the mall, restaurants, and movies. They make us laugh, and they care for us. They share their secrets with us, and they protect and defend us as well.

Occasionally, all the positive traits they bring deceive us because we fail to notice the negative ones. That same person you call a friend is the one who encourages you to sin. That same person you call a friend is the one who gossips and backbites about other people, and shares their secrets as well. That same person you call a friend is the one who applauds you on the removal of your hijab. That same person you call a friend is the one who takes you to nightclubs, hands you a drink, and tells you to try this drug. That same person you call a friend encourages you to avoid the mosque and pray. That same person you call a friend does not stop you when you curse, listen to inappropriate music, or when you're about to do something wrong, like meeting up with a man or a woman privately. Rather, they feed your curiosity and tell you, "What's the worst that is going to happen?" That same person you call a friend reminds you of your sins! That same person you call a friend is the one who is helping the Chief Deceiver, Shaytan, pull you away from Allah (swt). That same person you call your friend is NOT REALLY YOUR FRIEND.

To narrow it down as simple as it can be, if your friend is not helping you guard against evil and reminding you of Allah (swt), then do not call him or her your friend. I am not implying to shun people out of your life at this very moment! Sure, try to help them, but you must know when to cut them off if they choose to not cooperate, because even if you don't participate with their sinful actions, staying long enough in a sinful environment will eventually affect you and slowly overcome you. Don't place yourself near a fire and ask why you're getting burned all the time.

[31] Attributed to Imam Ali (as)

Passage 2

When a friend points out the faults of their friend, is that considered judging or advising?

The Imam (as) states,[32] "A true friend is one who upon seeing a fault gives you advice." Before giving advice to your friend you must take into consideration your intention, approach, and the setting. We have to set our intention for the sake of helping our friend to gain nearness to Allah (swt). However, if our intention is not that then we shouldn't do anything. Second, approach is very important; we never want to proceed aggressively and make our friend feel belittled. Instead of asking someone, "Did you pray?" Ask them, "Would you like to join me for prayer?" If they say, "maybe later," or something similar, leave it there, that's all, you did your part. Lastly, the setting must always be in private, between them and you only, and not in public whatsoever.

On the other hand, if I feel like my friend is judging me when he says I am just trying to help you, then the problem isn't with my friend, but it is within me. Sometimes, when someone tells us we need to fix something we quickly become defensive, because our ego doesn't accept anyone criticizing us. When we really destroy our ego, everything changes because we no longer see our friend as a threat. Think about it, your friend is telling you something that is going to benefit you. What is the problem? Instead, we should truly thank them. They went out of their way to help you. If we view it in a negative way, we should also take into consideration the whispers of the Chief

Deceiver, Shaytan. Shaytan can come and whisper, "Hey this guy is judging you, watch out! Does he think he is more religious than you because he prays on time?"

If you sin in front of your friend and they don't try to stop you, rather they encourage you...they're not your true friend.

[32]Attributed to Imam Ali (as)

Passage 3

It is one thing to be loyal to a friend when he or she is going through hardship, but it is a whole other thing to stay loyal to them while they're hurting themselves. Take drug abuse for example. The loyalty culture in today's society has to change. If one knows that their friend is using drugs they're expected to stay quiet. If they do otherwise, not only will they lose their friend's trust, but the relationship as a whole. This is why many people stay quiet while knowing that their friend is abusing drugs; there is an internal conflict.

We have to change this. We have to teach our children at a young age that if they know their friends are abusing drugs, they must inform their parents immediately before it becomes too late to prevent them from addiction. It is better to lose a friendship than to lose a soul! We can't be loyal to our friends when they're hurting themselves. If you know someone who is abusing drugs, inform their family and get them the help they need.

Reflection 88

Spiritual High

"Religious high," it's interesting isn't it? You know, that state we all go through when we are first introduced to Islam. We quickly try to absorb all the information we can in a short period of time. We attend lectures, stream lectures, read books, and so on. We make these drastic changes in the way we walk, talk, and dress. We even change our friends; we take it in all at once! We shoot up like a rocket, but within a few months to a year, many of us come crashing down like a comet. Back to earth and back to our old ways!

We see this happening to many of us, but why? Can it be because of the influence of those around us, or is it because the ornaments of this deceiving world appear mesmerizing? Or is it because life becomes too difficult, and society offers a more convenient outlet than Islam? Or is it because the straight path is too restrictive and dull? Or maybe it's because that's where the crowd was going at that time? Or maybe it was because we saw false propaganda about Islam, and believed it?

You see, the message of Islam reached us, but what many of us did wrong is we took this treasure and spent it all in one day. We didn't try to preserve it throughout our lifetime because we viewed it as an option instead of a way of life. We treated it as a phase instead of an awakening! It is sad because many of us leave before we get to really feel Allah (swt), and that connection is what makes one stay.

That connection is what motivates one to worship Allah (swt) like the Prophet (saww) and AhlulBayt (as)! That connection is what drives an individual to prepare themselves for the reappearance of Imam Mahdi (atfs). The greatest gift this world can offer is the worship of Allah (swt). Everything else is an illusion and temporary...

Reflection 89

Heartbreak

Passage 1

There are many people who are involved in forbidden relationships, and they justify their relationship by saying, "Our parents know." So they flirt and get intimate with each other, and it's okay because "our parents know." Surely, Allah (swt) has ordained different rules than our parents.

Now, many times such relationships crumble, and it leaves both individuals heartbroken, sad, and depressed. You see, when any foundation begins in a corrupt manner the chances of it lasting are very slim. However, the focus of this reflection isn't about being involved in a prohibited relationship. Rather, it is about the aftermath of such a relationship.

Anyway, as the couple "breaks up," the first thing they begin to do is blame. They blame each other and say, "You promised me, and told me…!" Second, they start blaming their friends and saying, "Why didn't you warn me that he or she was a bad person, and only wanted…!" Lastly, they start blaming Allah (swt) and saying, "Why God, why don't you want me to be with the person I love…why, why, why?!" It's easy for some to shove everything under a rug and act as if nothing has happened, but for others it may take years if not more to forget what happened. They dwell on the relationship until it gets to the point of not caring. They mistake carelessness for closure!

True closure comes when we stop blaming others and start blaming ourselves, and own up to our mistakes. Saying, "It's my fault," is one of the hardest things to do! "It's my fault for getting into a relationship which I knew was wrong, and is against what Islam says. It's my fault for befriending friends who were the ones that encouraged me to get into such a relationship instead of stopping me, and warning me that it is wrong. It is my fault for ignoring all of Allah's (swt) signs, and realizing that it's not that He (swt) didn't want me to be with the person I thought I loved, but rather He (swt) was trying to save me from losing this world and the hereafter." To be clear, I am not saying a person deserves to be heartbroken, sad, and depressed if they were engaged in such a relationship. Rather, I am saying to trace back your steps, and hold yourself accountable to all the times you went against the rules of Allah (swt), and you will know why you have been distressed.

Passage 2

Have you ever noticed it is only when couples "break up" that they become motivated to put the best version of themselves out there? It's very interesting when we think about it because in a sense it feels like they're not truly doing it for themselves, but rather to get back at one another.

This is wrong because your motivation is fueled by revenge, and not by loving yourself. Revenge can come in many different forms, but the revenge tank can't last forever. Eventually it runs out, which may lead an individual to go back to their old ways.

To end, prior to break ups, what is unfortunate is people tend to purposely "let go" of themselves when they get married. Even though some couples say, "we should love each other no matter what," I still believe letting yourself go because you're in a state of comfort with your spouse isn't ideal. And maybe if past couples tried to become the best version of themselves on all levels, they probably could've prevented a break up. Become the best version of yourself for yourself!

Reflection 90

Repetition

Passage 1

Then what? After you complete your education and start your career, then what? After you get married and start a family, then what? After you travel the world and purchase your dream home and car, then what? After you obtain what your heart desires, then what? We never take into consideration the "then what," why? We live in a mechanical society; do this, do that, go to work, raise your kids, vacation, and repeat for the years to come, then die. I am not trying to preach to become your own "boss," and live your life on your own terms. This reflection isn't about motivating you to make money, rather it's about to get us to reflect on the "then what." We must take the time to sit with ourselves and map out our future, not only in this world, but the hereafter as well. Have you ever witnessed anyone that has gone on to live forever? None of us can deny death, nor can we hide from it, or run away from it. It is just a matter of time!

With that being said, because we have this knowledge, how should we proceed with our lives? Do we continue to be unmindful and follow our desires, or do we seek the straight path and the truth? I mean, how many times are we going to use the excuse, "I didn't know," to continue our non-God conscious behavior. Such an excuse will not hold up during Judgment Day! Allah (swt) states, "And verily We shall recount their whole story with knowledge, for We were never absent (at any time or place)" *Quran, (7:7). How terrifying is that? Your whole life will be brought up in front of you. Let that sink in! This isn't another reminder; this is trying to encourage change. Answer the "then what" now. Know where you're heading, because once you do your decision making will change. You will not only decide for this world anymore, but you will also decide for your next as well. The Imam (as) states, [33] "Why is it that you're so excited when you get so little from this world, but there is no remorse in you when you lose so

153

much from the hereafter." Create a life that you will be proud of, not embarrassed of.

* Quran English Translation by Yusuf Ali
[33] Attributed to Imam Ali (as)

Passage 2

Death is a sensitive topic, not really a subject we would discuss over a cup of coffee with friends. I wonder why we avoid such a reality? Maybe it's because of the way we look and feel; for instance, an individual that is young assumes they have all the time in the world, but what they fail to realize is that their beautiful hair, skin, and strength is just an illusion. The lifespan of a human being doesn't depend on how a person looks and feels, or a life threatening disease, but rather it is solely on a fixed term set by Allah (swt).

We have to reprogram our minds to shift our behavior. Meaning, if we are convinced tomorrow is guaranteed we will continue to delay the actions that bring us closer to Allah (swt). It's not until we believe that our very next breath isn't promised that the will to change becomes a priority.

Life is repetitive, choose your repetition wisely. However, the only way to break the cycle of repetition is to commit to Allah (swt); on the path to Allah (swt) one is not only planning for this world, but also constructing their hereafter as well. Allah (swt) states in the *Quran, "The Death from which you flee will truly overtake you" (62:8). You will die, but don't just die, die with a sense of tranquility.

* Quran English Translation by Yusuf Ali

Reflection 91

Ego

Passage 1

Here is a secret...the truth is, doing our Islamic duties is very beneficial for our souls, but if we don't destroy our ego we will encounter many difficulties on our spiritual journey. This matter is hardly brought up, but it's the reason many people fail when trying to fully submit to Allah (swt).

Our egoistic nature is very dangerous if we don't put an end to it. Our ego is what will stand in the way between us and Allah (swt). Sometimes we mistake egoism with confidence, but they're two different things. For example, suppose I have an exam coming up, I am confident I am going to do well because I have been preparing for it for some time. This is confidence; you invest in yourself to put the best version of yourself out. On the other hand, ego would be like saying, "I didn't study for this exam, but I am right! Even when I am wrong, I am right!" It is out of arrogance and pride. Another example about the ego, suppose an egotistic person was born into a wealthy family, and they meet someone who isn't well off or comes from a broken home. Instead of understanding their situation, they begin to criticize their actions. They say, "Why does he or she do that, and dress that way? I can never imagine acting the way they do." They compare themselves to people who aren't on the same religious, social, and financial level as them.

Perform acts that will break your ego, acts that you won't normally do. To think you're better than the person next to you because of your "status" is egotistic. Remember, your ego only does what's best for YOU. A king lies in the same dirt as a poor person when they die.

Passage 2

When we analyze our "ego," we realize that even when it comes to suffering it becomes defensive at times.

Meaning, sometimes when we speak with individuals and they express what they're going through, they tend to follow up with, "No one understands me, or gets it," right? Even when it comes to affliction, the ego wants to make it a competition. That is why the ego convinces them that they're the only individual going through this pain, and no one else has ever experienced it before, but why is that?

Because this is how the ego works. It likes to be on top and alone when it comes to everything, but in such cases it is unpleasant because it prevents individuals from seeking the proper help they need. Only the ego can make us believe that out of billions of people, we are unique and going through a complex problem that has no solution.

The best way to destroy the ego is to do the opposite of what it suggests...

Reflection 92

Charity

Why is it that when it comes to giving a portion of our wealth we become stingy? When it comes to an Islamic cause we have many questions to ask, yet we are quick to contribute to our materialistic desires. Allah (swt) states in the *Quran, "If you give alms openly, it is well, and if you hide it and give it to the poor, it is better for you; and this will do away with some of your evil deeds; and Allah is aware of what you do" (2:271). Not to say no one donates to charity, countless people do, but with questionable intentions, in my opinion. This may be why their contribution doesn't go far, because they're giving part of their wealth for the wrong reasons, and Allah (swt) knows this. They give their wealth for themselves and not truly for the sake of the cause. Meaning, when you ask someone, "Why are you giving such a large amount to charity?" Obviously they respond with, "I want to help." However, sometimes they say, "I don't want to look cheap." Such intention is dishonest because they're giving for the sake of their ego to impress others; it is not done purely for Allah (swt). Which type of aid do you think travels further? An individual donating 1000 dollars for their ego, or one who donates 1 dollar strictly for the sake of Allah (swt)?

To end, were you ever about to give to charity, then out of nowhere you became discouraged because you remembered you have a bill to pay. You hear whispers saying, "You really need this, this whole 5 dollars can really make a difference in your life, put it back in your pocket, and walk away," or "this homeless guy is about to buy alcohol with your money, don't give him," or "these Shaykhs are all corrupt, and are trying to rob us." This is Shaytan trying to convince us that giving to charity is undesirable, because he wants us to settle with him in the hereafter. Look at the verse above, Shaytan does not want us to wash away our evil deeds. If an opportunity of charity comes your way, take advantage of it if you're able to; such blessings are not sent to us by coincidence. Surely, Allah (swt) sends mankind many opportunities to gain nearness to Him (swt).

* Quran English Translation by Muhammad Habib Shakir

Reflection 93

Clothes

Passage 1

Interesting is the criticism men receive when they gaze at a woman in a lustful way due to her immodest or tight fit clothes. We notice that when a woman exposes herself and a man "hits on her," he is called a pervert, pig, or someone who cannot "control themselves." The man is at fault completely, and the common excuse that most women state is, "I dress like this for myself, and not anyone else." To be clear I am not trying to justify anyone's actions, but rather I want to introduce a different perspective by Allah (swt) to entertain our thoughts.

Now, we aren't here to question or judge anyone's intentions, but let's be truthful with each other. Scientifically, naturally, etc., men are attracted to women and vice versa. Obviously this is how mankind was created. When a woman reveals herself, she automatically draws attention to herself whether she intends to or not. This is clear! With that being said, this may result in the man sinning because he "checked her out," when he should have been lowering his gaze like Allah (swt) states in the Quran. However, for one to lower his gaze and "control himself" requires God consciousness. At this point many people are probably asking, "Why do I have to worry about the actions of men," and "are you saying I am the reason that is causing men to sin?" To answer the first question, why do you look at them as ordinary men and not your brothers in faith. Don't you want to protect your brothers?

Think of it as being "tag team partners." For instance, suppose a woman tries on a revealing tight outfit, she is convinced that she looks beautiful and whatnot, but she pauses for a moment and reflects. She comes to a conclusion and tells herself, "I might look good in this outfit, but this might be problematic and might affect others." So she sacrifices her desires to protect others. This is one of the highest forms of Taqwa (God consciousness) in my opinion, when someone not only takes themselves into consideration, but also others. As for the second

158

question, it is naive to blame others for our sins, but to reach a strong state of Taqwa requires time and effort. In the meantime let's help each other out by being more thoughtful. Let's not make it hard on each other while trying to seek the straight path. Let's be that one less thing people have to worry about instead of being their trial. Let's protect each other! Note: This concept also applies to men as well...

Passage 2

Brothers and sisters, modesty doesn't mean just to cover up, but also to refrain from wearing skin tight clothes that outline the shape of our bodies.

We shouldn't defeat the purpose of being modest by wearing something that is provocative, even if it is long.

Physical modesty is very important for our spiritual journey! When [34] Shaheed Ibrahim Hadi was told by a friend that his style and body had become so attractive that two girls were following him to the gym, he became upset; he wasn't filled with joy. So the following day, Ibrahiam Hadi came to the gym wearing a long shirt and loose pants, baggy clothes.

Be mindful of what you wear and how you wear it. Protect yourself and those around you by displaying proper modesty!

[34] Jamaludeen, Sayyid Haydar, translator. *Peace Be Upon Ibrahim, Memories from the Life of Shaheed Ibrahim Hadi* . Vol. 1, Wilayah Publications.

Reflection 94

Red Cape

Passage 1

Red cape…many of us desperately want to wear it. We want to save the world! It is not until we waste a great amount of time that we realize this world was not meant to be saved, rather we have to find a way to save ourselves from this world.

Do not try to liberate, free, and unshackle others when your own soul is caged in this world. You want to eagerly save someone? Save yourself! Saving someone should not only be practiced at a hospital with doctors, nurses, and others. On the contrary, as much as a cardiologist knows about the heart, they cannot heal a corrupt one. Not all injuries require medical attention!

Just because you cannot see your soul doesn't mean it is not battered, wounded, and damaged! That "I am going to change the world" attitude isn't that marvelous, because such an outlook distracts one from the attention they very much need. This is where many of us get confused; we think Allah (swt) created us to be heroes! Allah (swt) does not need our heroism. Allah (swt) wants us to obey and serve Him (swt)! For example, suppose during the day a man ends world hunger, but by night he is wicked and evil, what does that do for Allah (swt)? Imam Ali (as) goes as far as saying that there is a universe within us, not a world, but a universe! So if there is something greater than the world within us, why are we focused on the wrong things? Meaning, what if this "saving attitude" wasn't meant for the public, but instead for YOU?!

Passage 2

The greatest contribution an individual can offer to society is to become God conscious to the fullest of their capabilities…

Some of us think we are aiding society, but just as we give with one hand, we take with the other! It is like a corrupt man who funds a drug rehabilitation center, but is also the one that sells drugs to people.

This is why we have to become God conscious to the fullest, because not only will it change our status, but also our children's, and their children, and so on. Generations will be changed! I stress the fullest because we want to be the best in our careers, in our education, and so on...why not with our religion?

Reflection 95

She Makes More

Many men are discouraged by the thought of their potential wife or current wife earning a higher salary than them. We find this mentality occurring excessively in some cultures. You're labeled as "less of a man" if your wife makes more money than you. I have asked numerous brothers before, "Why don't you try speaking to so and so?" And many of them always give me the same response, "She's a doctor, pharmacist, lawyer, etc., she makes much more money than I do." For many men this is the deciding factor, unfortunately.

When you ask them, "What do you mean?" They say, "When a woman makes more money than you, there is a possibility she might hold it over your head." Countless men don't want to put themselves in a situation where their wife might tell them, "Hey! I pay for this bill, or the majority of this one. You can't tell me what to do!" They don't want to lose that sense of assertiveness that comes with being a "man." Is this wrong? Most definitely! In Islam it is required of the man to be the provider for his family. However, in some circumstances the wife might need to step in due to hardship. Should that make one feel less of a man? Of course not! There is a difference between what a man is in society/culture, and what a man is in Islam. The scenario I relayed above has egoism written all over it. So what if your wife makes more money than you?! If she begins to feel prideful, or if he begins to put her down to protect his "manhood," then surely the couple failed miserably, and lacked understanding of their roles. They also were bonded by egoism instead of Allah (swt) in my opinion.

In Islam there is a tale for everything. We aren't left to walk blindly. If we move with a pure God conscious heart, we will be guided. Narrations state that the Messenger of Allah (saww), the Prophet Muhammad (saww) married Lady Khadija (as). She was very wealthy, while the Prophet didn't have much at the time. She dedicated her whole wealth to Islam! Do you think she held anything over the Prophet's head, and made him feel less of a man?

No, because she understood her role and was convinced of it; she was bonded to the Prophet (saww) by a foundation that only knew Allah (swt). The Prophet goes as far as saying that there were two factors that helped Islam survive and grow. One of them was the wealth of Lady Khadija! To end, if your wife makes more money than you do, don't feel threatened. Rather, come together and find ways to better Islam.

Reflection 96

Just Pray

Passage 1

How many times do we remember Allah (swt) per year just from prayer:

5 daily prayers (x) 1 day = 5 prayers.
5 daily prayers (x) 7 days = 35 prayers.
5 daily prayers (x) 365 days = 1,825 prayers.

TO BE MORE DETAILED:

1. How many times do we say, Takbiratul Ihram (Allaahu Akbar) to begin each prayer per year?
    a. 1,825 Takbiratul Ihrams per year.
2. How many Rakaats do we perform per week?
    a. 17 per day (x) 7 days = 119 Rakaats per week.
    b. Per year? 17 per day (x) 365 days = 6,205 Rakaats per year.
3. How many times are we in Sujud per year?
    a. 6,205 Rakaats per year (x) 2 Sujud per each Rakaat = 12,410 Sujud per year.
4. From Fajr to Isha prayer, the first two Rakaats we are required to recite two Surahs from the Quran. So for 17 Rakaats, we recite 20 Surahs that include "Al-Fatiha, Al-Ikhlas, etc."
    a. 20 Surahs per day (x) 365 days = 7,300 Surahs per year.
5. How many Tashahhuds (Testimony of Faith) do we recite per year?
    a. 9 per day (x) 365 days = 3,285 Tashahhuds per year.
6. Taslim (Salutation)?
    a. 1,825 Taslims per year.

When we recite "Tasbih Syeda Fatima Zahra (as)":
1. Allahu Akbar = 34 times after each of the 5 daily prayers?
    34 (x) 5 = 170 (x) 365 days = 62,050 Allahu Akbars per year.

164

2. Alhamdulillah = 33 times after each of the 5 daily prayers?
33 (x) 5 = 165 (x) 365 days = 60,225 Alhamdulillahs per year.
3. SubhanAllah = 33 times after each of the 5 daily prayers?
33 (x) 5 = 165 (x) 365 days = 60,225 SubhanAllahs per year.

Just Pray!

Passage 2

One mistake that many of us make is, when we aren't feeling our Islamic duties we think our relationship with Allah (swt) is tainted; we automatically connect the two.

For example, when we find it hard to pray we think maybe it's because we are becoming distant from Allah (swt), and Allah (swt) doesn't favor us anymore, and whatnot.

When in reality it's not that complex at all. You may feel this way because that day you were tired, you're lacking energy, probably didn't get enough sleep, but that doesn't mean your relationship with Allah (swt) has been compromised. If you told me, "I stopped praying," then that's a different story, but if you say, "I am having a hard time getting through these prayers today," it's okay; you're a human being, just get it done and try not to overthink it.

To end, if a husband had a bad day and is having a hard time speaking to his wife, does that mean he loves her less? Of course not, go easy on yourself, be realistic!

Passage 3

Tips to concentrate during prayer:

- Pray in a different room than where your phone is.
- Use ear plugs to block out surrounding noise.

- Pray on time, and try to stay on "wudu." I noticed that one of the most challenging processes of prayer is performing wudu.
- Don't start an activity or an important conversation around prayer, because we will either delay prayer or think about the conversation during prayer.
- Stay focused on the words you're reciting, and not what comes after it. Also, understand the meaning of what is being said.
- Don't overthink it, just do your duty to the best of your ability and go on with your day.
- Think of prayer as a tool to remind you of Allah (swt), not as a chore. Anyone can pray, but the question is, do your actions follow your prayers outside of prayer?
- Fall in love with Allah (swt), because then prayer becomes easier and you begin to wait for it.

Just Pray!

Reflection 97

Drama & Rumors

Passage 1

The problem with many of us is we don't search for the truth, rather we look for a story, and a dramatic one! This strong desire we have for drama is poor. We follow the hype as if it's a treasure map. When we see the gossip fire, we don't put it out; rather we sit around it, and try to warm ourselves with the flames. Think about it, you're getting excited by people's misery.

Drama is not only limited to, "he said, she said," or "he did, she did." Allah (swt) states in the *Quran, "O you who believe! avoid most of suspicion, for surely suspicion in some cases is a sin, and do not spy nor let some of you backbite others. Does one of you like to eat the flesh of his dead brother? But you abhor it; and be careful of (your duty to) Allah, surely Allah is Oft-returning (to mercy), Merciful" (49:12). Yeah, that doesn't sound too pleasant!

Anyway, the type of drama I am referring to is the one that deals with religion. The drama where we attend settings not to learn, but to watch a heated argumentative debate, or not to seek justice, but rather to witness and encourage a crowd to become rowdy. We try to provoke one another more than assisting each other. If one is knowledgeable and they're able to see right through drama, and differentiate between truth and falsehood, then good for them. But here is where the issue lies, not everyone has attained such knowledge yet. For example, take the youth in our community, the young brothers and sisters. Take their perspective into consideration for a moment! When they look at a mosque, or sit in on a religious gathering and observe all the commotion, and hear the corruption, what do you think their take on religion will be?

A younger brother once told me, "Why should I go to the mosque? There is drama there, the religious people don't even have it right, what's left for me?" Sometimes we think we are doing good, but our idea of good might cause more trouble and can affect others greatly. You cannot expect everyone else to have it right just because you have it right. Don't become a wild horse, tame yourself! There is a time and place to speak, and a time and place to stay quiet. We have to stop feeding drama as if it's a hungry lion, and start realizing who is being AFFECTED by it in the long run. Nonetheless, to our youth the role models of Islam are the Prophet Muhammad (saww) and AhlulBayt (as). If you see or hear someone doing wrong, it is they who did wrong, it wasn't Islam that was wrong! Separate the two...

* Quran English Translation by Muhammad Habib Shakir

Passage 2

A rumor is like an explosive that can be diffused, but that is not always the route taken. I guess many of us are more impressed with a bang. Like a gun, a rumor can also destroy a person. The only difference is, one is instant, and the other is a lifetime of pain. The stance Islam takes against rumors is praiseworthy; when we read the Quran we notice that Allah (swt) articulates many circumstances to our benefit, to protect us.

Let's take one of the most awful actions for THIS example... adultery. How many of us have heard the infamous beginning line to a rumor, "I heard he/she did...?" Or "I can't believe he/she did...!" Right, I am sure many of us. Here is what the *Quran states, "And those who accuse chaste women and then do not produce four witnesses - lash them with eighty lashes and do not accept from them testimony ever after. And those are the defiantly disobedient" (24:4). So, suppose I wanted to start a rumor about a woman and say, "You know so and so, she cheated on her husband." According to the verse I am not even allowed to utter such comments unless I have four witnesses present with me, which is nearly impossible in many cases. If I do utter these comments without the witnesses, I should not only get punished, but my credibility will forever be untrustworthy.

Rumors should not be taken lightly; we shouldn't gossip about anyone because we heard it "through the grapevine." Where is our PROOF? Next time, if our friends happen to entertain us with gossip, instead of saying, "Tell me more," we must stop them in their tracks. We cannot smear people's reputation and dignity for a few laughs. How small minded can a human being be that a rumor without verification excites them?! People commit suicide because of false rumors, isn't that enough for us to keep our mouths sealed? Even if we know the truth, we should diffuse it instead of share it; we must protect each other even if we don't know each other.

* Quran English Translation by Sahih International

Reflection 98

Hollywood

Many of us want to live out our lives like Hollywood stars, right? We want to look like them! We want to talk like them! We want their cars, homes, and clothes!

However, numerous Hollywood stars have committed suicide. That's mind boggling because they have all the money, materialistic things, friends, family, and access to the best doctors, surgeons, trainers, entertainment, etc. Yet, they chose to kill themselves...what is wrong with the equation?

Hollywood is excellent at creating standards, and they know these standards cannot be attained by the majority. For example, they tell us we are supposed to look a certain way. Yet, the stars who look this type of way have these trainers, surgeons, nutritionists, hair stylists, makeup artists all waiting on the snap of their fingers. Or Hollywood says your relationship should always be "lovey-dovey," because they show us a few good scenes in the movies, but right when we encounter conflict in our relationships, we are of the belief that it is a failure. It is incomparable...

They have created a false deception even for their stars, because after their stars have experienced all of what Hollywood has to offer, they're still unfulfilled. Think about it, Hollywood tells us to be fulfilled one has to have this and do that, but the equation is flawed because of the countless suicides. So, why are we chasing such a lifestyle and ignoring all the evident proof?

Reflection 99

Laid OFF

Where is the blessing? It is hard to find it at times. Perspective is very important; how we look at things can either make us or break us. For example, take an individual who just lost their job. This person is obviously frustrated and upset because they just got laid off, and they're constantly thinking about their next move and whatnot. They ask themselves, "How will I support my family now?" The blessing here that they're not detecting is that they still have their mind. With this mind, they're able to come up with a new plan on how to move forward. Moreover, suppose they cannot land another desk job like they once had. They're able to shift over to manual labor because they have functioning hands and legs.

You see, we don't even take these kinds of blessings into consideration. They don't even cross our minds. We think we are entitled to have an active brain and running body. We believe that this is what we deserve. Basically, Allah (swt) OWES us these things. This is incorrect! Once we start counting these blessings, no matter how small, our perspective will change for the better. We will become more humble, and we will become more appreciative, but first we must discover our blessings. Blessings are not like shooting stars; they're not rare to locate. Reflect and you will find more than you asked for.

Flaunting

Social media isn't that bad you know, there is a lot of good that comes out of being on social media. We get to stay connected with family and friends. Also, we can use such a vast platform to raise awareness on different issues, and we are able to gain knowledge as well.

But unfortunately, with the good comes the bad. In today's social media we see many of us "flaunting." There was once a time where men and women were very reserved, but nowadays such behavior has faded away. Today, men and women adore the idea of publicly displaying themselves. As if we are trophies on shelves...

Every bit of our lives has to be shared, from what we eat to how we dress, to what we drive and to where we vacation. The fact that we don't take the less fortunate into consideration before we upload a picture of our glamorous lives is absurd. For example, gender reveals are the new thing, right? What about the women who cannot have children due to complications? How do you think they feel after seeing a gender reveal event?

Moreover, the practice of self-love is important, but there's a difference between "I love myself," and showing the world you love yourself. Meaning, we have many people who are obsessed with themselves. So, they have to upload a picture of themselves to get reassured by the public that they're beautiful. Prophet Yusuf (as) was very handsome as well, to the point when he walked by a group of working women, they accidentally cut their fingers because they were mesmerized by his appearance, but Prophet Yusuf (as) tried to hide his beauty. Many of us don't try to hide our beauty, we SEDUCTIVELY show it off.

For what? For the same 100+ likes and comments? Is it worth it? To show off your body, clothes, and different poses for the same group of people who offer you nothing? Do you not take into consideration that you're sinning? Do you not take into consideration that you might be the cause of someone's sins? Do you take into consideration what the person who is looking at your picture is thinking of? Don't forget, the mind wanders far and wickedly when it is not conscious of Allah (swt). Let's try to be more reserved brothers and sisters, and more thoughtful. We are not trophies! We are humans…

Reflection 101

Legacy

Passage 1

Sometimes we get stuck; we don't know what path to take. Do we go left or right? Do we invest all our time for this world, or strive for the hereafter? When you look at history you learn that great empires once existed in this world. From the Roman Dynasty to the Ottoman. These empires were wealthy and powerful. They were led by kings and queens that thought no one could topple and overcome their great empire, but as time passed, they passed as well. As Imam Ali (as) said, [35] "Where are the kings that were proudly dictating? Till the pourer of death poured death upon them." They invested all of their time here only to find out that one day they will be gone.

What's unfortunate is we are blessed with all of these signs, yet we still ignore them. We are obsessed in building our own legacy and our own "mini empires" here, to the point we neglect Allah (swt). Allah (swt) states in the *Quran, "Indeed, We have warned you of a near punishment on the Day when a man will observe what his hands have put forth and the disbeliever will say, 'Oh, I wish that I were dust'" (78:40)! Imagine, we're this special human being with a brain, heart, and body, but a disbeliever wants to opt out of being a human being, because Judgment Day gets so unbearable for them that they wish to be dust instead. From a human to dust! When you think of such a scenario, it is mind boggling. Let's not be of those who disbelieved. Let's not neglect Allah (swt). Let's strive for the hereafter!

* Quran English Translation by Sahih International
[35] From "The Soul Cries" by Imam Ali (as)

174

Passage 2

Do you know what is a sign of character maturity? Being able to accept criticism without feeling the need to defend yourself.

We have to stop reacting and start listening…

It's okay to be wrong!

Reflection 102

Cancer

We wouldn't think sickness is a blessing until we look at it from a different perspective. Suppose an individual is diagnosed with cancer. Immediately he becomes distressed. He is hurt and saddened because now he is dealing with a life threatening illness. Prior to his diagnosis he was an arrogant individual; he was a sinner. He didn't really take Allah (swt) into consideration, nor did he follow what Islam asked of him.

However, after his discovery of cancer he became more dependent on Allah (swt), became more obedient. He started to follow the religion and avoid sins. The sickness humbled him. You see, sure sickness causes pain to the individual and his family and friends, but such affliction might have been the best thing for the individual because it brought him closer to Allah (swt). To understand this life we must start looking at it from different perspectives.

Reflection 103

Ashura

When we reflect about the legacy of Ashura, what comes to mind? Perhaps a tale about a man who went to war with the oppressors of his time when all odds were against him. Or maybe a lesson in sacrifice for the sake of Allah (swt), or how an enemy became an ally before battle. As we commemorate Ashura we can't help but envision fallen heroes, burning tents, and thirsty children crying out for water.

What is the theme of Ashura? For many it is death. But how so when Aba Abdillah's (as) message lives on until today? Whenever I think about Ashura many words come to mind to define it, but one word in particular arises more than the rest. That word is tolerance! My theme for Ashura is tolerance.

Ashura revealed to me how much an individual is able to handle when tough trials are pouring. Through Ashura I discovered the maximum tolerance threshold of men and women who have complete faith in Allah (swt). We should no longer fear the day we lose a loved one, or the moment we are tried with an illness. Nor should we be frightened by hunger and poverty, or the burden of anxiety and depression, because with patience and persistence in Allah (swt), we too can see "nothing but beauty."

Which beauty on the day of Ashura shall we disclose? Shall we speak of the act of unity by a Christian man, or the soldier who was deemed for hellfire but repented before taking his last breath, guaranteeing him heaven? How about an uncle who suppressed his desires by refusing to quench his thirst on the river bank, or his nephew who was entirely detached from this world to the point that he humbly marched to his own death, because he knew it would be "sweeter than honey?" Let's not forget about the lady who displayed marvelous leadership as she rallied the survivors together.

Ashura radiates light, but such light cannot be perceived unless we follow the path that guides us to Allah (swt)! What is your theme for Ashura?

Reflection 104

Divorce

It is reported that Imam Ja'far al-Sadiq (as) states, [36] "Among that which Allah (swt) has made permissible there is nothing He (swt) hates more than divorce," and [36] "divorce shakes the very Throne of God." However, in some cases divorce is needed. In my opinion, there was a time where divorce was the last option, but nowadays it feels like it is the first. Many newlyweds are separating from each other within a year or less. How a couple transitions from, "I love you" to "I can't stand you" is mind boggling. Clearly society has changed over time! Couples used to tolerate each other more in the past; maybe because they didn't deal with the idea that anyone is "replaceable." With social media this concept has evolved.

Many couples are entering marriage with an unstable mindset. Meaning, the thought of divorce is already lingering in the back of their minds before they say, "I do." They know if their significant other doesn't comply with what they want, or if hardship arises, they can easily replace their spouse. It is unfortunate, but this is the sad reality! Speak to people and they will tell you, "Why do I have to put up with her or him, I can easily find anyone else; I have so many followers on Instagram, and friends on Facebook." Statistics state that one in three marriages fail because of social media.

In my humble opinion, as I reflected on the topic further I realized this was the main difference between our generation and the past. Our fathers and mothers lived in harder circumstances than us, and problems poured upon them like rain, but somehow the majority of them made it work. They forced each other to adapt to one another because they had very few options. Having many options isn't necessarily always a good thing, because it can cause great confusion and put us in a state of mental paralysis. This is what many of us are dealing with nowadays!

With that being said, before entering a marriage couples have to communicate with one another. Love alone isn't enough to start a family! Rather, there has to be compatibility as well. We also have to change our definition of love; we have many people thinking love is texting someone "happy birthday" at 12 a.m. on the day the person was born, or liking the same shows. We have many couples who have known each other for over 10 years before marriage, but right when they move in with each other they say their farewells. It has been said that we truly don't know an individual until we live with them. Meaning, it doesn't matter if you went to all the restaurants in the world together, your true selves come out under one roof. This is what we have to be prepared for, the good and the bad.

Where many couples fail is they start comparing their present marriage to their past engagement, or their pre-engagement time; they become concerned when they learn of the differences. How is such a comparison fair and logically correct? It is not, you go from seeing someone a couple hours to 24 hours a day. There will be times where your spouse will be sad, mad, anxious, depressed, and so on. Couples have to create specific guidelines for what calls for a divorce before marriage, and strongly adhere to it. For example, adultery, abuse, certain addictions after refusing help, but leaving dishes in the sink or clothes on the floor is not divorce worthy, in my opinion.

Lastly, know the individual as much as you can before marrying them. Basically, if you want someone who is religiously oriented, then look for such a person before marriage. Don't wait until marriage to search inside of your spouse for what you desire. It is said that the first year of marriage is the toughest, but if you keep Allah (swt) and Islam at the core, you can overcome anything. For example, if you're going through a financial crisis, don't be so quick to get frustrated with the situation. Rather say, surely Allah (swt) tries the believers.

[36] Amini, Ibrahim. "Divorce in Islam." *Al-Islam.org*, Ahlul Bayt Digital Islamic Library Project, 12 Feb. 2015.

Reflection 105

This Life

Passage 1

Is the life that you're living a trial or a blessing?

Lately I have been reflecting on whether the life we live is a trial or a blessing. What life am I referring to? Here in the west where the majority of us don't have to worry about bombs, hunger, power outages, etc. I asked myself, "What makes me so special that Allah (swt) created me here?" While my brothers and sisters across the world live in poverty and fear. From a blessing perspective it did not make sense, but it did from a trial standpoint.

With that being said, the *Quran is filled with countless verses about trying mankind, "It is He who has created death and life to put you to the test and see which of you is most virtuous in your deeds. He is Majestic and All-forgiving" (67:2). Also, the Imam (as) states, [37] "Life consists of two days, one for you, one against you, for both days are a test for you." After coming across worthy information I told myself, I was not born here by chance or coincidence. I was put here specifically to be tried!

By this assumption, I felt like Allah (swt) was telling me, "Okay Nadr, I put you in the west where you don't have to worry about this and that, how will you answer? Will you obey and serve Me (swt), or will you follow your desires, because I have others that are being tried harder than you, but they still find time for Me (swt)!"

The only blessing in this life is being able to realize Allah (swt) in everything. Some blessings can be a curse! Many people have wealth, and they perceive their wealth as a blessing, but such wealth was the very reason they distanced themselves from Allah (swt). What if they observed their wealth as a trial? Others were blessed with good health, but it wasn't until they were tried with poor health that they discovered Allah (swt). Being able to get up, move around, and use your mind, this is a trial as well because there are people who are incapable of these things. What makes you better than them? Recognize this life as a trial, and many things will start making sense. Trials will turn into blessings once Allah (swt) is incorporated.

* Quran English Translation by Muhammad Sarwar
[37]Attributed to Imam Ali (as)

Passage 2

Dear Me,

Your expectation on life is what is causing you hardship. You're searching for eternal happiness in a place that simply doesn't offer it! You're dumbfounded every time life doesn't go your way, but why though? Didn't Allah (swt) warn you that He will try you...

Instead of preparing for trials, you believed that these trials and tribulations are a form of punishment. So, you decided to rebel, and lost hope in Him (swt)! You're showing the world that you found happiness through your deceiving smile, but you know that you're dark and dead on the inside because you left the only source of light that was truly charging you.

I wish you would've stayed because after hardship comes ease, but only for a moment because a trial is just around the corner to be seized. Because what is a trial? An opportunity to become closer to Him (swt)!

Reflection 106

Congratulations

The issue with society is they mostly show gratitude to those who accomplish worldly affairs. For example, accumulating wealth, or earning a high degree, etc. We as individuals have to begin showing more gratitude towards ourselves and others; unfortunately, we belittle many actions.

For example, praying on time. If we go one month without delaying prayer, or a year without skipping prayer, we should celebrate such accomplishments. In addition, if a young or older sister puts on a hijab, she should be recognized. Of course this shouldn't be done in a boastful way, but more of taking notice of one's progression. Why should we only celebrate worldly affairs? We should acknowledge events that benefit us in this world and the hereafter as well.

Reflection 107

The Media

Islam's battles have declined externally in my opinion. Meaning, the media's strategy was to associate violence with Islam, but as time went on, a different story was told by Muslims. Muslims showed the world that Islam is peaceful, and not violent. Today the battles Islam faces are internal, from within. The media is trying to normalize acts that are forbidden in Islam. For instance, we see TV series, movies, music videos, etc., that star women, right? It is difficult to point out anyone's faith on TV, but now, what is the media doing? They're introducing women with hijab on shows, and the hijabi actresses are indulging in forbidden relationships, parties, and so on.

For example, I once came across a show where a hijabi actress was hanging out with a male who was in a relationship, and they were seen by the man's girlfriend. What does this symbolize? Cheating. Take a moment and look at the picture from an outside perspective. How do you think the outside world views this? You and I might know the truth, but those who don't know are going to associate such actions with Islam, because hijab is the flag bearer of Islam.

That being said, no longer will the outside world say, "This actress did this on yesterday's episode." Instead, they will say, "the MUSLIM actress did...Islam must allow this type of behavior." Again, they're trying to normalize forbidden acts in Islam through the media. The battle is no longer with violence, but it is to promote liberal Islam, to destroy a religion from within.

Reflection 108

Opinions

To share our opinion is our right, but knowing when not to share it is just as important. Why? Because too many opinions result in a great amount of confusion. There are matters in this world where our opinions are simply NOT needed, especially when it comes to Islam. For example, the infamous question constantly asked, "What age do you think a girl should wear a hijab?" Many of us respond with, "Not at nine, that is way too young; she does not understand such a commitment yet." For this issue, what we think or don't think doesn't matter here because the decree is already set in stone. Furthermore, some of us express that several rules within Islam are outdated, and are not compatible with our current time.

However, do we ever ask who set these rules? Allah (swt)! When the Prophet Muhammad (saww) began to spread Islam, he did not preach based on what he thought was right and wrong. In fact, Allah (swt) directly states in the *Quran, "Your companion [Prophet Muhammad (S)] does not err, nor does he go astray; Nor does he speak out of desire. It is naught but revelation that is revealed, The Lord of Mighty Power has taught him" (53:2-5).

If the Prophet (saww) is known as the City of Knowledge, and he does not speak out of desire, nor does he make mistakes, and whatever he states are mere revelations from Allah (swt), and Allah (swt) cannot be bound by time, how then can we say some rules are outdated? Islam wasn't created for a certain time, but it is for all times...

Know when to share your opinion and when not to. Reason being, many of us without hesitation openly say we disagree with this and that part of Islam, okay fine, but do we at least know WHO we are disagreeing with? That being said, **Quran, "It is not for a believing man or a believing woman, when Allah and His Messenger have decided a matter, that they should [thereafter] have any choice about their affair. And whoever disobeys Allah and His Messenger has certainly strayed into clear error" (33:36). If we are having trouble fully submitting to Allah (swt), we must visit our egotistic-animalistic nature, and eliminate it.

* Quran English Translation by Muhammad Habib Shakir
** Quran English Translation by Sahih International

Reflection 109

That Feeling

Passage 1

Am I better than yesterday or worse? I ask myself this question, and I realize that finding the straight path wasn't difficult, but the real challenge lies in staying there. In Islam consistency is very important, but many times it is overlooked; Allah (swt) can guide us to Islam, but accepting and following it solely depends on our freewill.

Do you remember how you felt when Islam was first introduced to you? Several years ago I remember I was excited to learn about Allah (swt), the Quran, the Prophets (as), the Imams (as), Ashura, etc., and to build a real brotherhood with those who viewed life the same way I did; for a good year or so I felt lighthearted and spiritual trying to absorb everything I can at once, and truly trying to connect with Allah (swt). Later on I learned that the feeling of infatuation is always associated with something "new." Meaning, was I really excited about seeking the straight path, or was it because the straight path was something new? For example, do you remember how you felt when you first bought your new car compared to how you feel about your car now? What ends up happening to that feeling? It fades away over time. Essentially this happens to many of us while trying to seek the straight path. Once we stop feeling "spiritual," we think there is a problem, and we try to find different alternatives. There is no problem!

Being a practicing Muslim is more than just a feeling. Truly connecting with Allah (swt) takes time, consistency, and realizing that there is no such thing as a finish line within this journey. Maintaining consistency is difficult because new challenges arise every day. We must ask ourselves, how can we improve?! Do you think someone who prays knows Allah (swt) the same as someone who doesn't? Do you think someone who observes hijab knows Allah (swt) the same as someone who doesn't? Do you think someone who lowers their gaze knows Allah (swt) the same as someone who doesn't? Do you think someone who earns a halal income knows Allah (swt) the same as someone who doesn't? Do you think a just leader knows Allah (swt) the same as an oppressor?

Don't chase a feeling, but chase what Allah (swt) asks of you, and the rest will follow.

Passage 2

Sometimes we care too much about "a feeling" when it comes to our relationship with Allah (swt). If we feel spiritual we believe that we are close to Allah (swt), and if we don't then it must mean we are far away.

That shouldn't be the determining factor; your relationship with Allah (swt) should depend on your actions. For example, are you praying on time? Are you working towards observing modest Islamic attire? Did you stop listening to bad music? How are you with the opposite gender? Are you lowering your gaze or are you flirting? How are you towards your parents? Do you curse? Are you quickly getting angry? How are you reacting when it comes to trials? Are you nagging or accepting? When sins present themselves, do you quickly capitalize on them or do you fight them off?

Reflection 110

The Future

The future…for some it is exciting, while for others it is distressful. The question that comes to mind is, how can something that is hypothetical, non-existing, and an illusion cause so much intimidation? Think about it, the future is only a figment of our imagination, consisting of what we want or think might happen as time goes on. To overcome this problem we must train our minds to stay in the "now." Think of right now, in the past weren't you contemplating this very moment? Look how things turned out. Was it worth putting yourself through mental stress? Of course not, but we are the type of individuals who aren't easily convinced; we need to experience it to believe, we aren't able to just rely on Allah (swt).

In addition, the future becomes nerve-wracking when we think it is guaranteed, but ask yourself, what makes you so certain you're going to live until tomorrow? Because you're in good health? What is causing you to worry? Is it the fear of failure, or not being financially stable, or not being able to live up to society's standards? If you fail…so what, you try again! If you're not financially stable…so what, living paycheck to paycheck is not wrong! If you're not living up to society's standards… so what? Why are you going to force yourself to do something to please others? If you're not capable of doing something, it doesn't mean you're a failure. The point is, there is always a solution, so why fear?

The most important task of your life should always be what you're currently doing right now; put all your focus and energy into this very moment. No one is saying don't plan for the future. Plan for it, but don't live there. Constantly thinking about the future is a distraction, even if it's exciting. How do you expect to be the best version of yourself when your mind is living in the year 2021 while you're still in 2019? Lastly, when we say the expression, "Do your part and let Allah (swt) do his," please let Allah (swt) do his part. Sometimes mankind tries to do everything. Taking all factors into consideration, you might not be able to master the future, but you can master the present…one second at a time.

Reflection 111

Stingy

Among us there are many who become "stingy" when it comes to religion! Meaning, if a scholar or an organization charges a fee for their program, we become shocked and begin to say, "Look at them trying to profit off religion; religion should always be free, it is God's word." Right? However, these same people aren't stingy when it comes to their homes and cars, their designer clothes and purses, their vacations and foods. But SubhanAllah, when it comes to Islam…"Where does the money go; can we even trust this organization? Isn't this scholar corrupt?" The questions are ridiculous and endless.

Even though Islam is priceless, when we come across a flyer for an organization that is holding a course for 25 dollars, let's not be so quick to judge. Rather, let's understand that such a fee doesn't get "pocketed," there are many costs, not everything associated with religion is for free. The information might be, but there are real expenses, such as, equipment, electricity, gas, water, internet, rent, etc. A center isn't magically maintained by a team of volunteers every day; that is someone's actual job. The point is, that 25 dollars gets distributed towards payments we don't even think about. Moreover, why do we become irritated when it comes to paying scholars, but we pay top dollar for doctors? Is it because we quickly see the results of our physical health? How about our spiritual health?

Lastly, there is a responsibility in Islam that many people are skeptical about, and avoid to partake in. I am referring to Khums. What is Khums? It is a mandatory obligation for Muslims to pay one-fifth or 20% of their acquired wealth towards a specific cause. For example, assume my Khums payment is due on January 1st; suppose on January 1, 2019, I had 0 dollars in my bank account; throughout the year I made money, spent and saved it. Fast forward to January 1, 2020, I have 100 dollars in my bank account from last year's earnings that I saved, that 100 dollars is subject to Khums. Meaning, of that 100 dollars I have to give 20 dollars away; we don't actually give the money to anyone, there is an actual system in place. Allah (swt) states in the *Quran, "And know that whatever thing you gain, a fifth of it is for Allah" (8:41). This is just a brief introduction and explanation of Khums. For more detailed information, please refer to a scholar and do your own research; a credible website is al-Islam.org. The concept of Khums is eloquent because it teaches us detachment! With detachment follows a decrease in corruption, and an increase in justice.

* Quran English Translation by Muhammad Habib Shakir

Reflection 112

Masturbation & Porn

This isn't ordinarily a topic that is discussed publicly. In fact, many people shy away from this uncomfortable subject because it is embarrassing, but it must be addressed, even though it is a personal matter. The issue that I am referring to is an addiction that has and still is destroying humanity. From society's perspective it is considered healthy with several benefits, but Islamically it is considered a disease. That being said, it is not only drugs and alcohol that can cause an individual to crumble, but so does stimulating one's self sexually and watching adult films. Sure, the effects of these terrible acts might not present themselves outwardly right away, but internally, such acts are extremely damaging.

Having said that, I start with a narration about an encounter with Imam Ja'far al-Sadiq (as). For those who believe it is impossible to put an end to this terrible act, think again! Once a person came to Imam al-Sadiq (as) and said this about someone, [38] "Poor man has been involuntarily afflicted by a sexual perversion!" The Imam (as) asked, "What do you mean? Does he commit it in the presence of others also?!" The individual replied with, "No." The Imam (as) said, "So, it proves that he does it voluntarily and willingly." Meaning, mankind always has an option in this case because they choose WHEN and WHERE to do such an act, freely. In addition, Surah al-Mu'minun (The Faithful) in the *Quran describes the believers that are successful, and of the conditions is, "And those who guard their private parts" (23:5). Sayyid Kamal Faqih Imani states, [39] "The verse implies that the fourth attribute of the believers is chastity, which is self-control and abstinence from every kind of sexual impropriety. It means that they guard themselves from lewdness..."

In this part of the reflection we will examine some passages from Ayatollah Naser Makarem Shirazi's book, [38]*Sexual Problems of Youths*. He speaks about the harms of masturbation, and gives instructions to avoid such a sin. It is noted that when specialists analyze such an act, they tend to overlook the side effects of masturbation when it becomes an addiction, and that is why some physicians claim there is no harm, but that is false; for example, [38] "Smoking a narcotic may not be very harmful once," but what about in the long run? Also, it is important to keep in mind that such a practice is easily accessible, and does not require much means, and that is why it deserves extra attention. Per Ayatollah Naser Makarem Shirazi, he states that physicians and researchers claim, [38] "That most diseases related to the genital system, retina and choroids are caused by masturbation." Furthermore, this evil habit [38] causes: the face to lose color, gray circles around the eyes, anemia, weakening of physical and spiritual power, dizziness, imagining voices and noises, backache, forgetfulness, lack of appetite, anorexia, indigestion, asthma, envy, grief and boredom, deep sadness, seclusion and loneliness, weakness and laziness, lack of sharpness and thought, weakness in the eyes and ears, worry, and anxiety.

On the bright side, there is hope and many cures to such diseases. Here are [38] ten instructions to avoid such sin:

1. Avoid all artificial stimulations like pornography, magazines, books, television shows, and movies. (I suggest putting website restrictions on your phones, laptops, tablets, etc. Even if you're not struggling with this; it is better to be cautious and safe than sorry. Parental control should be for all ages.)
2. Prepare a full time program daily.
3. Focus on sports.
4. Replace one habit with another.
5. Absolute avoidance of loneliness.
6. Marry at first opportunity - even if it is engagement.
7. Suggestion and strengthening of will power - Meaning, [38] "The addicted individuals should regularly suggest to themselves that they can give up this ugly habit completely," and one shouldn't neglect [38] "reading psychological books written for stabilization and growth of character and strengthening of will power."
8. Absolute abstinence - be committed!
9. Improve general nourishment and diet.

10. Seek help from the power of faith and religious beliefs - know that Allah (swt) sees and hears you in every state you're in; you are never alone.

Know your trigger points; it is easier to fight off small battles than a large war. To conclude, the pornography industry is filled with individuals who are fully driven by their animalistic nature. Pornography has destroyed many marriages. Why? Such wickedness degrades men and women. People are watching fake, made-up abusive fantasies, and are trying to implement it within their marriages. When expectation and satisfaction is not met, partners begin to neglect one another, which eventually leads to separation. If you have a problem, seek help, and treat it like any other addiction.

[38] Shirazi, Naser Makarem. "Sexual Problems of Youths-Sexual Perversions." *Al-Islam.org*, Ahlul Bayt Digital Islamic Library Project, 9 Jan. 2013.
[39] Imani, Sayyid Kamal Faqih. "An Enlightening Commentary into the Light of the Holy Qur'an Vol. 11." Translated by Sayyid Abbas Sadr-'ameli, *Al-Islam.org*, Ahlul Bayt Digital Islamic Library Project , 4 Jan. 2020.
* Quran English Translation by Quran Hadi

Reflection 113

Testing His Seriousness

Sisters,

Would you like to save some time and find out if a guy is seriously interested in you, has good intentions, and is not messing around? Ask for this one simple request! Have them ask your father or guardian for permission to get to know you. It doesn't mean you're getting married; it is just a strategic method to filter out who is being real and not.

Also, no, it doesn't mean you're rushing either; it means you're protecting yourself and taking control of your life. People say, "Go with the flow and see where it goes." Naw, ain't nobody got time for that.

Reflection 114

I Want to Get to Know Her

Getting to know someone for a potential relationship is considered difficult, but in all seriousness it doesn't have to be if we are blunt, straightforward, direct, or whatever we want to call it. In this regard, before you decide to start this process ask yourself, "Am I ready for a relationship, commitment, responsibilities, etc.?" To be clear, I am not referring to financial stability, but rather mental readiness. If you're not, it's best you stop right there in your tracks, because if you don't you will be the root cause of someone's pain. That pain could have easily been avoided had you taken control of your self-centered soul, and looked beyond the situation at hand. I wish it was that easy, but we humans like to make things difficult.

For the sake of clarity I am going to approach this post from a male's perspective, because such actions are primarily done by men, but that doesn't mean some women don't do this either. Anyway, here is what really happens. A guy notices a girl, and she really interests him, but deep down he knows he is not ready. So, instead of telling himself "stop," he convinces himself that he has to capitalize on such an opportunity, because there might not be another chance with her. Why? Because that is how people driven by their animalistic nature move. Egotistically, they think every opportunity belongs to them. That right there is the definition of selfishness! It takes a God conscious individual to tell the soul, "Settle down, she might be great and all, but you're not ready. What is best is to wish her well, and move on." But that is not always the case, as we know.

Nevertheless, they begin to talk. Fast forward, they're now both really into each other. So the girl asks, "What are we?" The guy responds with, "Let's just go with the flow." More time passes and the girl asks, "Where is this going?" The guy realizes it is getting serious, so now he shows indecisiveness; he begins to tell her, "I care for you and I think you're amazing, and I am interested in you, but I just don't know." He says all these things, but doesn't provide her with any direction. At this point the girl is emotionally invested, and the guy probably is too, but does that even matter if there isn't any direction? Avoid these situations at all costs. Because if you attach yourself to a relationship like this, all it will ever be is a merry-go-round, you will just be going in circles for days; there has to be growth. If a person cannot provide some type of growth, don't waste your time. Sisters, in a previous reflection we said, to test a guy's seriousness, request of them to ask your guardian for permission to get to know you. Also ask, "Are you mentally ready for a relationship?" Brothers, ask this question too.

Indecisiveness is a problem; address it before you try to speak to someone for a relationship. "I don't know" is an excuse covering up one's real and true intentions, and is not an answer. In my humble opinion, I am a firm believer that everyone knows what they really want from day one, and we should all be able to truthfully answer every question asked. IF YOU'RE NOT READY OR MENTALLY READY, DON'T APPROACH ANYONE! To end, it is okay to admit that you're not ready, but what is not okay is leading someone on while knowing you could've prevented it; this is true selfishness. If you want to "mess around," go buy a toy, but don't play with human beings.

Reflection 115

Logistics

I hate to bring up this topic, but this is an important matter to reflect on. This post carries on from the, "I want to get to know her" post. When you want to get to know someone, please figure out the logistics around you before you try to make a move, so you may avoid pain and wasted time. The logistics I am referring to is with your parents! What tends to happen in many cases is two people speak for a good amount of time, and when the guy or girl tries to bring it up to their parents, the parents don't accept due to poor reasons! The parents will either say, "You're too young," or "finish school first," or "you're not financially ready," or "we dislike that nationality or village," etc.

That being said, the potential couple is forced to go their separate ways. Realistically not many people are willing to take a stance against their parents, despite how much they feel for someone. Communicate with your parents and see where they stand on this subject, be open with them; let them know of your plans beforehand, even if you're not speaking to anyone, just get an idea! This isn't something we can "wing." People's emotions and time are at stake.

Also, I am embarrassed to even bring up the subject of nationality, because it is sad that some parents still reject a potential spouse on the basis of where he or she is from. Forget nationality, the potential spouse can be from the same country, some parents will still reject based on the village they're from; I did not believe this until I witnessed it happen firsthand to someone. They got turned down due to generational stereotypes; that's mind boggling! Tell your parents when evaluating a spouse, the only thing that should matter is their relationship with Allah (swt).

Reflection 116

Worldly Fear

Where does fear originate from? Allah (swt) states in the *Quran, "It is only the Shaytan that causes you to fear from his friends, but do not fear them, and fear Me if you are believers" (3:175). From this verse we can distinguish that there are two types of fear, the fear of Allah (swt), and the fear of Shaytan; our ultimate goal is to fear Allah (swt), only. In my humble opinion, the difference between these two kinds of fear is that when we fear Shaytan we might be physically free, but mentally we are imprisoned, however, fearing only Allah (swt) provides us true freedom on both spectrums.

To be clear, this reflection is going to focus on fear spread by Shaytan; fear is a tactic by Shaytan that doesn't require any weapons. Also, fear can cause as much damage, if not more, than any major war because it prevents human beings from reaching their full potential by disrupting their connection with Allah (swt). Many of us aren't aware what Shaytan is capable of; Shaytan can hijack our thoughts by his whispers without us even realizing. For example, Shaytan can approach someone about a righteous topic, and whisper to them, "Don't support that, or go there, or post about it, you will end up losing your job and they might come after you, etc." When we lack faith in Allah (swt), such thoughts can overcome us, and instead of battling Shaytan privately, we end up relaying his message to our family and friends. At that point without even knowing it we are doing Shaytans job, completely free of charge.

When we deeply reflect on it, it is terrifying because in a sense we can become Shaytan's puppets, but there is hope, which is acting on what we already know is true. What is true is that regardless of how much we want to "play it safe," trials are unavoidable! Allah (swt) states in the *Quran, "And We will most certainly try you with somewhat of fear and hunger and loss of property and lives and fruits" (2:155). For instance, assume I refrained from standing up against oppression because I fear I might lose my job, who is to say I might not lose it anyway for a totally different reason within time? In general, how many people do you know that took all precautionary measures about a situation, did everything perfectly and as they were told, they "crossed their t's and dotted their i's," and still "loss" poured on them like rain. A question to reflect on is, suppose I did what Allah (swt) asks of me, and I lost my job, do I blame myself for standing up against oppression, or do I look at it as a trial from Allah (swt)?

We have to stop thinking Allah (swt) only exists at the mosque or near our prayer mats; He (swt) controls the universe. Mentally take yourself to your greatest fear, and overcome it through Allah (swt); this is not going to happen overnight, it will require time and work. Please note this world is temporary, and it is the lowest realm. Meaning, the only true loss here is not obeying and serving Allah (swt) correctly! Do not live your life in fear, not even an ounce; don't give Shaytan even a seed's size of your thoughts. Don't be afraid of poverty nor hunger, seek refuge only in Allah (swt), and accept any trial that you're blessed with. The ultimate fear for many of us is death. Why? Because we assume it is the end, but in reality it is the beginning. If we overcome the fear of death, what other types of fear can we be threatened with?

* Quran English Translation by Muhammad Habib Shakir

Reflection 117

I Am Getting Married

They say, "It is what every girl dreams of; it is wrong to put restrictions on a wedding." They say, "I will not come to your wedding if there isn't music and dancing." They say, "We are practicing our religion all year round, it's okay if we have one day for us, Allah (swt) will understand and forgive," and so on. I'm sure many of us can relate to such unpleasant comments if we are planning to have a wedding centered on what Islam allows and forbids.

That being said, I am not sure why we think we get a free pass during our wedding day, as if Allah (swt) turns a blind eye. If anything this is a trial; do we have a wedding based on what culture and tradition states, or do we follow religion? It takes great courage and will power to take a stance against the "norm," and it is difficult, especially when everyone is in our ears; what is even more intense is when our parents don't support our vision. Allah (swt) warns us in the *Quran, "And if you obey most of those in the earth, they will lead you astray from Allah's way" (6:116). What is ironic is even when we do listen to people, they will still find something to criticize, especially when it comes to weddings.

Nevertheless, it is crucial we stand firm if we are put in such a predicament, and if you're planning to have a wedding that includes music and dancing, I kindly ask you to entertain the following message. Seeking ultimate closeness to Allah (swt) comes at a cost, and the fee is as stated in the *Quran, "By no means shall you attain to righteousness until you spend (benevolently) out of what you love" (3:92). This is where many people put an end to their journey to Allah (swt); they're not willing to sacrifice what they love most, so they accept settling. Likewise, in the case of music and dancing at weddings, we also have to give up what we love too, but it should be effortless because such type of love is "haram," even if it is a long life dream of an individual.

Furthermore, keep in mind when choosing to have a wedding with music and dancing, we are voluntarily creating a haram venue that could've been easily avoided. I am sure we can all agree that men and women who are non-mahram dancing among each other to club style music isn't allowed in Islam. Let's not even mention: the lustful gazing, immodesty, and "accidental" touching that takes place in the middle of the dance floor when everyone is clumped together; this is aside from the excessive extravagance and wastefulness that occurs during weddings.

Anyway, on the Day of Judgment how will we answer to Allah (swt) when He (swt) questions us about our actions?! Ask yourself, is it worth it to have such a wedding that is only four to five hours long, that contains many sins, to please the creation? There might not be any physical harm from such an event, but what about our spiritual soul? Hosting such occasions may damage our spiritual soul without even knowing it. On the other hand, think about your children. Assume you've progressed in religion over time, and realized that these types of weddings are wrong; it will still be pretty hard to convince your children to refrain from such weddings when you had one like it. Lead by example from now, even if you are not married, nor have children!

The idea of this post isn't meant to antagonize anyone, but the intention is to introduce a different perspective that many of us overlook. We do have the free will to create a friendly, fun, and acceptable environment without music and dancing. I understand some people are okay with such "haram fun," but it shouldn't be at the cost of the believers; every action we take can either bring us closer to Allah (swt) or away. With that in mind, to make this process easier, select a spouse that has similar views as you, and don't hire a singer or DJ; they're the nucleus. We have to change the "norm," and pave the correct way for the next generation.

* Quran English Translation by Muhammad Habib Shakir

Reflection 118

Vaccine

This disease (COVID-19) has taken the lives of a number of people, which is causing many of us to become anxious and fearful; in these circumstances it's important to look at the facts. The number one reality is that your death is written. Assume this pandemic didn't occur, who is to say these people wouldn't have died anyway, but in a different manner? For example, it's noted that individuals with no underlying health issues have died from this disease. What does that tell us? Death doesn't depend on a disease; when it's time, it's time. To be clear, just because our death is written, it doesn't mean we shouldn't still take the necessary measures to protect ourselves and those around us.

However, we shouldn't let the current crisis blind us; we have to stay grounded, and understand the true meaning of this world. This world is simply a trial. It's evident that the current situation is escalating, but that doesn't mean we should lose hope in Allah (swt); He (swt) is the only one that can save us. Is He (swt) not the vaccine for all burdens?

1. Did Allah (swt) not split the sea for Prophet Musa (as) and his followers, and save them from Pharaoh?
2. Did Allah (swt) not save Prophet Ibrahim (as) from the burning fire?
3. Did Allah (swt) not save Prophet Nuh (as) from the great floods?
4. Did Allah (swt) not save Prophet Isa (as) from crucifixion?

*Quran,

"And if Allah touch you with affliction, there is none to take it off but He" (6:17).

Say, "O Allah, (please) relieve this community from the (current) grief through presenting him." Who is he? Imam Mahdi (atfs).

* Quran English Translation by Muhammad Habib Shakir

Reflection 119

Pandemic

Passage 1

It is not far-fetched that Allah (swt) can eliminate a generation within a blink of an eye; just research the history of past generations. Before we dive into that, it is crucial to understand the "why?" Why does Allah (swt) test us? The *Quran states, "And We tested them with good [times] and bad that perhaps they would return [to obedience]" (7:168). In a sense, trials cleanse the soul so that individuals may wake up, and seek the straight path, but many of us don't view trials like that. Instead, we are under the assumption that Allah (swt) is punishing us; we have to differentiate between a trial and a punishment. We have to go back to the people of the past, what was the outcome of past generations who were disobedient? The *Quran states, "Have they not seen how many generations We destroyed before them which We had established upon the earth as We have not established you? And We sent [rain from] the sky upon them in showers and made rivers flow beneath them; then We destroyed them for their sins and brought forth after them a generation of others" (6:6). The punishment was swift, and Allah (swt) quickly replaced such wicked generations.

To be clear, I am not in any way, shape, or form claiming that Allah (swt) is trying to eliminate us through a virus. Not I nor anyone else has such knowledge, but for the sake of reflecting, let's entertain our thoughts. Nevertheless, if that was the case for past generations, is what we are currently facing possibly a punishment? The **Quran states, "If Allah were to punish men for their wrong-doing, He would not leave, on the (earth), a single living creature: but He gives them respite for a stated Term: When their Term expires, they would not be able to delay (the punishment) for a single hour, just as they would not be able to anticipate it (for a single hour)" (16:61). Does that mean we get a "free pass," and can do whatever we want? The *Quran states, "Has it not become clear to those who inherited the earth after its [previous] people that if We willed, We could afflict them for their sins? But We

204

seal over their hearts so they do not hear" (7:100). Do you know what is worse than an immediate punishment? A sealed heart due to excessive sinning, and a lack of obedience and servitude to Allah (swt)!

It's time. It's time to wake up from our long slumber. An individual becomes awakened only when he or she connects to Allah (swt), other than that, they might be physically moving, but in reality they're asleep. We sit here and say with certainty, "This pandemic is going to pass," it's okay to be hopeful. I have personally said it, but is it a guarantee? We really don't know, just like we would've never guessed a tiny virus would leave "our" advanced world quarantined, and inactivated. Maybe this pandemic does pass, but who is to say we are not going to pass with it? Meaning, I am sure the people who have already died from the illness once thought that this will all pass, and they will get the chance to go back to their "normal lives," but instead death claimed them. Allah (swt) is not punishing us, He (swt) is giving us an opportunity; why would we want to go back to a norm that doesn't know Allah (swt)? This world belongs to Allah (swt); it does not belong to our desires, ambitions, and ego. This virus is not our greatest danger, but a sealed heart is. Protect your heart by becoming God conscious; it's time to seek and stay on the straight path together.

* Quran English Translation by Sahih International
** Quran English Translation by Yusuf Ali

Passage 2

The recent outbreak of the "coronavirus disease" has left many people taking precautionary measures to protect themselves. When we reflect on such a situation, one cannot help but realize that we focus greatly on physical harm, but neglect the spiritual soul. For instance, a diseased heart caused by sinning is more destructive than any illness; if only we have the same mindset towards sinning as we do towards COVID-19, only then will we be successful. The irony is, when death takes a soul, no health or physical sickness follows an individual to the grave, but a diseased heart does. May Allah (swt) have mercy on all of us!

Reflection 120

Our Freewill

Your relationship with Allah (swt) did not develop out of coincidence; a number of people might believe that Allah (swt) has preferred some over others, but this is untrue. Our relationship with Allah (swt) simply depends on our freewill! For instance, the actions we took, take, and will take can either bring us closer to Allah (swt), or away from Allah (swt). For example:

1. If you choose to pray, you will become closer to Allah (swt).
2. If you choose to wear a hijab, you will become closer to Allah (swt).
3. If you choose to lower your gaze and not flirt with the opposite gender, you will become closer to Allah (swt).
4. If you choose to donate to charity, you will become closer to Allah (swt).
5. If you choose to worship Allah (swt) like the Prophet Muhammad (saww) and AhlulBayt (as), you will become closer to Allah (swt), and so on.

The point is, creating and maintaining a relationship with Allah (swt) depends on our decisions.

The reward for making strategic decisions is that our mind and spirit will create and implement a defense mechanism, and a reminder tool. Meaning, when this world tries to suck us in, our "super powers" will kick in, and pull us right back to reality, but the only way to reap such benefits is to do things the right way on a consistent basis. The quickest way to lose our powers is to sin.

It is important to note, sure our surroundings and how we were brought up play their roles, but only to an extent; it all goes back to YOU. Do you want to commit to the straight path, or not, and if you do, to what degree? I think this is where many of us struggle, this is why we have one foot on the straight path, and one foot off. We think if we fully pledge ourselves to Allah (swt), then we are putting ourselves in a cage, and that is why numerous individuals choose to follow a progressive and liberal version of Islam instead. Such a philosophy is deceiving because it is designed by society. Such a path will not take us to Allah (swt); it will even stunt our spiritual growth. There is only ONE path to Allah (swt). It is to worship Allah (swt) like the Prophet Muhammad (saww) and AhlulBayt (as). Ask yourself, what "type" of Islam am I following? Once you realize this, and understand where you're going, only then can you make changes and improve.

The Imam (as) states, [40] "There are two kinds of people here: One is the kind of those who have sold their souls for eternal damnation, the other is of those who have purchased their souls and freed them from damnation."

[40] Attributed to Imam Ali (as)

Reflection 121

Care

One of the greatest worries we contemplate is, "Who is going to take care of or look after my parents or children if something happens to me." The simple answer is Allah (swt)!

It took me a while to understand this concept, and it wasn't until I was blessed to sit in a Special Education class. I noticed two students who both suffered from cognitive disabilities, but one was more severe than the other. As the day went on, I was mesmerized as I observed the actions of the student whose condition was less severe. He was practically caring for his friend, as if it was his job; he would assist him with his schoolwork, take him to lunch, and help him get his food. When it was time to go home he would wait for him and take him to the bus stop, etc.

It is as if Allah (swt) assigned this student to care for his friend at school every day. The point is, such worries are not for us to overthink and stress over. Many of us worry about our parents if something happens to us, and ask, who will take care of them? Did Allah (swt) not care for them when we weren't in the picture? Allah (swt) has special agents in this world to care for others! An example of this is when local organizations come together and feed those who are less fortunate. Do we think people do this out of goodwill? No, it's Allah (swt)! He (swt) does wonders through people.

It is [41] narrated that when Prophet Yusuf (as) was in prison, he asked a cell-mate to lobby for him with the King of the time. Afterwards, Archangel Gabriel descends near Yusuf and kicks the ground which causes a long narrow opening that reaches the seventh layer of the earth. Gabriel said, "O'Yusuf, take a look at the seventh layer beneath the earth, what do you see?" "A small stone," Yusuf replied. Then Gabriel made an opening in the stone and said, "What do you see inside?" "A minute worm," Yusuf replied. "Who bestows sustenance to this worm," asked Gabriel? "The Lord of the Worlds (swt)," replied Yusuf. Gabriel said, "Your Lord says, He had not ignored a small worm in the seventh layer of the earth, how could you think that He has abandoned you… why did you ask the man (the cell-mate) such a request?"

Allah (swt) tells us in the *Quran, "Not a leaf falls, but He (swt) knows of it" (6:59). A leaf! Let your mind and heart rest, surely Allah (swt) is looking after us. Everyone is accounted for, be it a human being or the smallest creature. Let's leave these matters to Allah (swt). Allah (swt) states in the *Quran, "The example of those who take allies other than Allah is like that of the spider who takes a home. And indeed, the weakest of homes is the home of the spider" (29:41). We seek refuge in the Lord of the Worlds (swt).

[41] Majlisi, Muhammad Baqir. "An Account of Ya'qub and Yusuf." *Al-Islam.org*, Ahlul Bayt Digital Islamic Library Project , 26 Dec. 2017.
* Quran English Translation by Sahih International

Reflection 122

Love vs. Attachment

What determines if you love someone? Sometimes we confuse love with attachment. Meaning we think we are in love, but we might just be attached to an individual because they filled in a void, or uplifted us in a positive manner. For many of us, under our "proclaimed" mask of love is nothing but attachment. Why do we convince ourselves that we are in love, even if we are in danger physically and/or mentally? In my humble opinion, the confusion between love vs. attachment stems from the following:

1. **Movies, TV series, novelties, etc.** - During our youth, these tools have planted seeds in our minds describing what true love is, and across the board they all have similar storylines. The overall picture they paint is that despite how tough a situation becomes, we should never give up on "love," we must always fight for it, but what they fail to express is the toll it takes on an individual. We have generations of people thinking true love is fighting then making up. This is their definition of love, but surely it is a dramatic addiction between couples, and they're of the belief that their bond is becoming stronger, but in reality, it is a ticking time bomb. In addition, one question to keep in mind is, does true love evolve from illicit relationships? Meaning, movies for example depict that it is possible for true love to occur outside of a marriage, but such relationships are "haram," yet we still try to imitate them. In this case, we are attached to an idea of what true love is through poor short entertainment, made-up of actors and actresses.

2. **Insecurities, lack of confidence, low self-esteem, etc.** - If you don't love yourself, you will certainly get attached to anyone that will make you feel good in any way, even if it is in a negative way. Someone can come and spit out complete "garbage," or nonsense, and you can be head over heels for them. Why is that? Because you didn't give yourself the

210

proper attention. It is important to work on self-love, but with an appropriate method. Meaning, society says accept "you" the way you exactly are, but that never sat well with me because some things within us can be changed by our freewill. If it is changeable, we should take the proper action to better ourselves; for example, if my weight is the reason why I am feeling down, why should I accept it and say I love myself? If I can make a change, I should work hard and strive for a transformation through a healthy balanced process, and not an extreme one. However, if it is something I cannot change, then I should refer to the verse in the *Quran where Allah (swt) states, "He it is Who shapes you in the wombs as He likes" (3:6). I should reflect and try to develop contentment. The examples mentioned above were from a physical perspective, but from a mental aspect, the best and most efficient way to change is to become God conscious; a negative mind doesn't stand a chance against Taqwa.

3. **Infatuation**- Words like this are dangerous! Infatuation means to have a passionate, but short-lived attraction towards someone. Many individuals have fallen victim to infatuation, and still haven't recovered from such an experience, even if a great amount of time has passed. Reason being, they confuse such strong feelings with love. They're fully convinced that it's love, so they will do anything to defend it despite what others are telling them; an infatuated person completely becomes blind, and begins to move with their emotions, forgoing their logic. Infatuation takes place when we think love at first sight is true. However, this intense feeling we adore probably originates from how a person looks, or their eloquent speech, but is it love? I say this with confidence, no! This confusion between infatuation and love requires clarification; we must note that for true love to develop, it requires more than an overnight meet and greet.

4. **Experiences**- Sometimes attachment develops between two people after they share an emotional experience; take a tragedy

for instance. A tragedy can unite two individuals together under one umbrella quickly, but it also can be deceiving because there are many emotions involved. Sometimes we think it's a good idea to get to know someone when we are feeling sad because we find comfort in them, but when we become better we realize that this person might not be who we want to be with. This is why it is important to make decisions with a clear mind, and never when we are too happy or sad. I found that the best time to make decisions is in the morning during Fajr prayer. On the other hand, take someone who just got out of a bad relationship, but they didn't give themselves the proper time to heal. Instead of spending time alone they decide to get to know someone new, which makes them feel better, but the problem with this scenario is feeling better is dependent on someone new, and not from within. Take a bandage for example, a bandage covers a wound, but does it heal it? No. What happens when we rip off a bandage? Pain! That minor "pain" symbolizes letting people come and go into our lives before healing because we don't like the feeling of loneliness, so we cling on to anything to feel temporarily okay. How does any wound heal? From within, taking good care and time with it. Mental and emotional wounds should be cared for just like physical injuries.

5. **Reflection**- In a recent poll, it was asked if social media has made it easier or harder getting to know someone for a serious relationship. The majority of people answered harder! Truth be told, social media has created a false image of what a person can be; individuals tend to portray their best versions on these sites, which always creates unrealistic expectations. A picture is worth a thousand words, but reality is worth much more, there's the good and there's the bad. Meaning, people tend to get attached to what they see, and when they realize what they once saw doesn't exist 24/7, they tend to discontinue communication. This is easily being done nowadays, but why? Because social media has given people the power to replace one another within a click of button, but what is being undermined? Value. It is true, social media has made it easier for us to connect with people, but

this process of connection has become overwhelming for many because of the excessive amount of users. We are no longer limited to a handful of people; for instance, an individual can connect to someone from a different continent. Past generations did not deal with such circumstances; the easiest way to paralyze a human being is to give them many options. What eventually happens is we ignore such a realm until we cannot anymore. Lastly, with social media there's excitement, instead of trying to love an actual person, people love the process of getting to know an individual more. The friend requests, the likes, the comments, the indirect quotes and pictures, the attention! This is what people are attached to now, and once it fades away with one person, it's all about how can I start it back up with someone else? To overcome this problem, it is important to set our intention for marriage, be specific to what we truly want in a significant other, and most importantly to lower our gaze, especially on social media.

Many of us think we are in love, but really we might just be attached to a routine, so we accept things the way they are. What is true love? It is loving someone through Allah (swt), whether it is your parents, spouse, siblings, children, friends, etc. Reason being, this love is pure because not only do you take the person into consideration, but you're taking Allah (swt) as well. For instance, if I love my parents through Allah (swt), I am going to serve them to the best of my capabilities because it pleases Allah (swt). Loving people through Allah (swt) encourages one to do things they never thought they would; it inspires them to go the extra mile for others even if they're complete strangers. It is not ideal to love someone from only our nature; if our souls aren't nourished properly by Allah (swt) we can easily become vicious. Take for example those who claim to "love" their spouse, but abuse them, or children who claim to "love" their parents, but neglect them, or a mother who claims to "love" her children, but drowns them. Furthermore, suppose the person we "love" doesn't abuse us, they're kind and well behaved, we have good communication, we click together and whatnot, but they encourage us to sin. The same person that loves us can be the reason we feel distant from Allah (swt). Is this considered true love? You tell me; on a surface level everything might look perfect, but what about on a spiritual level, which is more important, and which will follow us to the hereafter? Good is not good unless you're good with Allah (swt). To be clear, I am not telling you to leave your spouse if they encourage you to sin, but rather communicate, implement change, take stances, and direct yourselves to Allah (swt). The overall point is, if you want to experience true love, love through Allah (swt); it's much greater.

* Quran English Translation by Muhammad Habib Shakir

Reflection 123

Confidence vs. Anxiety

When we view this world from a different perspective, can it be that what we presumably think is right is really wrong, and what is wrong is really right? In this reflection, we are going to dissect various examples to entertain our thoughts.

To dive right into it, how important is confidence? If we ask anyone, they will say it's a crucial character trait; it's a powerful tool that helps us maneuver through our lives sufficiently. What is one way to build confidence? Exercising and improving one's self-image. What some of us end up doing when we feel confident with ourselves is we start feeling the need to share it with the world. For example, we start posting pictures of ourselves with tighter clothes, or sharing ourselves working out on social media. Hypothetically, can we say insecurities and lack of confidence protected us from sinning, but confidence in a sense led us to sin? There are boundaries between mahrams and non-mahrams. It is understandable that many people's intentions are not ill, and it is to promote a healthier lifestyle, but it is important to always consider if our actions align with what Allah (swt) allows and doesn't. Now, are we saying to avoid becoming confident? Of course not, but can you handle what comes with confidence? Are you going to use this quality to serve Allah (swt) or your desires?

On the other hand, sometimes anxiety is seemingly described to be a deficiency. The irony is I once asked an individual about what stopped them from committing a sin, and they responded with, "I became anxious." It was an eye-opening response because in many cases being anxious is known to be somewhat of a flaw according to society, but in the case of this individual, it stopped them from sinning. Now are we saying to stay anxious and not to try to overcome anxiety? No, but if we only measure ourselves based on the scale of what humanity deems is right and wrong, then we are missing the bigger picture. Maybe being anxious is a blessing from Allah (swt), and may prevent us from sinning; maybe if we weren't anxious, we would be more inclined to sin without hesitation. Maybe when we reach a high level of God consciousness, Allah (swt) will remove anxiety from our hearts and minds because He (swt) now knows we are ready to lead our lives with a pure purpose.

Let's use more common examples. Sometimes Allah (swt) may not bless us with what we want because it may take us away from Him (swt). For instance, money, it's good and needed, but how many people do you know that lost their way once they became wealthy? They stopped pursuing the straight path, created new addictions, and gave into materialism excessively. Now are we saying don't try to become wealthy? No, but can you handle what comes with money? Furthermore, education is a must; what is better than knowledge? So why is it that some individuals become Atheist or arrogant after gaining knowledge? Now are we saying don't become educated? No, but can you handle the power of knowledge? Social media is a powerful instrument; there are many benefits to social media, but at the present time, sins come to us through social media; we don't have to search for them. Now are we saying not to have social media? No, but if we see pictures of drugs and alcohol, are we going to feel tempted to give in? If we see pictures of half-naked men and women, are we going to lower our gaze? If we come across music pages, are we going to keep on scrolling? If we take pictures of ourselves, and we know they're immodest, are we still going to feel the need to share them? Social media didn't exist in the past, but trap doors for sinning always did, and they can come in many different forms.

To end, what we may think is good might be a poisonous snake, and what we may think is bad might be a hidden treasure if handled properly. However, the overall idea isn't to search for reptiles and diamonds in our lives, but rather it is to introduce a different outlook; furthermore, it is to discover if any matter at hand is really bringing us closer to Allah (swt) or not, and if not, we must learn to incorporate Allah (swt) in everything, despite how insignificant we may think it is.

Reflection 124

It's My Fault

"It's my fault!" No one likes to utter these words; it's tough to blame ourselves! What is easier is dropping our baggage at someone else's doorstep, pointing the finger at them, and saying, "It's your fault." For example, they asked her, "Why is your heart broken?" It's his fault, she said. They asked him, "Why are you on drugs?" I hang out with the wrong group of people, he said. "Why don't you exercise?" I have no time; I work long hours. "Why don't you pray?" I was never taught how to pray. "Why did you abuse her?" She ticked me off. Finally, they asked, "Why are you the way you are?" He/she said, "Because my life sucks, and Allah (swt) doesn't like me." Please note that all examples described in this post can happen to either a male or female, they're not specific to one gender; but for the sake of clarity, I am going to focus on one gender per example if needed, to avoid any confusion.

1. In many relationships when individuals experience a great amount of suffering, the first person they blame is the person they were once with. They never tend to take a step back and think for a moment, and ask themselves if they brought this pain onto themselves. Before many people begin "dating," they kind of have an idea who the type of person they're speaking to is by doing their own background check, or asking someone about them. They know deep down this person is NOT good for them, but this certain personality, or "bad boy," or "sweet talker," intrigues them, it excites them.

So, instead of pausing and thinking things through, they follow their whim. When the damage is done, the first person she blames is him. So, I asked, "Did you know dating is forbidden in Islam?" She said, "Yes." "Did you know flirting is not permissible in Islam?" She said, "Yes." "Did you know hugging, kissing, touching and getting intimate with someone before getting engaged or married is haram?" She said, "Yes." "Did you have a feeling he was not good for you from the beginning?" She said, "Yes!" Finally I asked, "Why did you take your chances with him then?" She admitted and said, "It's my fault, I should've never put myself in a situation that I knew was wrong from the beginning, and even if I didn't know it was wrong, if I had just followed what Islam permits and doesn't, I could've saved myself from a great amount of heartache." Please understand, I am not saying that the guy played no part in this scenario, but what I am saying is if we retrace our steps, we can realize where we went wrong.

2. He told me I am on drugs because I hang around the wrong group of people. So, I asked him, "Are these individuals forcing you to chill with them?" He said, "No, but we have a good time." Then I asked him, "Before you guys meet up, do you know that the place you're about to go to is harmful?" He said, "Yes, but you know how it is." I asked, "Are you able to make new friends?" He said, "Yes, but they're boring." Finally I said, "You're on drugs because you want to be on them; it has nothing to do with your friends." He said, "I think you're right; it's my fault, not my friends."

3. They told me I don't exercise because I am too busy. I asked them, "How many hours are in a week?" They said, "168 hours." I asked, "How many hours do you sleep in a day?" They said, "Eight hours a day." So that means you have 112 hours left in your week. I asked, "How many hours do you work in a week?" They replied, "It varies, 40-50 hours a week, sometimes 70, 10 hours a day." I said, "Even though the average person works only 40 hours a week, for this scenario, we are going to take the maximum hours you have ever worked in a week, 70 hours, right? Subtract 70 from 112 and what does that give you?" They said, "42 hours." Finally I asked, "Of those 42 hours, why can't you dedicate just three hours per week to exercise?" They said, "You're right, it's our fault; it seems that we are not that busy after all." Mind you, an average individual doesn't work 70 hours a week, they work 40. An average person actually has 72

hours of leisure time, and yet they still claim being "too busy" is what prevents them from improving their overall health.

4. They told me I don't pray because no one has ever taught me. So I asked, "Have you ever tried teaching yourself through online videos, or going to a local center, and asking someone for help?" They said, "No, I haven't; it's my fault, I should take advantage of the endless resources around me, especially nowadays living in a technology driven world where I can access everything through my smartphone."

5. He told me I hit her because she ticked me off. So I asked him, "Do you consider yourself an angry individual?" He said, "Not really, sometimes." I asked, "Were you violent growing up?" He laughed and said, "We used to get into many fights for fun." I asked, "What gives you the right to abuse her?" He said, "I lost it." Finally I asked, "Would you get violent with someone bigger and stronger than you?" He said, "I don't think so." So I said, "You can control your anger, but you choose when and when not to." He said, "I think I need help, and it is my fault for taking advantage of those who I overpower. If I am able to control my anger in certain situations, I should be able to control it in all situations."

6. They said my life sucks and Allah (swt) doesn't like me. I asked, "What do you mean?" "Allah (swt) has put me in such unbearable situations, and I feel like nothing ever goes my way," they said. I asked, "Well, have you taken the time to understand the truth of this world?" They said, "What are you talking about?" I said, "To be clear this world isn't meant for you and I, to have life go our way; its sole purpose is to TEST us. So yes you're put in these situations so you may evolve and become dependent only on Allah (swt). Let me ask you this, did the Prophet Muhammad (saww) go through hardship?" They said, "Yes, according to what I know; what I am going through is nothing compared to what he (saww) went through."

I said, "This is not a matter of comparing problems, but he (saww) is known to be the beloved friend of Allah (swt), and yet trials were poured on him (saww) like a rainy day. Do you think Allah (swt) disliked the Prophet (saww)?" They said, "I see where you're coming from; it's my fault for not taking the time to understand why I am in this world. For a while I was so focused on the center of the picture; I think I should step back and see the whole picture, and reflect on the importance of cause and effect."

The reason behind this post is to hold ourselves accountable. When we live our lives always blaming a certain situation or others, all we're doing is making up excuses, and going in circles. When we say, "It's my fault," sincerely, what does that do? Our mind registers it as something not good, and prevents us from taking that action again, and begins to offer solutions. However, if we don't do that, the mind will continue feeding the narrative because it doesn't see anything wrong with it. In addition, what many of us fail to realize is, when we don't own up to our actions the act will always linger through our thoughts from time to time; it is not until we do own up to them that they get filed away, and we barely think about them at all. One last important point I would like to mention is, saying it's my fault is truly the first step to forgiving yourself; I know that sounds cliché, but it is true. Once we forgive ourselves the thoughts that constantly haunt us will disintegrate.

Reflection 125

Addicted to Being Sad

Being in a state of extreme sadness can become addictive, and unfortunately many of us have gotten used to such a state without even knowing it. It's not that we aren't trying to become better, but it's more about the fact that leaving our comfort zone can be frightening. When we are in our comfort zone we already know what to expect, we already know how bad things can get. It's easy handling whatever comes our way because we are familiar with how "rock bottom" feels. This is why we see many people attached to being sad, even though they have all the resources to cross to the other side, and leave such a state.

Moreover, to be clear, this type of sadness is viewed as a way of life instead of a temporary emotion. Meaning, I know some of us will not be able to relate to this, but it does happen, especially for those who have experienced a great amount of suffering. Having said that, the question we must answer is, how can we get out of this state and protect ourselves from re-entering or entering it? Let's say our extreme sadness is caused by losing someone, this individual might be our lover. Now, what the common person does is when they lose something, they try to replace it, but where they go wrong is what they replace it with.

For instance, if we lose someone we tend to replace him or her with someone else. It's an equal replacement, but instead we are supposed to replace them with something greater; this is how we truly overcome any situation. It is a simple concept to say, but it is challenging to apply. If we do apply it the reward is endless, and will help us leave such an addictive state for good. In fact, we might not ever experience such intense sadness again if we do. Now, this part is for everyone, whether you have experienced a deep sense of hurt or not.

[42] "I sat at the gate of my heart, and let no one in, except Allah (swt)." This is the greater replacement I am referring to. Imagine this, you're sitting in a lobby, the door in front of you is for people to enter, and the door behind you is where Allah (swt) is (your heart). This door

221

is locked and no one can enter it. Now, if I begin to let people enter through the door behind me, that is when I have failed. If I keep them in the lobby, I will succeed. We tend to experience deep hurt at times because our love for others exceeds the love we have for Allah (swt), and that is why we see people sometimes lose their minds when they lose someone. Now, let's be careful, I am no longer referring just to a lover anymore, everyone and anything must stay in that lobby, whether it is your parents, children, friends, houses, and cars! To end, when we reprogram our hearts in this way, we are more inclined to seek growth, because we are now powered by an energy that is boundless, we are no longer frightened of the unknown. Instead, we become ready to cross to the other side, and strive for the betterment of our souls. It's important to understand why some people that have everything in this world still suffer from extreme addictive sadness...

*Quran,

"And whoever turns away from My remembrance - indeed, he will have a depressed [i.e., difficult] life" (20:124).

* Quran English Translation by Sahih International
[42]Attributed to Imam Ali (as)

Reflection 126

Mutah

In the name of Allah (swt), The Most Gracious and The Most Merciful.

All praise belongs to Allah (swt).

I seek refuge with Allah (swt) from the accursed Shaytan.

This post is about Mutah, also known as temporary marriage. Before we begin, we must note that this post is NOT going to highlight where Mutah can be found in the Quran and narrations, or why one group believes in it and the other doesn't, or if it is only allowed to be practiced in the time of war and traveling, and so on. If you would like more information on the authenticity, history, and how Mutah is exactly practiced, and who you can and cannot do Mutah with, refer to your Marja', respected scholars, and credible resources.

Having said that, I am writing this post on the basis that I agree with the system of Mutah, because it is permitted by the Prophet Muhammad (saww) and AhlulBayt (as). Meaning, I am not trying to make an argument for Mutah, or make a debate out of it in any form, because I am already convinced with it. Rather, I am just trying to introduce it from a different perspective so we may entertain our thoughts. I mention this because it's important to know where this post clearly stands so we may avoid any confusion. Let's begin…

Submission

Mutah is a sensitive topic, but it is an important matter to discuss because it may be the deciding factor between connecting to Allah (swt) entirely or not. First off, we are going to look at it from a spiritual perspective. When we say, "I disagree with Mutah," do we ever sit down and ask ourselves who we are disagreeing with? Probably not, instead we get all emotional and heated, and start calling it "halal prostitution" and whatnot. We tend to behave the same way when we find out Islam allows men to marry four women, but that is for another discussion. So, when we accept parts of religion and despise and take stances on other parts, what are we really doing? Sure it is nice to share our opinions, but in reality we are taking a stance against Allah (swt). When we say, "I disagree," we are indirectly saying we know more than Allah (swt), The All-Knowing. Do we ever think about it in that way?

Never, because when we look at life we view it in a way that is best for US only, and neglect everyone and anything else. You see, Allah (swt) doesn't do that; He (swt) offers solutions for every possible situation mankind may encounter. Instead of saying, "I disagree with Mutah" out of emotions, try saying, "I don't have all the information on it yet, and I will try to learn more about it." Mutah is an OPTION for mankind to protect them from sinning, same with the concept of four wives; they're options. Meaning, you can say, "Yes, this is for me," or "no, this isn't for me." It is not like prayer, prayer is mandatory. The overall point to understand here is, we might not realize it, but when we resent parts of religion, we are creating barriers between us and Allah (swt). To overcome these barriers we must educate ourselves, and know that just because we accept Mutah, it doesn't mean we have to personally implement it in our lives. However, accepting it will help us become closer to Allah (swt) because we are completely submitting to Allah (swt).

Why can't we stand Mutah?

Because we believe Mutah is a "loophole" to sleep around, which is mind boggling to me because we are overlooking the real problem. Before we dive into that point, we must briefly explain what Mutah is? Unfortunately, sexual intercourse is automatically a synonym for Mutah nowadays. However, that is untrue, they're completely two different things. People can engage in a Mutah marriage without doing anything (more to come on this later). Briefly, Mutah is what makes two non-mahrams halal/permissible among each other through reciting a formula in the presence of Allah (swt), which includes a dowry and an expiration date, and whatever they decide to do after is THEIR decision, not Mutah's, Mutah doesn't make decisions.

The question that arises is why are we so furious with a formula… with a sentence, a couple of words? What is mind boggling is people actually believe that an abusive nature of human beings (by abusive, I mean someone who takes advantage of Mutah) originates from what Allah (swt) permits and doesn't. I must ask, why don't we ever point the finger at the people who have deceiving intentions, and are moving according to their animalistic nature? Suppose Mutah didn't exist, how sure are we that those animalistic driven individuals will act differently? Let's be honest with ourselves, is Mutah really the deciding factor for such behavior? The argument some of us make is, some individuals cannot control themselves because they have Mutah as an option, but how is that true? When we study people in other cultures or religions, they don't know what Mutah is, and they probably never heard of it, but their animalistic behavior is still the same.

To be clear, I am not saying anyone that engages in Mutah is dominated by their animalistic nature, but what I am saying is, such animalistic driven people claim that what they're doing is halal… and yes engaging in Mutah is halal, but what they tend to forget is lying, being manipulative, and intentionally hurting anyone to achieve their goal is a sin. For the longest time, Mutah has been used as a scapegoat by those who cannot own up to their animalistic nature; that is the real problem. Allah (swt) creates solutions, not mistakes! When something gets abused, know mankind has entered the room, and it's from their nature, and NOT FROM Islam. Having said that, I am not sure why our focus is always on Mutah…instead, we should be focusing on ourselves, and learn how to put our excessive animalistic nature in check. Sometimes we act as if this is a Muslim problem only. No, this is a human being problem.

Emotions

What is one of the main differences between permanent marriage and temporary marriage (Mutah)? Mutah ends after the expiration date has been reached. I mention this because sometimes people belittle and disrespect their spouse in a Mutah marriage because they view it as a downgrade, and not only that, they go as far as exposing him or her when the Mutah marriage has concluded, which is a great sin by the way. To avoid confusion, the last sentence isn't referring to an individual who is in a permanent and temporary marriage at the same time. The overall point is, if anyone engages in a Mutah marriage, they should treat the person they are with the same exact way they would treat their permanent spouse, no difference.

Before anyone engages in a Mutah marriage they have to sit down with themselves and ask, can I handle such a commitment from an emotional side? They must clearly understand what they're getting themselves into, and understand all possibilities that come with Mutah. This is what many people tend to overlook, the emotional side of it, but in reality, emotions have nothing to do with Mutah, remember what we said earlier? Basically, all Mutah does is allow two non-mahrams to become permissible among each other. My point is, whatever the relationship is, Mutah or not, one should always consider their emotions. Don't just jump into things, think things through, and if practiced, be mature about it. Also, another argument that we make is that Mutah has hurt many women. This is untrue, Mutah cannot hurt anyone; the relationship between man and woman caused such hurt, just like any other relationship. No one ever says my marriage hurt me, or my marriage took advantage of me, or "dating" hurt me, or a friendship hurt me. Rather, we say he or she took advantage of me, or hurt me. How is it that when it comes to Mutah we say it's Mutah's fault. I hope at this point we are beginning to distinguish between Mutah and the actions of human beings.

Zina

I can't say who falls under this category, but it can be anyone. In addition, I cannot say we live in a perfect world and people don't do these things. I am a realist, and what I am about to address is very true. I am not going to try to sugarcoat anything because this is the reality of this world, and sometimes we cannot stop it, but we can suggest alternatives to prevent an individual from sinning. Sometimes, the difference between halal and haram is reciting one line and following a proper formula, and to us that might be absurd, but there is a bigger meaning behind it; it's a pure principle ordained by Allah (swt).

Zina, do you know what that is? It is unlawful sexual intercourse! People in our community are practicing Zina greatly. Would you rather have them practice Zina, or have lawful sexual intercourse after they used Mutah to become halal to each other? When we see people "dating" for years, I don't know what they're doing in private, but let's be honest, they're doing something. There is never an outrage against dating. This is where the frustration is. In fact, we encourage it and say, "They're in love, they're so cute together," and whatnot. So, what is the solution we should offer here? Should we accept the idea of dating, and all the sins that come with it? Even if it is not Zina, should we accept haram acts like kissing, hugging and flirting? So tell me, what would you propose to avoid Zina? Early marriage? Yes, I agree with you, but unfortunately many people don't want to get married young, or aren't capable of getting married at all. Let me hear something else? Suppress one's desires? If that is the case, we obviously haven't understood the natural human body yet. Here is the best one I heard, people should masturbate! So to avoid one sin, we must commit another sin? Makes sense, huh? I don't think many people are ever going to stop trying to fulfill their sexual desires, especially living in the west where sexualization is amplified.

When we boil it down, it is a matter of doing things the halal or haram way, and if we only view things from our eyes, we have failed. YOU might not be struggling, but perhaps the person next to you is. It is better to have an alternative than no alternative at all. It is not our business what people do, but it is important they know there is a halal option which prevents them from sinning.

Before Permanent Marriage/Engagement

This part is about using Mutah to get to know someone before permanent marriage/engagement comfortably. This idea is probably far-fetched, and looked down upon, especially by parents, but I think it is important to mention for the sake of it. The truth is, for some people, it's hard for them to show their true personality to a potential spouse because they don't want to fall into sin. For example, we cannot tell a potential spouse, "you're beautiful," even though that is considered a norm to say, and according to society is completely harmless. The reason we cannot say it is because we will think to ourselves, "Am I flirting here, did I just commit a sin?" So in a sense, we are always second guessing ourselves. A more relatable example is, some individuals who want to hug or hold hands with their potential spouse. If they do this without being lawful to them, they have committed a sin. How does Mutah come into play here? In some cases, to do Mutah with someone you need to ask the girl's father/guardian for permission, let's assume the father agrees.

The parties can create a Mutah contract with restrictions that only allows them to speak freely, hold hands, and hug, everything else is not allowed per this contract. Again, remember what we said earlier, people can engage in Mutah without doing anything, it can be just for speaking to one another comfortably; Mutah just creates a halal platform, everything else that happens is YOUR decision. But instead, let's just keep believing that having a "toulbeh," or publically asking for a girl's hand makes everything okay for the potential couple, and they can do whatever they want. To be clear, I am not claiming that doing Mutah is the ONLY proper way to get to know someone; it has been done before without Mutah, under parental supervision, in an appropriate setting. But I will say this though, what is sad is some people are so against Mutah that they would rather sin instead of doing Mutah. Meaning, they don't want Mutah to be on their resume or conscious, but they're okay if sinning is.

Divorcees

It would be unjust to mention this topic without mentioning women who are divorced. I have heard that their frustration is that some men only view them as a potential for Mutah marriage, and not a permanent marriage, which is unfortunate and a real problem in our community.

Anyone who gets divorced is not damaged goods, we have to destroy this mentality; this mentality is one thing I despise in our culture, and is not a part of Islam; I realized that in other cultures it is not like that. They don't shun divorced women, it is admirable. As the expression goes, people aren't pieces of meat; we have to treat each other better. If you want to engage in a Mutah marriage with someone, be honest with the individual, and tell them what you truly want from this Mutah marriage; don't sit there and lead them on, and promise false hope. Give them the option to make a decision with a clear mind before they're emotionally invested.

In addition, it is ironic that when it comes to "dating," if a woman breaks up with a man, other men are still inclined to speak to her for a permanent marriage, but if a woman goes through a marriage and gets divorced, she's automatically not worthy of a permanent marriage anymore. She only qualifies for a Mutah marriage for some, correct? The reason for this is because society believes that if a person has one failed marriage, they will have another one, history repeats itself. But how does that make sense? Assume a woman dated multiple guys before she got married, society never labels and solidifies her past relationships as failed anything, nor do they conclude that how she acted in her past relationships will reflect how she is in her future marriage. Why is it only when a woman gets divorced, society assumes that she isn't deemed fit anymore to be a part of a permanent marriage? It is possible that a couple got divorced because they just weren't compatible with one another, plain and simple. Here is what I have always wondered. Suppose a divorced woman didn't get married to her spouse, and instead dated him, then broke up with him, will she still get expelled by others? I doubt it, but I think the word divorce is given too much attention, and is what intimidates many people. "Breaking up" after dating is acceptable, but a divorce isn't? That is a double standard; be with someone for who they are!

In a Moment of Passion

In a moment of passion Mutah saved this individual from committing the great sin, Zina. This is a true story that was told to me.

In college, a woman began to flirt with this individual, to get to the point, she wanted a sexual relationship with this person. However, she did not meet the criteria for a Mutah marriage. Meaning, Mutah cannot be done with anyone; there are certain qualifications an individual must meet (refer to your Marja'). Anyway, whether they could've done Mutah and had such a relationship or not isn't the point. The point is, in many societies if such an opportunity presented itself for some men, they wouldn't think twice, or ask any questions, they would go with the flow. But for this particular person, he didn't go off his whim; there are divine rules he had to follow. Later, he went home and realized that was not a coincidence, but indeed a trial. So, we are here "hating" on Mutah when Mutah is out here saving people from sinning.

Furthermore, Mutah eliminates the unlawful moments of passion! For instance, affairs, a man sleeping with a married woman. A man who practices Mutah properly knows that such a woman doesn't fit the criteria to even approach; it automatically eliminates any curiosity of being with the woman in any way, because the man is bringing Allah (swt) into the equation from the beginning. This isn't about the man being a bad person, because there are many cases where the man is deemed to be a good person among society, and still commits such an act. Now, of course avoiding all this talk is what many of us would want, but that isn't realistic; these are real matters. We don't live in a utopia (perfect imaginary world). Another example that happens in the real world is, some women don't know who the father of their child is because she might've been involved with different men in a short period of time. Mutah eliminates this because if such a woman practices Mutah, after her Mutah marriage has concluded she has to observe an Iddah period before she can get involved with another man. During this waiting period she will be able to tell if she has gotten pregnant or not.

Many of us have expressed complete disapproval of Mutah, but have we ever thought of what options a divorced or widowed individual has that doesn't want to publically remarry? These are the individuals that are forgotten, and they're forgotten because society is emotionally driven, and we do not think of things logically sometimes. When it comes to any scenario, we put ourselves in the spotlight, and start spewing what is best for everyone, even if we have never experienced what others have. Anyway, such individuals probably want to avoid the traditional marriage route because maybe they're at an age where they're uncomfortable, or have older children, and would rather keep everything in private. Do they not have such rights? That being said, Mutah eliminates such potential awkward situations, and allows such individuals under these circumstances to marry in private, and Allah (swt) is their witness.

Conclusion

If there is anything I would like you to take away from this post, it is that Mutah is just a system that makes two non-mahrams halal among each other, only. Everything else that is associated with Mutah are decisions that men and women have taken. Over time they weren't fond of these decisions anymore, but they weren't brave enough to hold themselves accountable, instead they found it easier to blame religion.

Reflection 127

Men's Mental Health

Men's mental health is a special topic, a crucial one as well. Before we begin, it is important to note that I am not a medical professional. Meaning, this post is NOT intended to be medical advice! That being said, whoever is suffering from any type of mental illness should seek help. We shouldn't be ashamed of what others may think despite what certain cultures have said or still say, nor does it mean we lack faith in Allah (swt) if we do ask for help. Also, self-medicating should be avoided at all costs because this may cause accidental overdoses and addictions. So, what will this post entail? A humble opinion from my perspective as a male, and many others regarding our mental health.

Men Don't Cry

When we speak about mental health, society has given a great amount of attention to women, which is great, but rarely does it give any attention to men. To the point where we sometimes assume that only a certain gender suffers from mental battles, and they're the only ones in need of support. However, as we know that is false; depression, anxiety, bipolar disorder, etc., are all mental illnesses that HUMAN BEINGS suffer from. In a sense when it comes to this topic, society has allowed women to express themselves freely. It's welcomed, which I am all for, but for men, it is not equally the same. This is because if men express themselves in any type of way, whether it is mentally or emotionally, they're considered to be weak! There is a saying, "Men don't cry." Why are women allowed to cry, but men aren't? Why is it that when I cry, I am weak, but if a woman cries, she is in distress and needs help, and we have to comfort and care for her until she becomes better.

Crying is therapeutic; it is a release mechanism! It is a way to let out suffering, but instead men bottle everything up, which eventually leads them to explode, and this explosion can lead to severe depression, uncontrolled anxiety, and so on. Thankfully, we get a pass during

Ashura every year, we can cry in peace without any judgment! Once a brother told me, "I was not only crying for Imam Husayn (as), but I was also crying for my struggles as well, and it felt good to release such toxins out of my body because now my battles don't weigh as heavy on me anymore; I feel like my mind and body has reset." However, is that enough?

Emotions are Unattractive

There is a misconception about men, if a man shows his emotions he is considered to be extremely sensitive. I kid you not, this is not fabricated, and I am sure you have also heard such statements as well. In addition, it is known that many men avoid expressing themselves in front of their woman, do you know why? Because if he does, he is considered to be less attractive, a "turn off," and it is concluded that because of such expression, he will not be able or know how to care for her and protect her, which leads to separation sometimes.

Moreover, men who do show their emotions are not considered mentally strong, and if push comes to shove, they will collapse under pressure. This is a true dilemma men face! Why is it that if a man expresses himself, he is not considered a true man, why the association? I am not sure; it doesn't make sense, but what defines a man shouldn't depend on his emotional state in a moment of time. The overall message here is that when a man is not able to express themselves properly, it affects their mental health.

Violence

Why do many men resort to violence? Because they're always in a mode that is defensive; this is what they were taught. The concept of sitting down and talking it out rarely exists among men, especially in their youth; I say youth because the pressure of looking fragile among their peers is real. So, it's either I have to fight this kid if he disrespects me, or I will be forever labeled as a coward. What's ironic is, the reason many men don't resort to violence when they mature isn't because they're able to control themselves better, it's because they fear the consequences of the law. Suppose the law wasn't in place, I am pretty sure we will see chaos among all ages.

Basically, because men always have to put up a front, it affects their mental health since they cannot be themselves. We cannot tell human beings not to be a certain way, they have to be taught, and I think this is where we fail as a society. For instance, don't tell an individual to control their anger, teach them!

Pressure

When we speak about suicide, the rate of suicide among men is higher compared to women. According to the American Foundation for Suicide Preventation, [43] "In 2019, men died by suicide 3.63x more often than women." Of course all cases are different, but I think the pressure of life without proper support destroys an individual. For example, in some cultures getting married and starting a family can cause a great amount of pressure, not the actual marriage part, but the steps leading to it. There are so many expectations that parents set for a man; you have to do this, and have that before you can get the ball rolling, and if you fail at any point or don't meet their expectations, it is done. What does that do to a man?

It forces them to delay getting married, which is not ideal because human beings are in need of a companion. But the point is, when I spoke to many brothers they cited this scenario as one that weighs heavy on them mentally; they're eventually put in a situation where they either don't pursue the person they're interested in, or they're forced to give up, and this within itself takes a toll that sometimes lasts forever. They also mentioned the burden of finances; for example, if they're struggling financially they view themselves as failures, or they might lose their family. So, that is why some men begin to act irrationally and earn an unlawful income, because society puts so much emphasis on money and living luxuriously. So, in one spectrum they think they're doing good by providing for their family, but in reality, they're disobeying Allah (swt) and committing sins.

The proper support here is not to encourage someone to make an unlawful income, but to help them and those around them understand that this is a trial from Allah (swt), and eventually all trials come to an end, we just have to do our part. I'll be honest, real men aren't looking for an easy way out, they're just looking for support, and that is missing in many cases. Telling someone, "I got your back," goes a long way for a man! To decrease pressure, awareness must be spread. For example, value a person for who he is, not for his credentials, and try to be accepting of a modest and humble living, and overcome the fear of struggling.

To End

To my brothers, how can we change this narrative? Here is what I have found beneficial. Always be yourself, speak up, and learn when to say yes and no. If someone finds expressing yourself as unfit or unattractive, it is not that you're at fault, but it is they who are small minded. A great medicine for mental health is reflection, don't distract your thoughts by other thoughts, instead face them, find the root problem and offer a solution. There is always a solution, and sometimes letting go is a solution as well. I understand, maybe you can't cry, this is why it is important to implement other release mechanisms. Having said that, exercise, exercise, exercise, and not any kind of exercise, but resistance exercise is very productive for the mind.

Last but not least, sometimes you will have no one to vent to, or as the Imam (as) states, [44] "I put my fist into the earth, because the earth understands me more than the people do." For this reason you must befriend Allah (swt), because there are times all of creation will abandon you, but Allah (swt) never will.

[43] "Suicide Statistics." *American Foundation for Suicide Prevention*, American Foundation for Suicide Prevention, 9 Sept. 2021.

[44] Attributed to Imam Ali (as)

Reflection 128

An Individual's Image

An individual's image is very important, but to whom? Ideally, it should only be to Allah (swt) and themselves, but that's not always the case. Many of us genuinely care what other people think. When we try to seek any kind of change, it is inevitable that we are going to hear some noise, and what is unfortunate, it can come from those closest to us.

For example, if a person is trying to seek the straight path, don't remind them what they used to do 3-5 years ago! In addition, don't put labels on people; for instance, if someone is trying to work on their anger, and they have an incident where they become angry, don't say, "You'll forever be an angry person."

Help prevent situations, not provoke them. To end, if you're seeking change it's important you zone out everyone and only focus on Allah (swt), because if you don't, the brutal comments people make can hinder or halt your journey to change! Do you not deserve change?

Reflection 129

We Are Not Weak

Don't take advantage of someone you think is weak because of their mental or physical state! Allah (swt) can directly strengthen them at any time. They will surprise you, and they will be able to move on from any burdening situation they have been put through.

When you have lost hope in the creation, remember Allah (swt) is near, and all He (swt) has to say is,

"Be, and it becomes."

And your whole life can change!

Reflection 130

Mental Wounds

Treat your mental wounds like physical injuries!

Meaning, if you have a cut on your arm that's almost healed, what would happen if you scratch it? Most likely you'll re-aggravate it, and it will begin to hurt again.

Same thing with mental wounds; if you keep on talking about the same problem over and over, you will never fully heal. It is important to know when to speak about a challenging situation, and when to STOP speaking about it, completely! The fastest way a plant dies is when you stop watering it. Stop watering your thoughts with meaningless conversations with your family and friends that revolve around "what if" scenarios.

Reflection 131

Who Hired You?

Sometimes we give too much credit to human beings than we should; we think our fate lies in their hands. So, we start acting a certain way to impress them. For example, this happens a lot when people are interviewing for a job or school, or have an important meeting, etc. We have to be able to distinguish what Allah (swt) controls and what people do!

When you are granted any kind of interview, you don't have to go against your Islamic values thinking it will increase the chances of landing the job. If you get the job it is because Allah (swt) prescribed it for you, and if you don't, it is not meant to be. Allah (swt) states in the *Quran, "O mankind, what has deceived you concerning your Lord, the Generous, Who created you, proportioned you, and balanced you" (82:6-7)?

Your faith shouldn't be in the creation; Allah (swt) has been with you throughout your existence, do you really think He (swt) is going to let people determine the outcome of your life?

* Quran English Translation by Sahih International

Reflection 132

What Truly is Hell?

Over time one begins to realize that their greatest concern in this world is not trying to figure out how to enter heaven and avoid hell, but rather it is to construct a strong pure connection with Allah (swt) through obedience and servitude, by following the steps of the Prophet Muhammad (saww) and AhlulBayt (as).

Only then mankind understands that gaining nearness to Allah (swt) is a form of heaven, and becoming distant is HELL.

Reflection 133

Become a Healer

If someone is having a hard time letting go of "something," it means they're suffering. Help them get through it! Healing doesn't only take place at a hospital by operating on a physical body, but there is also the healing of the mind and heart through conversations.

Become a HEALER.

Reflection 134

Ding-Dong Ditch

How many of us are playing "Ding-Dong Ditch" with Allah (swt)? You know, we go to His door by praying for what we want, and right after He (swt) opens and answers, we run away!

Generally speaking, is this the proper way to get to know someone? Absolutely not! Enter the home of Allah (swt), spend time with Him (swt), and I guarantee that you will never want to leave.

Reflection 135

Self-Growth

When we analyze self-growth, progress determines if we are successful or not, despite how minor or major the steps are. For example, assume in:

Year 1- I didn't pray at all.
Year 2- I am learning to pray.
Year 3- I am praying, but only during Ramadan.
Year 4- I am praying, but STILL only during Ramadan.
Year 5- I am praying everyday.

From Year 1 to 3 there is growth, because over time the data reflects progress, but in Year 4 am I still growing? No, I am in a stagnant state because my routine didn't change; it's not until Year 5 that I begin to grow again. Many people state that, "It's okay if someone practices their religion only for 30 days each year, it is better than nothing." That might be true, but is there spiritual growth? This is what we tend to overlook.

To attain a high level of connection with Allah (swt), it requires us to always seek growth, we cannot stay stagnant.

Reflection 136

What is Our Duty?

We can sit here and speak all day about our duties as Muslims. The obvious are praying and fasting, but is that all? Definitely not, we must stand up and spread awareness against oppression.

Some of us live in a country that allows us to voice our opinion; we don't live in ancient Egypt, Pharaoh isn't around. Our First Amendment permits freedom of speech! I ask you, if we refuse to express our opinions in a country that ALLOWS US to, then where will we? Take advantage, for this is maybe our trial from Allah (swt). In Michigan, sometime during the year 2021, some individuals went heavily armed to the capitol to protest, and nothing happened to them. Obviously, in no shape or form should we imitate their actions, but we can spread smart eloquent messages verbally, through the pen, or a keyboard.

The only way to overcome "worldly fear" is to only fear Allah (swt). If we associate partners to whom we fear, we have failed, and we will stunt our spiritual growth. It's just mind boggling because every year we say, "We want to be with you O' Husayn (as)," but we refuse to speak about corrupt powers because of fear of what will happen to us. In reality NOTHING will happen, it is just fear mongering, but let's assume something did happen, Alhamdulillah, Allah (swt) is watching. Strengthen your heart through obedience!

Reflection 137

Without Allah (swt) vs. With Allah (swt)

Without Allah (swt) in our lives:

We are breathing, but we are drowning.
We are moving, but we are paralyzed.
We can see, but we are blind.
We can hear, but we are deaf.

With Allah (swt) in our lives:

We are drowning, but we can breathe.
We are paralyzed, but we can move.
We are blind, but we can see.
We are deaf, but we can hear.

Reflection 138

Greatest Worry & Least Concern

They asked, "What is your greatest worry?"

Living, because it may take me away from my Lord (swt).

They asked, "What is the least of your concerns?"

Dying, because it unites me with my Lord (swt).

Reflection 139

Belittling One's Problems

It is important not to belittle an individual's problems; for example, if someone expresses to you their struggles, don't compare it with those who are less fortunate and say, "At least you're not starving, or homeless like others." These comments are not solutions...

People sometimes assume that just because we live in a "first world country," we aren't allowed to have problems, and if we speak about them we are acting "spoiled," or are not humble enough. It's understandable that sometimes people say such phrases out of good intention like, "look at the bright side," but it is not always correct.

We must learn how to imprison our tongues, and free our ears.

Reflection 140

We Must Stay Patient

The story of Prophet Musa (as) and Khidr (as) is one to reflect on. Before their journey begins the *Quran states, "He (Khidr) said (to Musa): 'If you follow me. Then do not question me about anything until I myself speak to you about it'" (18:70).

1. During their trip, they come across a ship…Khidr puts a hole in it.
2. Later, they meet a boy…Khidr kills him.
3. Lastly, they reached a town where people refused them as guests; they found a wall that was about to collapse…Khidr restored it.

In the first two instances Prophet Musa (as) questioned Khidr, stating he has done grievous and horrible things, and in the last instance, Prophet Musa (as) said you could've taken a wage by fixing the wall.

I believe if any of us were there, we would react like Prophet Musa (as). Listen to the response of Khidr (as). According to the **Quran,

1. "As for the ship, it belonged to poor people working at sea. So I intended to cause a defect in it as there was after them a king who seized every [good] ship by force" (18:79).

2. "And as for the boy, his parents were believers, and we feared that he would overburden them by transgression and disbelief. So we intended that their Lord should substitute for them one better than him in purity and nearer to mercy" (18:80-81).

3. "And as for the wall, it belonged to two orphan boys in the city, and there was beneath it a treasure for them, and their father had

been righteous. So your Lord intended that they reach maturity and extract their treasure, as a mercy from your Lord" (18:82).

It is important to trust Allah (swt) at all times, despite how difficult a situation can become. Sure, at first glance things might look terrible, but Allah (swt) is the All-Knowing! We must stay patient…

* Quran English Translation by Muhammad Habib Shakir
** Quran English Translation by Sahih International

Reflection 141

Before You Show OFF

Don't be so quick to show off, and boast about your accomplishments and merits in a WORLD that doesn't give an equal opportunity to everyone. Stay humble!

Reflection 142

What is Stopping You?

1. What is stopping you from praying, fasting, and reading the Quran?

2. What is stopping you from wearing the hijab?

3. What is stopping you from quitting your addictions like: alcohol, drugs, pornography, etc.?

4. What is stopping you from giving up the nightlife, parties and clubs?

5. What is stopping you from lowering your gaze, and chasing multiple women?

6. What is stopping you from backbiting, and spreading drama?

7. What is stopping you from becoming God conscious?

Do you find fun and joy in such things? Is that why it's hard to give them up? But what if fully submitting to Allah (swt) is more entertaining? But it can't be, right? Because religion is presumably known to be "boring." But how would you know if you haven't purely tried?

The irony is, we assume we are free when we think we can do "whatever we want," but if you look closely, the reality is we are chained to our desires, and they dictate our every move.

It's only after reflection that we realize true freedom is reserved for those who have submitted and accepted to be governed by Allah (swt). It's mind blowing how that works because we are so used to freedom being described as not being under anyone's control, but in all scenarios in this world, true freedom relies on selling yourself to Allah (swt).

Reflection 143

Shaking Hands With the Opposite Gender

Passage 1

Recently I was put in a situation at work in which a woman tried to greet me with a handshake. Immediately I put my hand on my chest, and I apologized (because Islam doesn't allow for non-mahrams to come in physical contact with one another).

"I am sorry I don't shake hands due to religious purposes," I said. However, it wasn't always that easy; in the past such situations used to leave me anxious just thinking about them, to the point that I used to pray to Allah (swt) to not put me in such positions. Reason being, I didn't want to upset or make the individual feel embarrassed. After many encounters I realized such situations are inevitable. Instead, I started praying for courage because the tests began excessively, and it was time to get prepared. That being said, I had to make a decision; I decided I am only in this world to please Allah (swt), and whoever was to get offended with my actions was not my concern. My mistake was thinking Allah's (swt) creation lacked empathy. In fact, anytime I was put in such a situation people didn't get upset or offended, but rather THEY apologized and understood in the utmost respectful way.

Moral of this experience is to have faith in Allah (swt), and don't compromise your faith for a job, school interview, or anyone. A clear cohesive message with a smile goes a long way. People understand, but if they don't and you're at a loss, it's not your fault. Surely Allah (swt) is the best of planners, and with every trial there are blessings waiting to unfold. Be patient!

After I put my hand on my chest, a young boy came up to me with excitement and said, "I am not allowed to do that either." Be the difference, be more! Do everything for Allah (swt), do it for those around you; you'll never know who you might inspire.

Passage 2

I remember a few years ago I had a professional interview, and I was extremely conflicted on the inside because I didn't know how to greet the interviewer if she was a female. Should I shake her hand or should I not? Many thoughts were crossing my mind. One in particular was, if I don't shake her hand is this going to cost me the job?

So being as confused as I was, I decided to ask a scholar, and what he told me was profound. I am sharing this because if anyone else is put in such a predicament, they can find some motivation to do the right thing.

Anyway, the scholar didn't lead by saying it was automatically forbidden, and that was it. Instead the scholar said, before you even go to the interview, the result of whether you will get the job or not is already with Allah (swt). Also, keep in mind that sometimes an individual can do everything right according to the standards of society, and they still might not get the job.

The second part of what he said left me speechless. Be courageous when it comes to your beliefs!

Reflection 144

I Wanted to Leave Mid-Lecture

The other day I was watching a video and I heard Mike Tyson, a famous athlete, say, "Discipline…doing what you hate to do, but doing it like you love it." This quote reminded me of a personal experience that I would like to share.

I'll be honest, when I first began attending Islamic lectures I used to dread it. I would always look at the clock while shaking my foot up and down, thinking to myself, "When is this going to end?" I also felt like the scholars were purposely lecturing at a slow pace, which didn't make things any easier. I used to look around and see everyone paying close attention, and then there I was, contemplating leaving mid lecture, or always questioning why I came. One of the hardest things is forcing yourself to do something you truly don't want to do. That one hour on a Friday or Saturday night felt like a whole day!

We are taught that if there isn't an instant sense of love, spark or connection, then maybe we should consider walking away, right? At that time there was barely anything towards religion. I used to think, "Man, stick to the bare minimum, and call it a day." This is what happens to many individuals if they don't feel it or it doesn't click, they give up.

However, what I did see was the overall goal, and realized that this might not be something I like right now, but it is the best thing for me right now. Even after realizing this I would say, "I am still done," but I forced myself, and kept on forcing until one day, by Allah's (swt) will, my heart turned the corner, and I fell in love.

I no longer counted the seconds until the program was over, but rather I found a home, and I didn't want to ever leave my sanctuary. You see, Allah (swt) eventually enlightens the hearts of those who try, and keep on trying.

If you dislike praying, keep on praying.
If you dislike fasting, keep on fasting.
If you dislike reading the Quran, keep on reading.
If you dislike hijab, keep on wearing it.
If you dislike religion, keep on practicing.

Obviously, I am still nowhere near perfect, and have endless flaws, but I am still going to try, and you should too.

Reflection 145

When Our Friends Pressure Us to Side With Them

Sometimes in a friendship a friend may pressure us to "side with them" in a certain situation, even though deep down we know they're at fault or wrong, and if we don't then we are not loyal or aren't considered a true friend.

Have you ever been put in such a situation before? It's like what the heck am I supposed to do? Who made up these rules? This isn't okay; we see this happening quite often. Right is right, and wrong is wrong, despite who the person is, or how long we have known them! Always adopt and implement this principle.

Maybe the actions of your friend extremely hurt someone, and by taking their side to express your "loyalty" makes you no different from them. We shouldn't take ANY stance, we have to take the RIGHT stance. Learn to say the truth even against your own soul, and don't be worried about losing your friend, but be more mindful that Allah (swt) sees and hears everything.

*Quran,

50:17- When the two receivers [i.e., recording angels] receive, seated on the right and on the left.

50:18- Man does not utter any word except that with him is an observer prepared [to record].

To end, on the Day of Judgment, what will these Angels do?

50:23- And his companion, [the angel], will say, "This [record] is what is with me, prepared."

* Quran English Translation by Sahih International

Reflection 146

What if I Fail?

But what if you succeed?

I don't think anyone would regret trying and failing, but we can all agree that not trying at all will leave us in a state of regret. This can be said about anything! The reality is, there is no such thing as "failure," but it's all a learning experience. For example, suppose I lost a thousand dollars in a business, did I really lose it, or did I now learn how NOT to lose it if I am put in a similar situation in the future?

Don't let fear stop you from whatever you want to do, Allah (swt) is right there next to you; that mindset of trying to tackle the world with Allah (swt) is very powerful, but many people don't tap into it because of fear. One of my favorite sayings is, "innovate or die," we are all going to die, might as well try to shoot for change! Trying costs nothing, but always asking "what if," and not doing anything is a lifetime prison sentence, mentally.

*Quran,

"If Allah assists you, then there is none that can overcome you,..." (3:160).

* Quran English Translation by Muhammad Habib Shakir

Reflection 147

Crossing a Point of No Return

Hijab Example

Many times people accept that they've crossed a point of no return; they think that they have done so much that they're doomed.

Take for example a sister who removes her hijab! Just because she removed her hijab, it doesn't mean she's not allowed to wear it again, but she may become hesitant now because we as a society are harsh critics. This may affect a person's decision making without even knowing it. For instance, we might say, "What do you think this is a game?" We become discouraged! If someone regresses, we don't have the right to demoralize them in any way; rather, it is essential we ask, "How can we help you?" If you want to wear your hijab again, Bismillah! Go for it.

That being said, the relationship between Allah (swt) and a human being is critical. For those who feel they've regressed as a Muslim, and have a lacking connection with Allah (swt), it is never too late to reconnect with Allah (swt). Don't let the whispers of society rob you from building a strong relationship with Allah (swt). Be extremely selfish, and don't let anyone come in the way of it. If we are always going to worry about what he or she said, we won't get far; we only have to answer to Allah (swt). It is your life, take control! Become God conscious.

Reflection 148

Morning Prayer (Fajr)

We can all admit that waking up for morning prayer (Fajr) is challenging. What's ironic is we don't have a hard time waking up in the morning when there is a direct benefit to us. For example, for a job so we may get paid, or taking an exam to pass a class, or to workout so we can look and feel better. Why isn't morning prayer being prioritized when it's more beneficial than all these combined?

One of the pleasures of this world is sleeping, and even that we must detach ourselves from, and morning prayer helps do that. We're waking up in the middle of the night and putting cold water on ourselves, then offering two units of prayer to Allah (swt), and sometimes we cannot go back to sleep. What does this teach? Discipline! A *scholar once said, "Are we really committed to Allah (swt)? Okay, let's see, try getting up when you're most comfortable."

There are people who spend their whole lives struggling to get up for morning prayer, and then there are people who are awake during Fajr but don't pray. Change your perspective on it; tell yourself that this is a job, and if you don't get up there will be consequences. Tell yourself that morning prayer isn't an option. We would never skip anything that benefits our future in this world, why are we skipping something that benefits our hereafter?

* From a lecture by Hajj Khalil Jaffer.

Reflection 149

Can We Be Friends?

Question: Is it possible for men and women to have a friendship? By friendship I mean calling, texting, going out with each other, etc. I am not referring to a coworker, classmate, counselor and whatnot.

A few things to consider:

1. It is narrated by the Prophet (saww) [45] that when a man and woman are together in private, and aren't married or engaged, the third among them is Shaytan.

2. We cannot overlook the sins of flirting, gazing, touching, and hugging.

3. If you "grill" someone hard enough with questions, you will know their true intentions right away.

4. Adopt a cautious mentality, try to see things before they happen.

5. It is better to find comfort within your sister or brother in Islam than the opposite gender, especially when one is in an emotional state.

6. Sure, a friendship might lead to a relationship, but one question to reflect on is, how many friendships didn't lead to relationships, and led to misery instead?

[45] Attributed to the Prophet Muhammad (saww)

Reflection 150

Is Going to the Gym Haram?

Precautious Example

Is going to the gym haram? NO.

But is it possible that if we go to a gym, where there are an excessive amount of non-mahrams working out among each other, we will fall into sin? From the start, we can conclude that a gym setting that includes men and women is flawed because it increases the chances of sinning with the eyes.

Our job isn't to fix a flawed setting, but to recognize it and take precautionary measures. When we know a setting is flawed, we don't say let's take our chances. We have to be wiser! For example, it's not ideal to say, "I am going to a mixed gym, and I will try to lower my gaze." That is like saying I am going to try to put out a fire while I am standing in the middle of the fire. Our job is to avoid the fire!

What are the alternative solutions? Joining a same gender gym, or creating a simple home gym, etc. We have to be aware and know that we must nourish not only our physical bodies, but our spiritual souls as well. When it comes to any situation, the overall idea is to recognize a sin before living it.

Reflection 151

Why Doesn't Allah (swt) Answer Our Prayers?

Sometimes we become upset when Allah (swt) doesn't answer our prayers; we spend countless nights praying, but nothing changes.

What if the problem is what we are praying for? Think about it, what if what we are praying for is bad for us? The irony is that sometimes we know it's bad for us as well, but we become stubborn and say, "We want it and we don't care about the outcome."

Logically speaking, why would Allah (swt) grant you something that is going to hurt you? Allah (swt) is our protector; He (swt) is not going to set us up for failure. So if you're struggling with a situation like this, question what you're praying for, not Allah (swt). You question it by asking yourself if it brings you closer to Allah (swt) or not, and if not, let it go.

Reflection 152

You're Too Extreme

Why is it that when people want to correctly practice their religion they're referred to as "extreme?" Imagine trying to worship Allah (swt) like how the Prophet (saww) and AhlulBayt (as) did, and you're labeled as "too much." I wish it stops there, but many people go as far as saying this individual is: "whacking out," "backwards," "close-minded," "obsessed," "paranoid," "crazy," and more.

Truth be told, when people start labeling others who are getting closer to religion it is because they're afraid. Meaning, a sinner doesn't like to sin alone; sometimes a sinner justifies his or her sins by the number of people that are committing that sin with them. So when one of a sinner's friends decides to make a change and becomes closer to Allah (swt), they begin to mock them, but what they haven't realized is they're the ones who are "backwards." This is because they lived for so long in this world and never truly evolved. In their eyes they're the norm, but to Allah (swt) they're not the standard. Changing in the way of Allah (swt) comes at no cost, but making fun of people is costly.

Another aspect as to why people may insult others by name-calling is because they've seen or heard an individual do or say something out of the ordinary in the name of Islam, and this very individual might have a mental health problem which causes them to act a certain way, or is misinformed. Instead of giving them the benefit of the doubt, or offering to help this person, members of the community say, "He/she whacked out after they got into religion." In reality, Islam had nothing to do with it from the beginning. It's just that this individual might have a medical illness.

But people are so quick to say, "Religion has done this to them." What does this lead to? The whispers of Shaytan travel far; it discourages others from committing to the straight path because they start believing religion can really do that to an individual. If we may, let us all be extremely mindful of what rolls off our tongues.

Reflection 153

Do it For Yourself

Passage 1

There is this mindset, it's a common one where people live their lives to prove others wrong. For instance, when it comes to accomplishing their goals, what motivates them to do so are those who doubt them, or as we say, "the haters."

However, the problem is why are we motivated in such a way? Why does it take someone to tell us that we cannot do this for us to do it? This mentality is dreadful because it's a short term drive; it feeds the ego. It is not sustainable long term; what happens when you achieve those goals, does your mission end? Find a bigger purpose! Find a better drive...

- Prove it to yourself, LOVE YOURSELF!
- Do it for yourself! Are you not worthy? Or do you only feel worthy when you're recognized?
- Do it for Allah (swt)!

Say, "I AM DOING IT FOR ME, and I am going to do it NOW because tomorrow may not come!"

Passage 2

It is okay if no one notices.

If you're the only one that notices...

That is enough.

Reflection 154

Why Haven't We Reached Our Full Potential as a Community?

Passage 1

One thing I have noticed about our community is that we haven't really reached our full potential from a religious perspective. In fact, I think we are a community that stays stagnant, or in better terms, "goes in a circle." How is that possible?

This question has been on my mind for quite some time now. What I have realized is we are a community that treats the servitude towards Islam as a phase instead of a lifestyle. Meaning, the majority of individuals contribute to the cause of Islam when they're in high school or during their first couple years of college. Then later on as they become busier with their graduate programs, careers, or families, they completely stop playing their part. Their excuse is, "I don't have any time anymore," which is completely understandable and I am not here to call anyone out, but it is important to know what this causes.

This stunts the growth of the community because as the "old group" leaves to attend to the duties of life, the "new group" comes in, and in a way restarts everything. Change is good, but going from Point A to Point B then back to Point A is not, and we see this happening all the time. What's supposed to happen is that the "old group" must stay connected with the "new group" and work together, even if it is on a minimal basis. However, what happens is a "new group" comes in with lack of guidance, they do the same exact thing the people before them were doing but with their own creative approach for a couple years, and then they move on to attend to the duties of their life. This repeats for generations to come; that's the cycle.

To break this sequence we must constantly stay involved in the servitude of Islam regardless of how old we are, or how many children we have, or how demanding our jobs are, despite every single obstacle! It's easy for us to plan a weekend gathering with our friends, or vacation with our families, but why is it difficult to plan for our religious growth as a community? To be completely honest, our biggest mistake as a community is believing that contributing financially to Islam is more important than giving our time. It's amazing, Hamdillah, this community is filled with individuals who are willing to open their pockets for Islam, but are they willing to give their time and do the groundwork? That is the difference between "going in circles" and growing.

The first step to work with others is diminishing one's ego.

Passage 2

For a community to be successful religiously it needs support. Not only financial support, but individuals who are willing to lead by example. People are always so quick to donate to Islamic causes thinking that is what will resolve issues, but that's a small fraction of it. What Islam needs is PEOPLE who are willing to increase their consciousness of Allah (swt), suppress their evil desires, and serve. This is more valuable to Islam than money. Money is a short term fix, but enlightened individuals are the long term solution. Be the difference…

Reflection 155

About Our Eyes

Be Careful…

Don't let your eyes make your decisions for you!

Reflection 156

Why Do I Need to Pray?

"I am a good person, why do I need to pray?" How many of you heard this phrase before? Allah (swt) didn't only create us to strive for being good! We need to perfect our faith. What is the point of being good by day, but committing sins by night?

What is requested from us is to increase our faith! Assume you start a new job and your manager tells you, "To succeed in our company you must do this and that." What will happen to you if you ignore them?

Same thing with religion, Allah (swt) tells us in the *Quran, " Surely the most honorable of you with Allah is the one among you most careful (of his duty)" (49:13). Being good doesn't promise salvation; we have to be faithful as well. We also hear, "This person has a good heart." Okay...and? There's a rubric to life that's already been set by Allah (swt), what we have to do is follow it, not change it.

* Quran English Translation by Muhammad Habib Shakir

Reflection 157

Witnessing People Die Young

Witnessing people die at a young age used to upset me greatly, and it still does; it hurts, but not as much as seeing individuals living a sinner's life for a long period of time. Reason being, when death takes the soul of a young individual we say, "How sad, they didn't live their life to the fullest, and they're going to miss out on so many things, etc."

But who is to say the ones that are living long lives are gaining so much? When we understand the reality of this world we realize that a long life comes with a great amount of sins, hardship, and more if one is not God conscious. In no shape or form am I saying dying young is a good thing, but we have to wake up. Living a long life without obedience to Allah (swt) isn't ideal either.

I fear for myself because I cannot fathom meeting Allah (swt) with all the sins I have accumulated over the years. The brother or sister whose soul departed at a young age might meet Allah (swt) with a cleaner slate.

Reflection 158

Asking Allah (swt) For Help

Passage 1

One time I was sitting with my friend, and he was expressing to me how difficult it's been for him to lose weight because of how hard it is to exercise and limit his eating. I asked him, "Did you try asking Allah (swt) for help?"

He laughed and said, "Come on, I am not going to pray for something like that." It's unfortunate that we have this belief that we should only pray to Allah (swt) during crucial times, like a sickness or an exam.

On the contrary, we should pray to Allah (swt) for everything. For example, in my friend's situation we both reflected and agreed that only Allah (swt) can fuel our spiritual soul. Once fueled, this soul becomes motivated, and you'll find yourself having energy to do things you once couldn't.

Just pray, no matter how small or unimportant you think what you're praying for is. You will notice a difference!

Passage 2

Spend time with Allah (swt), and not only through prayer or reading the Quran! Actually sit down with Him (swt) and have a conversation. Tell Him (swt) what your concerns are and what you want. Sometimes we limit our interaction with Allah (swt) because we aren't fully convinced with His (swt) existence; if you lack certainty in Allah (swt) increase it through knowledge and action!

Put away your phone and just speak your heart out, and I promise you will see positive results within your life. We cannot see oxygen, but we depend on it to survive. Same thing with Allah (swt), just because we don't see Him (swt) it doesn't mean He (swt) is not there.

There was nothing I prayed for that Allah (swt) did not grant, so long as it was permissible.

Reflection 159

Speaking With an Atheist

During undergrad in one of my classes the topic of religion came up. As I was speaking to my classmate they stated that they were an Atheist, and I remember asking, "What do you believe happens to you after you die?" They said something along the lines of fading away into darkness, basically nothing. I was surprised how they accepted such an ideology; they took their "meaning" out of living. I tried processing such a belief, but it wasn't possible!

I am not sure why this memory came to mind today considering this class was almost several years ago, but I thought to myself, how many of us know and are confident of what will happen in the hereafter yet are still neglectful and lack preparation? Why are we investing the majority of our time for this world? If anything, my Atheist classmate confused the two realms; it is this world that is nothing.

*Quran,

"My people! this life of the world is only a (passing) enjoyment, and surely the hereafter is the abode to settle" (40:39).

* Quran English Translation by Muhammad Habib Shakir

Reflection 160

There Are Two Types of Individuals

Passage 1

There are those that when a problem befalls them they are only relieved when they find a solution to their problem.

Then there are those that when a problem befalls them they're automatically in a state of peace, because they know Allah (swt) controls all affairs; they embrace and welcome the process because they know Allah (swt) is hearing and watching everything. How they feel during the end (solution) is the same as how they felt in the beginning (problem). It doesn't phase them!

Now, how can we get to this point?

Passage 2

There are those who stay away from sin because people are watching, and those who stay away from sin because Allah (swt) is watching. Which one are you?

Reflection 161

A Couple Bad Years

The average lifespan of a human being is estimated to be anywhere from 70-80 years old. However, it's still important to note that we can die at any time, but for this scenario let's say we live up to 75 years old. That being said, one obstacle many of us face is we allow a few messed up years in our past to pave our future.

For example, many of us say, "I am the way I am because I messed up when I was younger during my teenage years or early twenties." In total, let's say this person had 10 "messed up" years on their profile from the ages 15 to 25. They did every kind of sin in the book! Having said that, they still have 50 years until they reach 75, right? I am also pushing it, some people don't even have 10 messed up years; it's probably anywhere from 1-3 years, in my opinion.

Anyway, instead of continuing down their sinful path they decided to make the intention to sincerely repent, and to begin to obey and serve Allah (swt) moving forward. Year 75 comes, they reflect on their journey and realize that they had 50 years of being good, and only several years not so good. The overall point is we are giving up on ourselves too early! Don't let a few bad decisions in your life chain you down and make you feel like you aren't worth loving and building a relationship with Allah (swt).

Reflection 162

Detachment

Passage 1

"Detachment" isn't solely meant for materialism, but it is also for those closest to us as well. We must cling to Allah (swt), only!

Detaching ourselves from our parents, children, siblings, spouses, etc., doesn't mean you love or care for them less; it's just knowing that one day we are going to lose this person, and having to prepare ourselves. What tends to happen to many people is they become deeply attached to an individual that when they do lose them, they lose themselves as well and are never able to recover. Many times people will prioritize those they are attached to over Allah (swt). For instance, children are a blessing but why does Allah (swt) refer to them as a trial? The *Quran states, "Your possessions and your children are only a trial, and Allah it is with Whom is a great reward" (64:15).

No one defines the concept of detachment better than Imam Husayn (as)! Was he (as) not a father, husband, and sibling? Did he not give up all those titles willingly because of his (as) love for Allah (swt)? It's hard to take action and strive on the straight path like the Prophet (saww) and AhlulBayt (as) when we are attached to the world and those within it. This concept isn't something that can be achieved overnight; detachment requires work because we are reprogramming our minds that nothing belongs to us, but our deeds. Think about it, we are just renting everything for a certain period of time; forever doesn't exist in a temporary world.

* Quran English Translation by Muhammad Habib Shakir

Passage 2

Why do we attach ourselves to people when history has proven to us that not love, nor children, or wealth can salvage a relationship sometimes.

Everyone leaves each other; it's just a matter of time. Come Judgment Day, Allah (swt) states in the *Quran, "The day on which a man shall fly from his brother, And his mother and his father, And his spouse and his son" (80:34-36).

How is that possible? How can a mother run away from her child? Yes, it's going to be that intense. We must detach ourselves from people, not in a way where you avoid someone, but rather that deep emotional connection that can be dangerous.

This world wasn't created to find love within the creation, but rather it was created to find love for the Creator (swt) through His (swt) creations. For example, I love my spouse because she protects me from sinning. Due to this my connection with Allah (swt) grows stronger!

* Quran English Translation by Muhammad Habib Shakir

Reflection 163

They're Religious

He is "religious," she is "religious," they're "religious," this term is thrown out a lot and to anyone. It puts individuals on a pedestal. Also, it comes off as if those who are "religious" are automatically considered to be close-minded, or are not aware of social struggles.

Why are we putting labels on one another? Speaking or writing about one's religion does not make an individual religious. Whoever claims they are religious is putting a heavy burden on themselves, and this title should only be reserved for the Prophet (saww) and AhlulBayt (as). They're the standard!

Because here's what happens, people end up following those who are labeled religious even if they're wrong. They will say, "So and so is religious, if they did this I can too." I have seen this happen many times and I also fell into this trap as well. Let's be careful and use better terms! Instead of saying, "I am religious," say, "I am practicing my religion."

Reflection 164

Be Honest With Yourself

It is important to be honest with ourselves because honesty sets a pure foundation, it also gives us direction. I am sure we all have heard many reasons for the, "I am not ready" phrase. Such remark is mainly used when it comes to certain practices of Islam. For example, it's a well-known expression when it comes to hijab. Sometimes people say, "I am not ready to wear a hijab because it might stunt my career goals," despite them personally knowing or hearing of women who have reached high positions while wearing a hijab.

This reflection isn't about the importance of hijab and why we should wear it; it is more about digging deeper under the words, "I am not ready." In my humble opinion, reflecting on myself, in some cases I have come to a conclusion that whenever I used the words, "I am not ready," I wasn't being truthful with myself. In fact it had nothing to do with readiness and everything to do with desire. I realized that I would say, "I am not ready" because I didn't want to give up the desires I am practicing. To be clear, there are good and bad desires; the desires I am referring to here are the ones that prevent us from building a strong relationship with Allah (swt) to its full potential.

That being said, when a sister still says, "I am not ready to wear a hijab" after having all the Islamic information about it on hand, and she is convinced of it, does it really have anything to do with readiness or is there a desire that is overpowering her to use that excuse? Maybe this desire originates from being attached to her hair, or certain types of clothes, or her physical appearance, or worldly affairs, and so on. Maybe a brother doesn't want to get into the practice of religion because he knows if he does he has to give up his nightlife, and it's not that he's not ready for religion, but it is more of he's not ready to give up chasing women, alcoholic drinks, drugs, and so on.

I am sure this might sound "bogus" to many of us, but if only we knew how powerful desire and attachment are, and the impact they play on our lives, especially when it comes to our Islamic duties. At the end of this, all we are trying to say is be HONEST with yourself. Say it how it is! It helps.

Reflection 165

Judging

Passage 1

If we disapprove of someone's actions, does that mean we are judging them? For instance, if I share a post that says brothers shouldn't be going to nightclubs, or sisters should observe proper physical hijab, and so on, by doing this, does that mean I am indirectly "taking shots" at individuals who do such things?

Definitely not, because I am not specifically targeting individuals personally. Meaning, I am not going to people's posts and publicly saying, "Hey what you're doing is wrong." Generally, what we are doing is preventing the idea of normalizing such things. Think about it, when we don't speak about such behavior, what will happen? We won't be able to distinguish between right and wrong anymore. This is why it's important we keep showing disapproval! Obviously in a kind and respectful way, but it's a must because if we don't a new norm will be created, and this norm will cause greater harm than good.

I am sure I am not alone in this, but in the past I have thought to myself if I was being too "judgmental" when it came to certain topics. Sometimes I refrain from speaking about them because I don't want to be labeled as a "villain." But then I realized it had nothing to do with being judgmental, but everything to do with not accepting what is being implemented and normalized nowadays because Allah (swt) disapproves of it.

If someone shares something and we find it offensive, before we become furious, maybe we should research what Allah (swt) says about it. We are not against YOU, but we are against what is trying to be normalized. What was once frowned upon is now being slowly accepted, be aware!

Passage 2

What is wrong with many of us is when we judge someone we judge them based on that one action they committed. There are many variables leading up to that action that we don't take into consideration. Instead of judging an individual try to understand them. Try to learn why they did what they did. Create a comfortable setting where people trust you and aren't worried about getting taken advantage of when they're hurt.

Reflection 166

Imam Mahdi (atfs)

My question to you is, suppose you know when you're going to die or you have knowledge when Imam Mahdi (atfs) will reappear, what would you change about your life? Before going on, pause for a moment and reflect...

If what comes to mind is stopping certain actions and becoming more obedient to Allah (swt), then that should tell you something. For instance, some will say they would begin praying or observing hijab, and others will say they would cut down on "influencing" others on social media. Meaning, if Imam Mahdi (atfs) has access to your social media, would you still be comfortable with the content you share? I can assure you the majority will not be. In fact, we will probably go on a "delete rampage." The problem with this equation is such eagerness to change only comes to fruition when what we think finally becomes a reality. Having said that, many of us never think about dying, we only think about death when we are put in unbearable situations like an illness. So, it's like one day I am going to die, then death comes and now I must change, but it is too late at that point.

To end, if Imam Mahdi (atfs) was to announce his (atfs) return tomorrow, many of us would be in panic mode, except who? Those who have been preparing, and who are those? They are those not waiting for death nor for the arrival of Imam Mahdi (atfs) to change, but rather their change solely relies on pleasing Allah (swt). It is mind blowing that we are so quick to change for death, but Allah (swt) created death, and Allah (swt) is the All-Seeing, All-Hearing, and is always next to us, yet, we don't change!

Reflection 167

Waiting

When it comes to relationships I warn you about the concept of "waiting for something better to come along."

Sometimes when looking for a potential partner, individuals might come across a great opportunity, someone who checks off all their boxes. Instead of taking advantage of the situation, they tell themselves, "Let me wait for something better to come along; if this person came so easily, someone else that might be better is bound to come along after some time."

Guess what eventually happens? No one better comes along and in most cases they end up settling and regretting. To make themselves feel a little bit better they say, "It just wasn't my naseeb." We all have heard such stories before, right? Not to put all the blame on social media, but I am sure it plays a role when it comes to this concept because connecting with new people is just a click away nowadays.

When good opportunities come your way they're not out of mere coincidence, ask yourself who sends them your way? Allah (swt)! Then ask yourself again, who does not want you to take advantage of good opportunities and to continue to delay important life goals? No one other than the whispers of the Chief Deceiver, Shaytan.

Supporting Haram

You know what I never understood? How Allah (swt) clearly states in the Quran that certain acts are forbidden, with complete clarity, yet some Muslims show support for such acts. It just doesn't make sense!

I think one of our biggest problems as human beings is we always feel the need to share our opinion. What is even more disturbing are the lengths we will go to justify certain acts that are haram, especially when they're committed by those closest to us. For instance, if I try to warn my brothers and sisters that a certain act is forbidden, they don't say, "Let's talk about it." In fact how they respond is intriguing; it is like they play a little "reverse psychology" to the point where they make you feel bad for even bringing up the topic.

Some of us don't like to be labeled as a "villain" because society has made it clear that if you disagree with any of our norms you're a bad person. When an individual is committing a sin accepted by society but is haram in Islam, we don't take a stance. Instead, we comfort them and rush to be "there for them." What we fail to understand is such support is leading them to their destruction in the hereafter, and you're playing a role! Yes, so your intention is to help them, correct? But have you looked at the bigger picture? Are you really helping or are you adding to their destruction when it counts? We are seeing this a lot; it's all over social media, go look through the comment sections! We see Muslim brothers and sisters that are VERY WELL VERSED in Islam supporting matters they know they shouldn't, and they know they're being hypocritical, yet they still show support, and I wish I knew why.

Has the message of Islam entered our hearts or is it only stuck on our tongues? The person you're supporting is openly sinning, right? So let them be, why are you showing support for their sins? We have to be careful with our actions! You do know you're going to stand before Allah (swt) and you're going to be questioned. Picture this, on the Day of Judgment you're asked, "So and so, why did you show support when you knew this was haram?" How will you respond then?

Pain

Don't lose your mind while trying to find a solution for your pain.

Maybe such pain is for the moment, for the day. Maybe it will be gone by tomorrow.

Instead, reflect on how many days you have gone without pain, because sometimes the solution to your pain is simply patience.

Reflection 170

Battling Fear as a Community

There are many silent killers that can destroy an individual's spirituality, one in particular is FEAR.

Fear is contagious! If we are not careful our own mind can imprison us by creating false illusions that don't exist. Many people's solution to fear is to isolate themselves from everything and anything, and they label this strategy as being "cautious." Having said that, these same people go around and spread public fear by saying phrases like, "If you post this, or go there, they will come after you." When you ask them for proof, they tell you about an extreme outlier that is not relevant at all.

Be careful of associating yourself with such individuals because they can crumble your spiritual foundation! They're under the assumption that they're wise, but in reality the whispers of Shaytan are deeply infused within them, to the point that they don't recognize that they're doing his job! Fear shouldn't stop us from standing with the oppressed and against the oppressors. This is why many individuals are on the sidelines, because they believe that if they take part in voicing their beliefs they will get in trouble with the law, despite knowing their First Amendment rights in the west.

As a community the solution to fear is not to isolate ourselves, but it is to become educated on knowing our rights! Let's take it even a step further, there are many lawyers in our community, if several of them united and created a committee to provide reassurance, that would be very helpful for our community to overcome such fear. Allah (swt) is the best of protectors, but it is also up to us to provide and offer creative solutions as well.

Even if nothing was to happen when we raise awareness, having such an organization in the corner of our community that are well versed in the law will automatically strengthen us! Is there any service that is better than the one in the way of Allah (swt)?

Reflection 171

Comfort

*"We should not settle down in this world as if we are going to stay here forever."

Comfort is poisonous! What is the threat that will stop you from standing with the oppressed and against the oppressors? What is your breaking point? Is it your family? Or is it your career? Perhaps it is your lifestyle? Maybe you think you're entitled to such a glamorous life because you worked so hard for it? When it comes to this world, own but don't let it own you...

Some of us don't rise because we are afraid of losing "it." What is "it?" It can be anything! But here is the irony, eventually you're going to lose it when death comes to claim you. Might as well lose it with some dignity IF you were going to lose it, but I doubt you're going to lose it anyway, because those who do or say anything in the way of Allah (swt) are automatically victorious!

A true believer has to prepare for everything; we are going to be put in uncomfortable situations, and that is when our faith is really going to be tested. We will fail if we find comfort in anything except Allah (swt). Here is the value of a believer...

**Quran,

"Prophet, mobilize the believers for the battle. It will take only twenty of your men who are steadfast (in prayer) to defeat two hundred unbelieving men. Your two hundred men would defeat their two thousand; the unbelievers have no understanding" (8:65).

* From a lecture by Hajj Khalil Jaffer.
** Quran English Translation by Muhammad Sarwar

What You Lost

Suppose what you lost brought you closer to Allah (swt)...

Then is it really a loss?

Reflection 173

Palestine

Passage 1

As Muslims and non-Muslims it is very important that we partake in events that express support for our Palestinian brothers and sisters. We must attend protests and try to raise awareness in any way we can.

You don't have to be a Palestinian to stand with Palestinians.
You don't have to be a Muslim to stand with Palestinians.
You don't have to be an Arab to stand with Palestinians.

You just have to be a human being; it is our duty as humans to stand with the oppressed, no questions asked! This isn't a political issue, it is a humanitarian one!

Standing with the oppressed is one way to strengthen your faith in Allah (swt), take advantage of the opportunity!

Passage 2

They asked, "Aren't you afraid of the consequences you may face when speaking against the oppressors?"

We said, "I wonder how my brothers and sisters feel under raining missiles."

Our lives aren't worth more than theirs…

Passage 3

What is occurring around the world is not a concern for certain nationalities only, but should be on the mind of every believer. We must stop caring and planning for only ourselves and our families. In a sense that is very selfish. Anyone who shares the ideology of standing up against oppression is automatically our brothers and sisters! Care and show support for those around the world the way you would care for your own mother.

Reflection 174

Allah's (swt) Command

If Allah (swt) orders a generation of people to complete a task and they refuse to, it doesn't mean the mission stops. Some of us may think that it is okay if we don't stand against oppressors, because eventually everything will just fade away and we can go back to our "normal lives." But what we fail to understand is that the order of Allah (swt) doesn't stop for anyone! If you and I don't get the job done, we will get replaced by those who can.

There is a **narration that always sends shivers down my spine despite how many times I have heard it, and not because it leaves me in awe, but because it is terrifying. The people of Prophet Musa (as) were slaves for generations until Prophet Musa (as) freed them from the Pharaohs, by Allah (swt). Over time, Allah (swt) ordered them to enter the promised land and fight their enemies, and victory would be guaranteed. Instead, according to the *Quran, "They said, 'O Moses, indeed we will not enter it, ever, as long as they are within it; so go, you and your Lord, and fight. Indeed, we are remaining right here'" (5:24).

So how did Allah (swt) respond? He punished them by making the promised land forbidden for them for 40 years, and then left them to wander the desert until they passed away. This brought about a whole new generation that was ready to go out and fight for their Lord (swt).

It leaves me terrified because I wonder if we are like the people of Musa (as) without realizing it, and is Allah (swt) in the process of replacing us without us even knowing it? How ironic, we are worried about jeopardizing our comfort in this world if we take certain stances, yet we neglect our comfort in the hereafter.

* Quran English Translation by Sahih International
** From a lecture by Hajj Khalil Jaffer.

Reflection 175

The Destruction of Society

Passage 1

Sometimes we may think that the destruction of society only comes from violence and drugs, but that's not the full truth...

Society can also be destroyed morally through beautiful words like love and equality.

There's a difference between standing against something out of pure hate, and standing against it because Allah (swt) ordered us to, and to be clear this isn't a matter of hate!

To Allah (swt) we belong, and to Him (swt) we shall return...

Passage 2

Be careful who you support; we hear many people say that all minorities should stick together because they all stand under the umbrella of oppression.

However, the issue is some minority groups totally go against what Islam states. That being said, just because a minority group is being mistreated, we cannot just stand in solidarity with them and say we support their decisions and they deserve such rights.

To be clear, it's important to note we are against the mistreatment of any human being, but to show support is a whole other thing. Such support might contradict our religious beliefs which will leave us stuck in a state of confusion.

This is why it's important to have structure in our lives. There is Islam first, and then everything else follows. If we live our lives putting everything next to Islam without that barrier or division, then get ready to face internal hardship.

Reflection 176

Negative Attitude

Why do we have this negative attitude towards Allah (swt)? Why do we think that if we do or say something in His (swt) way, we are going to get punished for it. For instance, if I speak against the oppressors I am going to lose my job, or if I greet the opposite gender with my hand on my chest during an interview I am not going to get the job.

I find this is something that many of us struggle with, and it is very wrong! We should adopt the mindset that if we do something for Allah (swt) our lives will IMPROVE! That's how I am thinking about it; if I do what is required of me then my life will become better, not worse. I know this not because of who I am, but because of who Allah (swt) is: The Giver of Gifts, The Provider, The Sustainer, The Most Generous, The Enricher, and The Source of Goodness.

Stop telling yourself that if I do this or that something "bad" might happen to me. Instead, ask yourself who you are doing it for. I have found more success in serving Allah (swt) than serving mankind.

Reflection 177

Shaytan-Ophobic

Here is where I think the confusion lies when we speak against LBGTQ+. People assume that we have formulated such opinions on our own, but what they fail to realize is these are Allah's (swt) divine rules, not ours!

They come and label us "judgy" and "negative," why exactly? For what reason? You see, they speak out of baseless opinions and emotions! In our case we don't do that! We are speaking using facts, Holy Scripture, and so on. We are not speaking for "entertainment."

Also, why do they compare sins and say, "We all sin differently." What is the logic behind that statement? So just because someone commits a sin, other sins automatically become justifiable? There's no value in such a statement; it is just hype. They have no direction! Let's encourage each other to stop sinning instead...

Then they have the nerve to say we are homophobic, but that's not true! The only type of phobic we are is Shaytan-Ophobic. We don't speak out of hate, we speak out of care! We speak so our words may touch the hearts of our brothers and sisters who do struggle with this; we speak so they may wake up and sincerely repent. Why do you speak? We try to offer solutions while you offer destruction to an individual's soul by condoning their actions.

The bottom line is, we dislike what Allah (swt) dislikes, and we love what Allah (swt) loves, that's it!

Reflection 178

Heart Hardening

Remember that one time you sinned and you felt regretful after? However, instead of fighting off that sin you decided to continue doing it.

Slowly you stopped feeling remorseful towards that specific sin. Rather, it became a part of your system and normal to do. When you feel regretful and remorseful, this may be a blessing from Allah (swt). When we stop feeling that way towards sins we should be very concerned.

Many of us say, "Is Allah (swt) really going to punish me if I do...?" Such a sentence is fueled by the whispers of Shaytan to keep us in our sin. How are we so certain He (swt) is not going to punish us?

Sometimes we may think that a physical punishment is the only type of punishment. We forget that our hearts hardening is a punishment of its own...

Reflection 179

Gambling

A new problem has emerged in our community; it's particularly popular among our brothers! This topic seems harmless because it recently became legal in our state, but just because society makes something lawful doesn't mean Islam does. Allah (swt) has the final word! The issue I am referring to is sports betting, better known as gambling.

We all like to make money; it is human nature, but how we earn it is more important. In the *Quran, Allah (swt) states:

- "They ask you about wine and gambling. Say: 'There is a great sin in both of them and (some) profits for people; but their sin is greater than their profit'" (2:219).
- "O' you who have Faith! Verily wine, gambling, idols, and (dividing by) arrows are an abomination of Satan's work, so avoid it, that you may be prosperous" (5:90).

[46] According to AhlulBayt (as):

- Imam Muhammad al-Baqir (as) states, "All kinds of games of betting are gambling. The sale, the purchase, and the use of all the tools of gambling are haram. It is only an act that Shaytan instigates you to do."
- Imam Ja'far al-Sadiq (as) states, "Allah pardons all the sinners in the month of Ramadan, except three kinds of people"... one of them being a gambler.

These sports betting websites and apps are designed to look friendly, but they're undoubtedly deceiving. Having access to them is made easy on purpose, but we must stay strong and not give into temptation. I understand that is hard to do sometimes, especially when someone is telling you they made a few hundred bucks in a couple of minutes. It is funny that they never mention their losses. We cannot give into sports betting now because football season is around the corner, I would hate anyone to lose their money betting on the Detroit Lions! It is already torture watching them, now imagine losing money while watching them...YIKES!

Lastly, gambling is an interesting sin because it increases your chances of losing everything in this world and everything in the hereafter, especially if it develops into an addiction. There is always a catch to "quick cash." Do not let desperation or an overly excited state cloud your judgment.

* Quran English Translation by Quran Hadi

[46] Shirazi, Sayyid Abdul Husayn Dastghaib. "Fourteenth Greater Sin: Gambling." *Al-Islam.org*, Ahlul Bayt Digital Islamic Library Project , 20 Oct. 2012.

Reflection 180

Strange

Strange, isn't it?

Nothing is guaranteed except death.

Yet we plan for everything except death!

Reflection 181

Ask Them

Before we want to get to know someone it is important to ask about them. We must do a little research! That being said, have you ever inquired about someone and the person you asked exposed the individual to a whole other level? They tell you everything they "heard," whether it is true or not. They even tell you what this person has done years ago, which is unfortunate because the person might've repented for it.

Do not be such an individual! We hear about such scenarios all the time and it is not fair. None of us have the right to expose other people in such a way. If someone asks you about an individual, keep your answers within the boundaries set by Islam. On a side note, personally I like to say, "Knowing what you're looking for, maybe it's in your best interest not to pursue him or her." But to sit there and completely destroy a person's reputation is wrong! We don't need to air people's laundry out for fun and get into details, because such conversations may lead to a pile of sins.

I understand you want to look out for your "boy" or "girl," but if they're concerned with someone's private life or past experiences in depth, encourage them to ask the individual straight up. Give the person a chance to explain themselves properly IF they want to.

Disclaimer: In no way is this post encouraging to withhold significant information that would protect someone from harm when inquiring about a potential spouse. Rather, be mindful of your answers and keep them within the boundaries of Islam. Please refer back to the jurists to determine what is considered within the boundaries of Islam.

Reflection 182

The People of Lut (as)

Passage 1

Sad, sad, sad! Unfortunately there is a false agenda being pushed, and terrible claims being made which need to be addressed because people will begin to believe them. We live in the digital age, and information on the internet can either benefit you or hurt you, depending on what you're looking for. However, if you search hard enough you will find whatever you desire, but the question we all seem to forget to ask is, "Is it credible?"

The first time I heard this narrative was back in 2017, and it is about the people of Prophet Lut (as). I also shared a post of an account that stated the same information last month; that account eventually removed its post, Alhamdulillah! Anyway, the claim states that the people of Lut (as) were punished because they were murderers, thieves, disbelievers, and so on. Basically they were not punished for taking part in homosexuality!

Such an argument would've been strong if Allah (swt) wasn't so clear in the Quran. Whoever is pushing this narrative is CLEARLY changing the meaning of the Quran, which is a grave sin. They're crossing red lines and if we don't answer back they will not stop, and they will continue to modify the Quran until it fits all their wants and needs, just like what others have done with the Bible.

Allah (swt) states in the *Quran,

"Lot told his people, 'Why do you commit such indecent acts that have never been committed by anyone before'" (7:80)? Let's reflect on this verse. What is Prophet Lut (as) referring to? Is he (as) really referring to killing and stealing? Because we can all agree that such crimes have been committed before his (as) time according to history.

What is this indecent act that no one has done before? The following verse answers it clearly, "You engage in lustful activities with men instead of women. You have become transgressing people" (7:81). Does Allah (swt) say murderers, thieves, or disbelievers here? No, because during Prophet Lut's (as) time sodomy between the same sex was not only a prominent issue, it was the main problem.

To end, not everyone with a brain should be allowed to draw their own conclusions when it comes to religion. Have you ever seen me holding a scalpel trying to perform surgery? No, because I am not a doctor; I know my boundaries. But when it comes to Islam, everyone seems to be an expert nowadays...

* Quran English Translation by Muhammad Sarwar

Passage 2

One of the main reasons homosexuality is accepted and highly promoted nowadays is because "the strategists" introduced it from the gateway of "LOVE." We live in a society where that word is very strong, and it tops everything and anything no matter what. According to society, if you love something you're supposed to do whatever it takes to attain it, but that is wrong. For the believers, Allah (swt) tops everything and anything! Allah (swt) draws our lines for what we can and cannot cross.

The mind and curiosity of an individual are very dangerous! If we don't stay within the boundaries of Allah (swt) we will also be more inclined to commit abnormal behavior. I have spoken to people before that told me they were once attracted to the same gender, but they never capitalized on it because it is haram. They kept on refusing such desire and eventually they overpowered it, and it is not even a thought anymore.

Some people claim that this is a matter of satisfaction. I ask you, someone who identifies as bisexual can be satisfied by the opposite sex, so why is it that they desire the same sex as well? Is this not greed when it comes to pleasure? I think there's a difference between desire and satisfaction. I think human beings can easily be satisfied, but they transgress to rebellious territory out of curiosity that is fueled by the desire of trying to discover how the unknown feels. That's how many people work when you tell them "NO," they want it more.

Many of us went to elementary school years ago, such an ideology wasn't present as much. So it wasn't really a concern, but now it is. It is becoming indoctrinated in our children's schools and through their TV shows. We have to speak up and offer solutions, because if we don't we are going to start believing such behavior is okay.

Reflection 183

The Perfect Moment

So what are you exactly waiting for? You know…to begin praying, to put on a hijab, to read the Quran, to go to Hajj, etc. Basically to fully commit to the straight path!

What is it? Are you waiting for the perfect moment? Because I can tell you right now such a "thing" doesn't exist, especially when it comes to practicing your religion. Waiting for the "perfect moment" is a trap set by Shaytan to keep putting our Islamic duties off.

In this case we just have to dive right into it, even if we are not ready. Being a Muslim is one of those things where we learn and adjust as we go.

Here is where many of us get confused. We are under the assumption that we have to stop doing "this and that" before we can commit to Allah (swt), but what we fail to realize is that taking that first step towards the straight path is what will help us stop doing "this and that." Do you see how that works?

Just do it! Think about it, there is no loss in practicing your religion, but there is great loss in waiting.

Reflection 184

Walk Behind Me

This is a pretty interesting story and something we are probably not used to, especially because we are taught to do the opposite!

I remember during my college days I stopped opening doors for women and letting them walk in front of me. Before you get upset with me, hear me out! Instead, I would open the door and walk in first, or if they were a few steps behind me I would hold the door open until they reached it, then I would walk in first. I did this on purpose. Now, according to society this is rude and disrespectful; we are not taught to do this. These aren't actions of a true gentleman or someone that is well mannered in general, correct?

That is what I thought also until I heard a well-known [47] narration about Prophet Musa (as). One day while Prophet Musa (as) was resting under a tree he noticed people pulling water from a well, and saw two girls with their animals standing aside waiting to get water. Prophet Musa (as) asked them their reason for coming and why they haven't acquired water yet. They said that their father is an old man, so they had to get water for the animals but couldn't until the shepherds were done. Prophet Musa (as) ended up taking on the task and got them the water.

When the girls returned to their father he asked why they were home early. The girls explained the situation, so he told them to call Prophet Musa (as) so he may reward him. They modestly approached Prophet Musa (as) and told him that their father wishes to speak to him. Before they began walking to their home Prophet Musa (as) tells the sisters to walk behind him and guide him, [47] because the sons of Ya'qub (as) never see females from behind.

SubhanAllah! That is some Taqwa...

[47] Majlisi, Muhammad Baqir. "An Account of Musa and Harun." *Al-Islam.org*, Ahlul Bayt Digital Islamic Library Project , 26 Dec. 2017.

Reflection 185

Who Has a Better Relationship With Allah (swt)?

Have you ever heard the phrase, "Someone who doesn't wear a hijab can have a better relationship with Allah (swt) than someone who does." This is a very popular discussion, but a dangerous one at the same time. In the grand scheme of things such a conversation is stating that it is possible to build a real relationship with Allah (swt) without fulfilling our Islamic duties. We have to reflect on the bigger picture here, the overall concept. To be clear this reflection has NOTHING to do with hijab.

Having said that, it is not our job to find out who may be closer to Allah (swt) by comparing the two individuals. Instead, what we all have to ask ourselves is, are we fully meeting the criteria that Allah (swt) has set forth to become closer to Him (swt)? What is the standard? The formula to become closer to Allah (swt) is to worship Him (swt) like the Prophet Muhammad (saww) and AhlulBayt (as). If we are not doing that then we all have work to do.

To end, let's try to avoid such conversations because there is no true legitimacy to them.

Reflection 186

The Test of Life

Have you ever taken an important test and needed more time? I am sure we can all relate to such a scenario. Test day comes along and you're having a hard time getting through the exam. You're stuck on multiple questions and find yourself running out of time. You begin to panic as your teacher says, "You have five more minutes left." You look down at your test and you're nowhere near done. Five minutes pass by and your teacher says, "Turn in your tests." You plead with her and beg her for more time, but she says NO while forcefully grabbing your test out of your hands. As you leave the classroom you see your friend in the hallway and ask them, "How did you do?" Your friend says, "Good, I was well prepared; I only needed half the time to finish the test."

Now, when our "test of life" is coming to an end, how many of us are going to plead with the Angel of Death and beg him for more time? How many of us will be prepared and let him take our souls effortlessly because we know what is to come is much better? The actions of today will dictate how you will be in that moment. We have to ask ourselves why is it that when it comes to fully committing to the straight path, we are indecisive. If anything such commitment is a guaranteed win; there is no loss or risk. Even if you're not convinced with it, but you do your part, it still benefits you in the long run. However, this Dunya doesn't offer you the same deal. Yet we cling on to it, for what?

Your final test is coming, prepare for it NOW. In school sometimes they allow us to make up an exam if we fail it, but in the "test of life," there is no make up. We only get one chance, and like your teacher, when you ask for more time in this life Allah (swt) will also say...

Reflection 187

Religious Family

They say there is a GREAT advantage being born into a family that practices their religion, however that is not totally true. To be a practicing Muslim is something we cannot inherit like money. My parents cannot leave behind their level of Taqwa (God consciousness). Sure my family can teach me about Islam, but is it going to give me a significant advantage over someone whose family didn't? Not at all, and we can prove this.

Just look around you. I am sure you know of individuals who come from pious families, but are the total opposite of them, and vice versa. Meaning there is no real advantage like how we make it seem. When it comes to practicing our religion the outcome depends solely on our actions. It is all about "who wants it," and that's the beauty of it! There is no 1%, no class system, it is accessible to everyone.

There is a difference between knowing and practicing, and I believe that is where many of us get confused. We can know everything about Islam, but if it is not followed by action it means nothing. Similarly we can know nothing about Islam, but if it is followed with an eager attitude to know and act, then Allah (swt) will directly bless us and guide us to the right resources to help us on our journey to Him (swt).

This eagerness is instilled within us all since birth; we can all tap into it, but many of us choose not to or we bury it under our worldly affairs. To end, let's stop making excuses for ourselves like, "I wasn't born into a religious family, my father doesn't pray, my mother doesn't wear a hijab, I didn't go to Islamic school, etc." You don't need any of those things, you just need to tap into your eagerness. You just need to take control of your freewill...

Reflection 188

Life Without Social Media

I wonder how life without social media would be! Would we still express ourselves the same way without an audience? Many of us are acting improperly on social media, and for what? Just to gain fame and wealth...

You want to be remembered, but at what cost? Selling your religion? Fine go for it, but you will only be known in your generation, you will be forgotten in the next like others were. People won't remember your name, but Allah (swt) will remember your actions. Just keep in mind that the *Quran states, "Do not be like those who forget about God. He will make them forget themselves. These are the sinful people" (59:19).

Undoubtedly, we have belittled and normalized many sins on social media. From inappropriate pictures to music, and so on. But it is okay, everyone is doing it, right? Do you know what is amusing to reflect about? Suppose social media didn't exist, how many sins could we have avoided? But that is not how life works; that is wishful thinking. The reality is there will always be different types of platforms that will test us, and our job is to find Allah (swt) in the midst of them. Instead, many of us are...! Yeah, you get the point.

* Quran English Translation by Muhammad Sarwar

Reflection 189

Losing Opportunities

They said, "If you speak about this or that you will lose many opportunities in life."

We said, "It wasn't until we spoke that life opportunities began to pour like rain. In fact, our mental and physical health improved, so did our sustenance."

You have misunderstood who your Lord (swt) is! Why is it that you believe if you do something for His (swt) sake you will be punished? This is not Allah (swt), this is your imagination. All our Lord (swt) does is reward, reward, and reward.

While you hide in the shadows of your mind others are reaping the full benefits of their Lord (swt), in this world and the hereafter. The only difference between you and them is that they perceive Allah (swt) as limitless, while you limit Him (swt)…

Reflection 190

It's an Every Moment Thing

When we read about prominent figures during the Prophet's (saww) time one becomes fascinated. These individuals were described to be true believers; they performed all their duties and more! We can almost conclude that they were the perfect role models, BUT as time went on they changed the trajectory of their lives…

You see, these same individuals that were once recognized as heroes in Islam later became enemies of Islam. They drove themselves straight to the pits of hell because they allowed their desires to overcome them. Having said that, I would like to bring attention to a relevant story I once heard from a lecture. Kumayl was once praising a Quran reciter's voice to Imam Ali (as), stating that it was beautiful and eloquent; in a future battle, this very individual fights against the Imam (as).

What does that tell us? The straight path isn't a game. Meaning, in a game when we reach a certain level we stop trying, we are done playing, right? The straight path is not like that! There isn't a specific level we are trying to reach. Instead, we are required to pursue the straight path every single moment that we are breathing, because if we don't we can easily switch sides over time.

To end, when it comes to the straight path we must build a wide and vast road by becoming God conscious. If we keep dabbling between truth and falsehood our road is going to be narrow, and when the road is narrow we can easily go over the edge.

Reflection 191

When We First Got into Religion

It's funny, when I first got into religion I didn't know that we weren't allowed to express certain emotions anymore. For instance, I remember when I was younger if I showed any type of anger someone would say, "Aren't you supposed to be religious?" I used to get bombarded with such comments.

It didn't stop there, such phrases were also used if I ever stood my ground when it came to certain situations. Basically, if someone disrespected me because "I am religious," I am supposed to let it go and turn the other cheek since Islam always preaches peace. It kind of felt crippling because I knew I was being taken advantage of, but I stayed quiet because society makes it seem like a religious individual is not allowed to behave a certain way, but that is incorrect.

For the longest time such an outlook caused a great amount of internal conflict because I would suppress my basic human emotions, and it hurt. Why would society question my religiosity when I got angry, and why did they make it seem like I am supposed to have it all figured out at such a young age just because I pray? I felt like they were holding me to an unrealistic standard as a teenager, and it was truly unfair and frustrating.

I write this post because I know many of us can relate, and to offer some truth to an "overplayed card." That being said, when we study Islam nowhere does it say getting angry is impermissible. Also, when researching about the lives of the Prophet (saww) and AhlulBayt (as), we learn that in certain situations they also expressed anger, but it was channeled through a proper form. It is not like they completely avoided such emotion. Moreover, if someone is channeling their anger through an improper form try to offer help instead of questioning their religiosity. We have to stop assuming that everyone is born knowing "how to do things." Meaning, instead of telling someone to do something, ask them first if they know how to do it. In this example you cannot tell someone to control their anger if they have never learned how to do so.

Lastly, I absolutely love how Imam Ali (as) treated individuals throughout history. For example, an oppressive tyrant tested him (as) and disrespected his caliphate multiple times. The Imam (as) tried to find a solution, but the tyrant wasn't having it. What did the Imam (as) do? Did he (as) continue to let the tyrant walk all over him? No, he (as) gave him multiple warnings, but the tyrant didn't listen and so he delivered the blow. This is also how we should be in our daily lives. Yeah, we will turn our cheek the first time and maybe the second, but after that there will be a proper response that fits the occasion.

Reflection 192

The Quran

When it comes to the Quran it is important we don't just rely on the verses we see on social media. The verses on the internet have been the same exact verses individuals have been sharing for the past couple of years; in total it is about ten different verses.

Yes those verses are beneficial, but this isn't an ideal relationship to have with the Quran. Imam Zayn al-Abidin (as) *states, "If everyone from the East to West was to die, I would not feel lonely if I had the Quran with me."

The Quran is a manual to our lives; it gives us a clear understanding of what this world is all about. When we are able to process such information life becomes easier because we know what to expect. For instance, society tells us to do anything to avoid suffering, but the Quran teaches us that no matter what we do suffering is inevitable, prepare for it.

Read and reflect…

* From a lecture by Hajj Khalil Jaffer.

Reflection 193

Focus On the Why

Have you ever asked yourself why you're committing a certain sin? Why is it that I know something is haram yet I still do it? Many of us neglect to ask why? What most of us do is we sin, we repent, and move on. We believe that repenting is the solution to stop sinning, but what we fail to realize is we are missing a big factor, and that is the part between sinning and repentance.

For instance, let's analyze someone who drinks; alcohol is Shaytan's preferred beverage. Unfortunately, such sin is very popular especially among some Muslims. What doesn't make sense is many Muslims know drinking is haram, and they know that there are severe consequences for such a sin, but they do it anyway. Why? Some say, "It is for fun." But how is it fun when a drinker doesn't remember what happened the next day. What is the real reason?

Also, why would someone put themselves in a state of intoxication knowing that there is a possibility they may get behind the wheel of a car and kill someone while drunk driving? I don't know about you, but that is a great risk to take; what are they trying to forget? It doesn't make sense in this world or for the hereafter...

Sometimes our lives can be terrifying! There is great pressure so we commit certain "haram habits" to get away for a little, but the reality is that is not a solution. It's a short term fix, and sure we might forget for the moment, but we still might have to pay our dues for committing such sin in the hereafter; this is what we tend to forget.

For this reason we have to begin asking why? Once we figure out the "why," putting a halt on sinning becomes easier because we have more information about ourselves. When it comes to anything in life when we know more about it we are inclined to address it with confidence. We say we know ourselves, but do we really? If we cannot answer why we are doing something haram while knowing it is haram, then we have to get out the pen and notepad and reflect.

Reflection 194

How to Stop Suffering

Many people don't like it when you tell them Allah (swt) is the solution to their problems. In fact, sometimes they will respond with, "Religion doesn't resolve everything."

I have noticed this narrative is being forced a lot nowadays. In a sense society is trying to push us away from depending on Allah (swt). In one aspect, they have become successful in doing this when it comes to our mental health. To be clear, I am not referring to individuals who are born with a condition, or those who have reached a condition that is severe, but more regarding the beginning stages of our suffering.

When someone is going through intense hardship they want to find a solution ASAP, and that is why when we bring up religion to them they become defensive. That is why some of us rely on alcohol or drugs for a quick fix, and then there are others who rely on medication, which isn't wrong at all.

That being said, I would like to suggest a different perspective to entertain our thoughts; in my humble opinion Allah (swt) and Islam alone can eliminate all of our problems, and offer a long term solution as well. Now I am not here to tell you to just have faith in Allah (swt) and keep the traffic moving, but when you implement these four factors (listed below) in your life you will be able to overcome any type of suffering. Many individuals who struggle and continue to struggle are always missing one or more, even all.

1. Having a clear understanding of what this world is about by using the Quran/Hadith and patience.
2. Doing the mandatory acts.
3. Staying away from sins despite how small they are.
4. Living in the NOW.

If you combine all of these together you're putting the best version of yourself out there; the first two are probably easy to accomplish, but it's 3 and 4 where many of us have a hard time. It is no mistake that the Imam (as) states, [48] "Your remedy is within you, but you don't sense it." This is the recipe! Stop focusing on what MAY happen. Instead, focus on what is happening.

[48] Attributed to Imam Ali (as)

Reflection 195

Playing a Game

You know when you're playing a game and someone beats you ten times in a row, and finally on the eleventh time you beat them, how do you feel after? Usually not that accomplished because it took you eleven tries to finally achieve your goal. Despite how much you gloat, you know deep down that your performance wasn't acceptable...

When reflecting about this scenario, it reminded me a lot about when we should begin to commit to the straight path. The obvious answer is from day one, but many of us delay such commitment until we are older, much older.

There is a huge difference between beating our "nafs" when we are young versus beating it when we are older. Beating it when we are older is like the game example above. Sure we finally did it, but it is not that satisfying because it was obvious that it was going to happen. There isn't much going on when we are older, when we are young it is more fruitful because we have so many options, and yet we still choose Allah (swt).

Reflection 196

The Right Tools

Reflecting about my life, there were many times where an objective had to be completed but I had no clue how to go about it. It wasn't until the time came to fulfill the goal that I was given the proper tools to execute it, whether it be mentally or physically. Can you relate to such a scenario?

For instance, I am sure most of us had some type of interview to go through in the past, or needed to do a presentation in front of an audience. Leading up to such occasions we tend to get distressed by going back and forth with ourselves wondering what will happen, right? Then SubhanAllah, right when we partake in the interview or presentation all those negative thoughts disappear, and we handle the situation as if we are professionals. This can be said about anything, and is not only limited to the examples mentioned above.

Sometimes certain tools in life aren't given before, but are given during the moment to overcome an obstacle. Why does this happen? In my humble opinion, if Allah (swt) was to give us such tools before then we would begin to find security in the tools, and not Allah (swt). Meaning, Allah (swt) gives us these tools in the moment because there is a lesson to take from it, and that is we have to begin trusting Allah (swt) from the beginning, not the end.

Trusting in Allah (swt) isn't done properly when things become evident, it is done correctly when we have absolutely no knowledge of what is going to happen, but feel comfort because Allah (swt) has our backs...

Reflection 197

Connecting With Allah (swt)

A connection evolves when the created fully submits to the Creator (swt). Sometimes we think we are connected to Allah (swt), but is Allah (swt) reciprocating that same connection back to us?

The thought that we can connect to Allah (swt) without doing our responsibilities is flawed. What are we really connected to then? Maybe to our ego, or Shaytan!

To connect to Allah (swt) we must submit to Him (swt), and the truest form of submission is through actions, not thoughts. It is only when we act that the veils between Allah (swt) and us will begin to diminish. If we want to reach the highest level of connection with Allah (swt) we must follow the steps of the Prophet Muhammad (saww) and AhlulBayt (as).

Have you ever met an individual who became a doctor without going to medical school? It is only when it comes to religion that we believe things are supposed to "magically" happen. No, if we want to connect to Allah (swt) we must work for it.

Reflection 198

Your Income

Passage 1

What is more important than making money is HOW we make it! Sometimes people justify their haram earnings by saying, "I am trying to provide for my family." This is not logical! Please research in Islam and ask the office of your respected scholar about what types of jobs and careers are and aren't permissible, and if the occupation isn't allowed stay away from it, despite how lucrative it may be.

We must keep in mind that wealth is nothing but a trial. The more we have the more we are accountable for.

Passage 2

Many people obtain their income in an illegal way: they sell drugs and alcohol, commit fraud, etc. What is more absurd is that they do it under the excuse of, "I have a family to support."

So your family expects you to engage in haram so you can provide them with what? A large house? Nice cars? Expensive clothes?

Why don't you all just lower your standards of living? Be humble. One doesn't participate in such actions because they love their family, but it is because they love their greedy souls; if they truly loved their family they wouldn't be filling their stomachs using haram money.

Reflection 199

Alhamdulillah

Many of us take the word "Alhamdulillah" out of context. For example, if we are facing a problem we are expected to say Alhamdulillah and move on with our day, and if we try to express our issues to others people assume we are complaining, right? How many of you have dealt with something like this?

That is wrong; Alhamdulillah doesn't mean to sew your mouth shut and hold everything in. We can be content with a problem and still speak to others about it if it is going to benefit us mentally, emotionally, physically, and if we are trying to seek a solution. Talking is therapeutic, and it doesn't make you less of a faithful person if you vent to someone.

Reflection 200

Corruption

In the medical field, when we discover a doctor is corrupt we don't stop going to doctors nor do we blame the industry as a whole.

However, in religion that is not the case; if we find out a scholar is corrupt we say, "All scholars are corrupt and religion is too," and we stop going to mosques, events, etc.

Why is that? Is it because we can quickly see the benefits of one field compared to the other? Just because an individual is corrupt it doesn't mean everyone and everything involved in such an entity is corrupt as well.

Impulsiveness

1. Impulsiveness leads to regret.
2. To not be impulsive one has to control their emotions.
3. To control our emotions we must live in the now.
4. To live in the now we must let go of the past and stop overthinking the future.
5. To let go of the past and stop overthinking the future we must be excited about the present.
6. To be excited about the present we must connect to Allah (swt).
7. To connect to Allah (swt) we must develop our Taqwa.
8. To develop our Taqwa we must obey and serve Allah (swt).
9. To obey and serve Allah (swt) we must act.
10. To act we must set our intention.

Reflection 202

Making Things Haram

It's not okay to make something that is halal haram to yourself and others because you happen to disagree with what Islam says about it, or it doesn't sit well with you emotionally. People think when they take such extra measures about certain topics they have more faith, but in reality they're oppressing themselves. Our job isn't to create new laws; if we disagree with something Islam permits, gain more knowledge on it instead of taking a stance.

Reflection 203

Changing For Someone

The problem with many of us is when it comes to change we do it sometimes because someone asked us to, especially when it comes to religion. It might be someone we care about greatly or a lover. For example, a girl asking her guy to start praying, and he does; or a guy asking his girl to put on a hijab, and she does.

What's wrong with such change is that if the person exits their lives there is a high possibility they might return back to their old ways, and such change is being done for the sake of pleasing the creation to keep them satisfied.

However, the question that arises is when Allah (swt) asks us to change, why don't we? Why are we quick to change for others, but for Him (swt) we are hesitant; is He (swt) not worth it? Change for Allah (swt) because this type of change will last forever. The issue with many of us is that it's hard for us to love Allah (swt) the way we love the creation.

Reflection 204

It's Haram

"It's haram," or "Allah (swt) doesn't allow it." We have to get used to saying these words when we want to refrain from doing something; we shouldn't feel embarrassed to say, "I don't want to do this because it's haram."

Sometimes we tend to shy away from saying something is "haram." Maybe it is because we don't want to be made fun of, or blasted with comments like "haram police." I personally experienced this with myself, someone would ask me to do something and instead of saying it's haram directly, I would say something else to avoid it.

We think we need to give people a lengthy explanation as to why we cannot do certain things. That is incorrect, we don't have to! Saying, "Allah (swt) doesn't allow it" is the greatest explanation, it should be sufficient.

Reflection 205

Thanksgiving

Thanksgiving is around the corner! I am sure many of us are excited to get with our families and eat tons of food.

However, it is important to note the history behind thanksgiving, and how our dear Native American brothers and sisters were slaughtered by the hands of oppressors. I am not here to ruin your "turkey vibes," or say don't get together, but have an open discussion with your families and friends, spread the truth, be aware, and say a prayer.

Pass along the right message to your children and the future generations to come! Don't feed them the lies our schools fed us. Yes, we know that "we celebrate thanksgiving because everyone is off and it's easy to come together, that's our intention." But still it doesn't hurt to mention a few words.

Imagine if most of mankind celebrated and feasted intentionally during Ashura while knowing what truly happened. How would you feel then?

Reflection 206

Insects

While I was working outside today I noticed a wasp struggling to move; it looked very vulnerable. Typically when we see insects we are quick to kill them, and it's very easy to take their lives. All it requires is some slippers and the rest is history, and we don't ever think about it again.

Then I thought to myself, is that how the Angel of Death views us? Is it that easy for him to take our souls? Maybe…

Reflection 207

Ghusl

I want to elaborate about "Ghusl," known as The Major Ablution.

One type of Ghusl is Janabat. Many of us are not aware of this mandatory act, but if we don't do it we are in a state of impurity, and are not allowed to touch the writing of the Quran or enter/stay at the mosque. By mosque, I am referring to the masjid/prayer area. In addition, prayer and fasting depend on Ghusl Janabat as well.

Ghusl Janabat becomes obligatory when either of the following occur:

1. Discharge of semen, whether the person is awake or had a wet dream.
2. Sexual intercourse.

Also, women are required to perform a type of Ghusl after their menstrual cycle as well. This minor reflection is meant to introduce "Ghusl." Please consult a scholar and credible resources to learn more about this topic and how to perform it.

Reflection 208

Threatening Your Family

So, there is one question that we all must reflect on; it's a challenging one and probably one of the hardest questions we will have to answer in our lives.

If your livelihood and family were threatened when taking a stance against injustice, would you still stand up against oppressors and corrupt powers? You fear that if you stand you will lose worldly possessions, but little did you know that your worldly possessions aren't a reward, but a trial indeed.

Reflection 209

Our Parents

We don't speak about this topic enough, but it is so important to have a good healthy relationship with our parents.

Some of us are so quick to get upset with our parents because they don't "understand" us, when in reality we should be the ones trying to understand them. Many of our parents are immigrants; they have come from countries that have experienced wars, poverty, famine, and so on. You and I, that were born here or came at a young age, we didn't live through that (even though I was in Lebanon in '06 during the war, but according to my parents that was "nothing" haha, anyway...).

Just because they're our parents we think such traumatic events didn't affect them, or because it happened a long time ago, they're good now. Be mindful; it's possible that your parents are very overprotective because they may have lost a loved one back home, or are still quietly suffering internally.

In addition, I noticed in our community many individuals only speak English while their parents only speak Arabic or their native language, this may create a language barrier, miscommunication, anger, etc. Take that into consideration when you speak to them (and learn your native language as well). Be gentle with your parents, be kind to them, and be patient. Serve them as much as you can!

Why is it important to serve our parents?

Imam Ja'far al-Sadiq (as) [49] narrates that a young man presented himself to the Holy Prophet (saww) and said that he wanted to participate in Jihad. The Holy Prophet (saww) told him:

"Certainly, go for Jihad in the way of Allah. If you are killed, you will be alive near Allah and be provided sustenance from Him. The recompense for your sacrifice would be with Allah. If you return alive, your sins would be washed off as if you were a newborn child."

This man said: "O Prophet of Allah, my parents are alive and they are aged and have great expectations from me. They do not like me to be away from them."

The Holy Prophet (saww) said:

"If that is so, then stay behind to serve your parents. By Allah in whose hands is my life, to serve parents for a day and night is equal to a year of Jihad."

[49] Shirazi, Sayyid Abdul Husayn Dastghaib. "Sixth Greater Sin: 'Aqq Al-Walidayn (Disobedience To Parents)." *Al-Islam.org*, Ahlul Bayt Digital Islamic Library Project 1995-2022, 31 Jan. 2022.

Reflection 210

Saying No

If we want to live a peaceful life we have to learn how to say no.

Sometimes we are not capable of doing something, but we say yes to it so we don't come off any type of way. Don't feel bad for saying no. Doing something when we aren't capable of doing it is not okay because we put ourselves under unnecessary pressure, and we begin to resent what we are doing.

Don't expect people to know how you're feeling; you're the master of that. Saying yes to everything isn't going to make you more likable. In fact, if you really want to know how someone feels about you, say no to them and see how they will respond.

To end, just because someone has their hand out, it doesn't automatically mean you're the one that has to come pick them up and "save them." Before you put yourself in any situation, think thoroughly about it, because some situations will bring more harm to you than the good you're trying to put in. Don't exhaust yourself, learn to say no! You will thank yourself in the future...

Reflection 211

They Asked

Passage 1

They asked, "Do you love this world?"
We said, "So long as it brings us closer to Allah (swt)."

Passage 2

I asked Allah (swt) for guidance…
He (swt) directed me to the path of the Prophet Muhammad (saww)
and AhlulBayt (as).
I followed their way, and only then did I truly find Allah (swt).

Passage 3

They asked them, "Who do you miss the most?
Is it your deceased parents, your estranged siblings,
or a past lover?"
They said, "My Lord (swt)! I feel very far from Him (swt)."

Passage 4

I went searching for Allah (swt).
I couldn't find Him (swt) anywhere.
Then I learned He (swt) is everywhere!

Reflection 212

Starting Our Lives

Amongst us are those who say, "I cannot wait to start my life." Implying that life does not start until an individual gets married, begins their career, etc. However, the reality of it is that our lives began right when we existed in the womb, but we choose to limit our vision. We tend to neglect the hereafter and focus more on this world.

That is why we wait for "worldly events" to feel some type of worth or satisfaction. If we broaden our vision and give more attention to our actions today, we will realize that with every step is an opportunity to build something special in the hereafter.

Reflection 213

Certainty

To have certainty that we are going to live until tomorrow is dangerous, because it doesn't push for change, it delays it. It's not until we realize that we can go at any time that we really think twice before making any decision. Program your mind to lose such certainty; if there is anything that was ever guaranteed it's our death. It is mind blowing that we know this and yet we neglect to prepare for it.

Reflection 214

What IF

When it comes to certain situations many of us struggle with the "what if analysis." You know, what if, what if, what if...

At this point we have two options, we can either run through the whole list of "what ifs," creating unnecessary anticipation, and then do what we have to do. Or save some time, skip that whole routine and dive right into it by trusting Allah (swt).

Reflection 215

That One Time

Remember that one time you were going through something extremely difficult? It could've been last week, month, or even a year ago. Remember when you asked yourself, "How am I going to get through this?" Then time passed and you felt better.

This is a reminder! If you're going through hardship now, remind yourself of those days you were once struggling, and how you overcame them. Hardship also has a prescribed time limit; it doesn't last forever. Stay patient and keep relying on Allah (swt), and without a doubt things are going to get better.

Reflection 216

Letting Go

Sometimes the solution to a problem is to simply let it go! However, many of us believe that the concept of letting go translates to giving up. That is why we continue to force things when they don't turn out as planned, which causes a great amount of stress.

This mindset of not giving up is good, but it also depends on the situation. Some of us use this mindset on the most mundane things. We have to distinguish what is worth it and what is not, and many times what we think is worth it is REALLY NOT. We have to learn to conserve our energy, use more logic and less emotions.

Reflection 217

Be Specific

When it comes to repentance, be specific what sin you're repenting for. For instance, don't just say, "Allah (swt) forgive me for my sins." Instead say, "Allah (swt) forgive me for backbiting," for example. It is important to be specific because it registers in our mind that this action is not good for us, but if we stay broad the mind is going to take a while to pick it up. It's important to train ourselves in this matter because it is like an extra layer of defense.

Reflection 218

Playing Favorites

When it comes to haram we cannot be biased, or play "favorites." Meaning, if someone we know is doing something haram we have to take a stance, and not show any type of support despite how close we may be to them. For instance, we tend to stay quiet if our parents, siblings, spouse, or best friend is doing something wrong! We look the other way, not sure why, but it is not okay. If you really care about someone, encourage them to sincerely repent.

Reflection 219

Paralyzing Yourself

The fastest way to paralyze yourself mentally is caring what others think about you; this will really slow you down. It is important we don't get lost in such thoughts; we have to train ourselves to stop caring, but that doesn't mean we stop caring what Allah (swt) thinks about us. Some of us make the mistake and stop caring for not only what others think, but also what Allah (swt) thinks, such a road only leads to destruction.

Reflection 220

Wearing Gold

Just a friendly reminder for the brothers, men are not allowed to wear gold; Islam doesn't permit it. This has been a common trend lately, especially among the youth. I know sometimes we want to look "flashy," but let's do it within the boundaries of what is permissible. Stick to silver! Even if our gold jewelry is fake, we should refrain from wearing it in my opinion, we shouldn't give the wrong impression.

Reflection 221

Feeling Worthy

The sad truth is that many of us only find value within ourselves when we accomplish worldly affairs. But this mentality is not correct. Being a human being alone should increase our value when we perceive ourselves, because we have great potential. Being obedient to Allah (swt), serving the world like the Prophet Muhammad (saww) and AhlulBayt (as) is what true value looks like. You shouldn't wait until you accomplished something worldly to feel worthy.

Reflection 222

Capitalism

Living in a capitalist driven society there are many opportunities that arise from time to time, but do we ever ask ourselves if such opportunity is permissible to partake in Islamically? Cannabis or "weed" dispensaries have become a popular business venture among our Muslim community.

When this industry was only available on the black market, "noble" community members used to criticize it, but now after the legalization of recreational marijuana, they have become the forerunners to open shops. They're supposed to be the champions of the community, the role models, but I guess when it comes to making money everything gets tossed out of the window.

In the public eye they say, "We are against drugs and we have to protect our youth," but behind the scenes they're the owners of these stores. What is shameful is that they allow the law of the land to govern their actions and not Allah (swt). They used to stay away from this line of work when it was illegal in fear of the consequences they may face from the law, but what about the consequences of the hereafter?

You know what is upsetting? Many people use the excuse of "providing for my family" to take part in such an endeavor, when in reality it is for their own greedy souls. Our Muslim community has a real drug problem, but now it isn't only from the consumer side, it is from production as well.

Trying to separate religion from business is a low form of intelligence. May Allah (swt) have mercy on our souls and help us understand what it truly means to be God conscious.

To end, a companion of the Imam (as) once came to him and said, [50] "I look at all the people around me, and they're doing so much good.

346

I have the correct faith, but my actions are so few. I cannot fast or pray the recommended nor am I able to give charity due to my poor status."

The Imam (as) responded with, "Do not say that! That is not how one is valued. The individuals around you might have many good deeds, but when the doors of committing sins are open, they quickly rush in without thinking. You might not have many good deeds, but you stop yourself from entering. You have Taqwa (God consciousness). You think before you do wrong. That is more precious to Allah (swt)."

[50] Attributed to Imam Ja'far al-Sadiq (as)

Reflection 223

Decision Making

Passage 1

Many times when we make a decision we try to look for some type of validation to make ourselves feel a bit better. For example, I was speaking to a parent once and they were telling me how their son was persistent about getting their blessing after being told no. Basically, this young man was seeking permission to go somewhere the parents advised against because they believed such a trip wasn't ideal from every perspective, especially Islamically. Even though he was at an age where he could've gone without asking anyone, he was still looking for some type of approval.

This is what happens with many of us. We don't like making decisions on our own, because if something was to go wrong we can easily justify it by saying, "I consulted so and so, and they said it was a good idea." So eventually I asked this brother why he desperately wanted his parents' approval. He said, "I don't want to do anything that might upset them." But if that was true we wouldn't be having this conversation. He obviously was looking for some type of validation for his actions to feel a little bit better about doing something that wasn't okay.

The point is, we have to own up to our decisions and know what comes with it. We cannot go around looking for people's approval before doing something just to feel a type of way.

Now, how should we come to a decision? A friendly suggestion:

1. What does Islam say about such action.
2. Do it based on the hereafter.
3. Weigh out the pros and cons, especially if sinning is involved.
4. Seek advice from those who are competent, experienced, and have your best interest at hand.

5. Make your decisions when your mind is in a state of peace. For instance, I like to make my decisions after Fajr prayer. I realized that is when I am most focused, and not emotionally driven.

Lastly, it's important that when you make a decision you try not to overthink it, because many times such thoughts can be fueled by the whispers of Shaytan.

Passage 2

Sometimes when we reflect on our past decisions we become overwhelmed. That shouldn't be the case! At the time you made your decision you were confident with it because you believed it was the best one. Just because the results didn't turn out the way you thought they were going to, doesn't mean you should become upset with yourself and carry a heavy burden forever.

The worst thing we can do is view such situations as a waste of time, or a grave mistake. Instead, we should change our approach and take them as learning lessons, because now we are mentally equipped with how to decipher and proceed in the future if we are put in similar circumstances. This piece of knowledge comes at a cost sometimes, and it might be the cost of suffering, but it's okay because what you become armed with is powerful and priceless if you use it.

Go easy on yourself and stay patient as well, because sometimes some of the worst decisions can lead to a garden blooming with beautiful flowers.

Reflection 224

Faith

Sometimes, believing only in yourself isn't enough. I personally gave up on myself countless times, but it was my faith in Allah (swt) that kept me going…

Faith is what reassures an individual that they're in good hands despite not knowing what is going to happen.

Strengthen your faith, for it was faith that split the sea for Prophet Musa (as).

Reflection 225

Political Positions

When it comes to running for a political position or any position for that matter, one instance in Islamic history always comes to mind. Imam Ali (as) being stripped of his (as) right to the caliphate after the death of the Prophet (saww).

However, later on it was narrated that he (as) was offered the position so long as he (as) pledged allegiance to those who stole his (as) God given right. The Imam (as) refused, and had to wait many years before he (as) eventually became caliph. There is a lot to learn from this scenario that we can implement in our lives, especially if we are those running for a public position.

Should we ever compromise our faith, dignity, and morals to fulfill a position? You tell me! If we would rank different positions, being caliph of an Islamic Ummah is probably number one, it is higher than any Presidential seat. Such a position comes with control of the treasury and army, but our beloved Imam (as) rejected it under such circumstances, and he (as) also criticizes it's worth as well.

What's unfortunate nowadays is that we have individuals selling their whole Islamic ideology for very minor positions, nothing that can compare to being a caliph. Instead of saying no, they take on such positions and convince themselves that they're doing it for the "greater good." Did Allah (swt) task them to do this? Did He (swt) send them revelation and say, "So and so compromise your faith so you can serve the people?"

Most likely not! Therefore, a question you have to ask yourself is, if such a position is going to cause me to compromise my faith, is it even worth it? We cannot think that because we live in the west it is okay to bend here and there. In this case the problem is not where we live because Allah (swt) is everywhere, it is with what we are trying to accomplish. We care deeply about public servitude, but we neglect servitude towards our own souls sometimes.

Reflection 226

Modeling the Hijab

Browsing through social media, it is obvious that the hijab is being modeled excessively nowadays. It's crucial that we condemn such behavior. We must speak against it and raise awareness, like how we do with any other issue that brings harm.

The hijab is being mistreated, and it is being used for personal gain! This isn't acceptable. The hijab belongs to Lady Fatima (as) and Zaynab (as); we must defend the hijab, especially the sisters. You have to fight for it...

From an Islamic perspective such actions are very problematic. Yet, we have more and more women taking part in it. Why is modeling the hijab becoming normalized? This type of representation is not needed because it's based on lies; it's deceiving because it is not what true hijab stands for. In fact, it is what true hijab is against...

To end, the "strategists" tried to destroy Islam by portraying it as a religion fueled by violence, but they failed miserably. So they moved on, and now they're trying to destroy it from within by pushing it through a secular system. As Muslims we must not give into this despite what they offer, because there will come a time where all of us will stand before Allah (swt).

Reflection 227

3-Phases

When we reflect on our journey to the straight path we notice that we go through different phases. The goal is to obey and serve Allah (swt) like the Prophet Muhammad (saww) and AhlulBayt (as), but do we ever come close? In my opinion, there are three phases we go through...

The first phase is made up of individuals who aren't really interested in religion. I am sure many of us have been there at some point. The harsh reality is that many of us stay in this phase and never experience any type of connection with Allah (swt) throughout our whole lives. My prayers go out to those who are struggling with such a phase.

The second phase are those who set their intention to gain nearness to Allah (swt). So they begin to do their Islamic duties, and all the necessary things that are going to make them feel spiritual. But at the same time they're still doing questionable things. They're standing between truth and falsehood. This is where most of us are stuck at!

Lastly, the third phase is the most important, but many of us never reach this stage because it requires us to give up what we love most, and come out of our comfort zone. Sometimes the things we love aren't suitable for a Muslim, and believe it or not they can be the smallest of the things, which can become the barrier between phase two and three. If we want to experience more of how it feels to obey and serve Allah (swt) like the Prophet Muhammad (saww) and AhlulBayt (as), we must make it a priority to get to this phase, and STAY THERE.

To experience Allah's (swt) best we have to research what Islam is okay and not okay with. Afterwards, we have to reflect on our day to day actions to understand what needs to be addressed. To us some actions might seem harmless, but to Islam they might be a sin.

We all have potential to be great believers, but many of us settle. As long as we are breathing we have to strive for greatness, especially when it comes to the straight path. Don't just look the part, sincerely be a part of the part!

Reflection 228

Alcohol

The consumption of alcohol is a real problem within our Muslim community. For some reason this sin has become a norm among many people, and isn't being addressed much. From a physical aspect, alcohol can damage many parts of our bodies, from our brain to our liver and so on. Even though many people know this, they still make a case for wine, claiming that it benefits the heart. I am sure many topics are deemed beneficial from a scientific perspective, but where does Islam stand on these matters? I think many people are under the impression that the consequences of consuming alcohol is just not being able to pray for 40 days, and this might be the reason why people aren't hesitant to drink because the tradeoff is minimal. The "40 days" statement is misleading. Never leave your prayers!

In reality, consuming alcohol is much more dangerous than we think. That being said, let's dive into the [51] narrations by the Prophet Muhammad (saww) and AhlulBayt (as) regarding alcohol, because sometimes saying it's just haram is not enough, which is understandable. I hope these narrations will help us stay away from this sin, and leave it if we are taking part in it.

If you would like to be deprived of the Prophet Muhammad's (saww) intercession, then consume alcohol, and if you would like to meet Allah (swt) as an idol worshiper, being addicted to alcohol will do that for you. Imam Ja'far al-Sadiq (as) states, [51] "Alcoholism is the mother of all sins. Liquor invites the drunkard to all sorts of indecencies. It destroys his intellect. So much so that under its influence he even fails to recognize his Lord. Whatever sin he encounters, he commits it. The alcoholics do not refrain from any such acts, which are against morality." People claim wine benefits the heart, but what is truly going on behind the scenes? Imam Ja'far al-Sadiq (as) states, [51] "Certainly even if a person swallows only a mouthful of wine, at that very moment, the angels, the Prophets and the righteous believers send their curses upon him." Also, [51] "When he drinks enough to make him intoxicated, the spirit of belief leaves his body, it is replaced by the dirty, accursed, devilish spirit."

We also have to be careful of the types of environments we sit in. The Prophet Muhammad (saww) states, [51] "Accursed, accursed is the one who sits at a table where wine is being served." Moreover, Imam Ja'far al-Sadiq (as) states, [51] "Do not sit with drunkards because when the curse descends it engulfs all the people in the company of the drunkards." When it comes to marriage, the Prophet Muhammad (saww) states, [51] "Allah (swt) has made me to pronounce wine as haram, after this pronouncement if someone still drinks wine, he is not fit to have his proposal for marriage accepted, when he proposes. If he seeks recommendation, he should not be recommended. If he says something he must not be believed. His testimony must not be accepted. Nothing should be kept in his trust." Furthermore, Imam Ja'far al-Sadiq (as) states, [51] "One who marries his well-behaved daughter to a drunkard; it is as if he has given her to adultery."

May we sincerely seek forgiveness from Allah (swt) and commit to the straight path!

---

[51] Shirazi, Sayyid Abul Husayn Dastghaib. "Thirteenth Greater Sin: Drinking Liquor." *Al-Islam.org*, Ahlul Bayt Digital Islamic Library Project 1995-2022, 31 Jan. 2022.

Reflection 229

Representing Islam

Some of us stop doing our Islamic duties because we believe we aren't representing Islam properly. We care too much about how we represent Islam than being actual Muslims. So we construct this narrative in our mind that to preserve Islam it's best that we don't commit to certain acts that are going to label us as Muslims. In a sense, it's like we are sacrificing ourselves for the greater good of Islam! But is that what is asked of us?

For instance, we might feel our actions contradict Islam, so we may stop praying or remove our hijab. Afterwards, we tend to convince ourselves that was the noble thing to do because we are protecting the image of Islam.

We aren't doing Islam a favor when we leave it. With or without us, Islam is already perfect! We have to use Islam to gain nearness to Allah (swt). Being a Muslim is a work in progress; it's a life journey. Some people may have a bad week or a bad month, or a bad year even, but that doesn't mean they should cancel themselves out completely. Allah (swt) never told us that the requirement to be a Muslim is to be perfect right off the bat; it was mankind that put this unnecessary pressure on themselves.

Yes, some of us might have extreme flaws, but I think Allah (swt) would want us to continue to pray instead of leaving prayer completely. To end, those thoughts that come to mind that tell us to leave our Islamic duties because we don't represent Islam properly may be fueled by the whispers of Shaytan. His main job is to take us away from Islam. So the only question left is, are we going to make it easy for him, or are we going to make it hard?

Reflection 230

Out of Pity

When it comes to getting to know someone, if you no longer want to continue, the proper way to end things is to be honest with them. But many of us don't do that! Instead, we take this heroic approach; we convince ourselves that we must continue to speak to them because we don't want to hurt them. When we do this, we aren't doing them any good. In fact, we are speaking to them out of pity, and this is one of the worst things we can do to an individual.

Speaking to someone because you feel sorry for them is a form of oppression in my opinion. This is why we shouldn't make decisions when we are extremely emotional. Sometimes when we first meet people we quickly promise them things, and then after some time we might realize they're not for us. It becomes extremely difficult to end things when you guaranteed them marriage a few weeks ago. Know yourself, and know what you're getting yourself into first!

However, for some people, because they made such promises they make it their duty to fulfill their obligation, thinking it is the righteous decision. But when we study the situation we realize they're really doing it for their ego, because had they been brave enough they would've understood that what they're doing is wrong, and put an end to things early. The reason I mention this is because of what tends to happen when we speak to someone out of pity. We begin to mistreat them, even though they may be the most amazing individual ever. This is because we feel forced and stuck, so they become our punching bag, and this can destroy an individual on all levels. No human being deserves this!

If you naturally and genuinely can't give yourself to another person, then end things, because they might find someone else who can. Don't rob them of that! If our actions are going to hurt someone, I think we can all agree that dealing with pain in the beginning stages is much different than when the stakes are high, and marriage and children are involved.

Reflection 231

Taqwa

Passage 1

Taqwa means to be God conscious. Let's reflect on this verb, how can we expand on its meaning? I believe one of the highest forms of Taqwa is realizing a sin and avoiding it before it manifests.

For example, if I know my group of friends casually take part in backbiting, I try to avoid them or begin to distance myself. Or if I know a certain setting will provoke me to sin with my eyes, I avoid it because it may be hard to lower my gaze, and so on.

Everyone has a different definition of success, but who are the most successful to Allah (swt)? Those who are God conscious.

Passage 2

I have been thinking about what it truly means to be God conscious, to have Taqwa. I realized that doing our Islamic duties doesn't necessarily mean we are God conscious. Being God conscious is an act within itself; it needs its own proper time and attention.

For example, prayer might force us to remember Allah (swt) because we are in a state of worship, but the question that arises is, are we going to remember Allah (swt) after we have finished praying? It is easy to remember Allah (swt) when you're required to remember Him (swt), but what about beyond our Islamic duties? This is a whole different challenge! We have to ask ourselves if we are truly putting in the effort to become God conscious?

Appendix

1. From "The Soul Cries" by Imam Ali (as)

2. Attributed to Imam Ali (as)

3. Ṭālib ʿAlī Ibn Abī. *Nahjul Balagha: Peak of Eloquence: Sermons, Letters and Sayings*. Tahrike Tarsile Qur'an, 2009. –p.139

4. Attributed to Imam Ali (as)

5. Attributed to Imam Ali (as)

6. "Diseases of the Soul: Pretending Virtuousness (Riya)." *Al-Islam. org*, 18 Aug. 2019.

7. Attributed to Imam Ali (as)

8. Attributed to Imam Hasan (as)

9. Ṭālib ʿAlī Ibn Abī. *Nahjul Balagha: Peak of Eloquence: Sermons, Letters and Sayings*. Tahrike Tarsile Qur'an, 2009. –p.487

10. Ṭālib ʿAlī Ibn Abī. *Nahjul Balagha: Peak of Eloquence: Sermons, Letters and Sayings*. Tahrike Tarsile Qur'an, 2009. –p.187

11. Shirazi, Sayyid Abdul Husayn Dastghaib. "The Thirty-Second Greater Sin: Isrāf." *Al-Islam.org*, Ahlul Bayt Digital Islamic Library Project, 18 Jan. 2013.

12. Ṭālib ʿAlī Ibn Abī. *Nahjul Balagha: Peak of Eloquence: Sermons, Letters and Sayings*. Tahrike Tarsile Qur'an, 2009. –p.316

13. Ṭālib ʿAlī Ibn Abī. *Nahjul Balagha: Peak of Eloquence: Sermons, Letters and Sayings*. Tahrike Tarsile Qur'an, 2009. –p.277

14. Rastani, Shaykh Amin. *Death and the Barzakh: Stages Between Dunya and Resurrection*. MIZAN INSTITUTE, 2018.-p. 7

15. Rizvi, Sayid Sa'eed Akhtar. "The Seven Responsibilities." *Al-Islam.org*, Ahlul Bayt Digital Islamic Library Project , 4 June 2015.

16. Attributed to Sayed Ruhollah Khomeini (ra)

17. Attributed to Imam Ali (as)

18. Ṭālib 'Alī Ibn Abī. *Nahjul Balagha: Peak of Eloquence: Sermons, Letters and Sayings*. Tahrike Tarsile Qur'an, 2009. –p.844

19. Ṭālib 'Alī Ibn Abī. *Nahjul Balagha: Peak of Eloquence: Sermons, Letters and Sayings*. Tahrike Tarsile Qur'an, 2009. –p.299

20. Attributed to Imam Ali (as)

21. Shirazi, Naser Makarem. "Discourse 13: Two Despised Characteristics: Eating Too Much and Looking at Others." *Al-Islam.org*, Ahlul Bayt Digital Islamic Library Project , 3 Oct. 2012.

22. Attributed to the Prophet Muhammad (saww)

23. Shirazi, Sayyid Abdul Husayn Dastghaib. "The Thirtieth Greater Sin: Not Helping the Oppressed." *Al-Islam.org*, Ahlul Bayt Digital Islamic Library Project, 18 Jan. 2013.

24. Attributed to Imam Ali (as)

25. Reyshari, Muhammadi. "Affliction." *Al-Islam.org*, Ahlul Bayt Digital Islamic Library Project, 18 Jan. 2020.

26. Qara'ati, Mushin. "Bowing Down {Ruku'} and Prostration {Sujud}." *Al-Islam.org*, Ahlul Bayt Digital Islamic Library Project, 13 Sept. 2015.

27. Ṭālib 'Alī Ibn Abī. *Nahjul Balagha: Peak of Eloquence: Sermons, Letters and Sayings*. Tahrike Tarsile Qur'an, 2009. –p.908

28. Ṭālib 'Alī Ibn Abī. *Nahjul Balagha: Peak of Eloquence: Sermons, Letters and Sayings*. Tahrike Tarsile Qur'an, 2009. –p.398

29. Attributed to Imam Ali (as) & Husayn (as)

30. Attributed to Imam Ali (as)

31. Attributed to Imam Ali (as)

32. Attributed to Imam Ali (as)

33. Attributed to Imam Ali (as)

34. Jamaludeen, Sayyid Haydar, translator. *Peace Be Upon Ibrahim, Memories from the Life of Shaheed Ibrahim Hadi* . Vol. 1, Wilayah Publications.

35. From "The Soul Cries" by Imam Ali (as)

36. Amini, Ibrahim. "Divorce in Islam." *Al-Islam.org*, Ahlul Bayt Digital Islamic Library Project, 12 Feb. 2015

37. Attributed to Imam Ali (as)

38. Shirazi, Naser Makarem. "Sexual Problems of Youths-Sexual Perversions." *Al-Islam.org*, Ahlul Bayt Digital Islamic Library Project, 9 Jan. 2013.

39. Imani, Sayyid Kamal Faqih. "An Enlightening Commentary into the Light of the Holy Qur'an Vol. 11." Translated by Sayyid Abbas Sadr-'ameli, *Al-Islam.org*, Ahlul Bayt Digital Islamic Library Project , 4 Jan. 2020.

40. Attributed to Imam Ali (as)

41. Majlisi, Muhammad Baqir. "An Account of Ya'qub and Yusuf." *Al-Islam.org*, Ahlul Bayt Digital Islamic Library Project , 26 Dec. 2017.

42. Attributed to Imam Ali (as)

43. "Suicide Statistics." *American Foundation for Suicide Prevention*, American Foundation for Suicide Prevention, 9 Sept. 2021.

44. Attributed to Imam Ali (as)

45. Attributed to the Prophet Muhammad (saww)

46. Shirazi, Sayyid Abdul Husayn Dastghaib. "Fourteenth Greater Sin: Gambling." *Al-Islam.org*, Ahlul Bayt Digital Islamic Library Project , 20 Oct. 2012.

47. Majlisi, Muhammad Baqir. "An Account of Musa and Harun." *Al-Islam.org*, Ahlul Bayt Digital Islamic Library Project , 26 Dec. 2017.

48. Attributed to Imam Ali (as)

49. Shirazi, Sayyid Abdul Husayn Dastghaib. "Sixth Greater Sin: 'Aqq Al-Walidayn (Disobedience To Parents)." *Al-Islam.org*, Ahlul Bayt Digital Islamic Library Project 1995-2022, 31 Jan. 2022.

50. Attributed to Imam Ja'far al-Sadiq (as)

51. Shirazi, Sayyid Abul Husayn Dastghaib. "Thirteenth Greater Sin: Drinking Liquor." *Al-Islam.org*, Ahlul Bayt Digital Islamic Library Project 1995-2022, 31 Jan. 2022.

The future might seem terrifying, but sometimes there is beauty in not knowing what is going to happen because one is compelled to depend on Allah (swt)!

For it is tawakkul that removes the worries of tomorrow...

www.ingramcontent.com/pod-product-compliance
Lightning Source LLC
Chambersburg PA
CBHW020836020726
47497CB00005B/1131